DEAR
ORSON WELLES
&
OTHER ESSAYS

About the Author

A globally acclaimed Scottish-Irish director, writer and wanderer, Mark Cousins was born in 1965, raised in Northern Ireland during the Troubles, and has lived in Scotland since the early 1980s. His 24 feature-length films (as well as 30 short films) and 40 hours of television – including *The Story of Film: An Odyssey*, *What is This Film Called Love?*, *Life May Be*, *A Story of Children and Film*, *Atomic*, *Stockholm My Love*, *I Am Belfast* and *The Eyes of Orson Welles* – have premiered in Cannes, Berlin, Sundance and Venice film festivals and have won the Prix Italia, a Peabody, the Persistence of Vision Award in San Francisco, the Maverick Award in Dublin, the Stanley Kubrick Award, and the European Film Academy Award for Innovative Storytelling as well as many other prizes. He has filmed in Iraq, Sarajevo during the siege, Iran, Mexico, across Asia and in America and Europe.

Mark Cousins is also the author of five books, including the acclaimed *The Story of Film* (Pavilion Books, 2004), *Imagining Reality: The Faber Book of Documentary* (Faber and Faber, 1996), *Widescreen: Watching. Real. People. Elsewhere* (Wallflower Press, 2008) and *The Story of Looking* (Canongate Books, 2017). He continues to live in Edinburgh.

DEAR
ORSON WELLES
&
OTHER ESSAYS

MARK COUSINS

THE IRISH PAGES PRESS
CLÓ AN MHÍL BHUÍ
2024

Dear Orson Welles & Other Essays
is first published in hardback on 28 May 2024.

The Irish Pages Press
129 Ormeau Road
Belfast BT7 1SH
Ireland

www.irishpages.org

Editors: Chris Agee, Jacob Agee and Milena Williamson

Typeset in 14/18 pt Monotype Perpetua.
Designed and composed by RV, Belfast. Printed by Bell & Bain, Glasgow.

A CIP catalogue record for this book
is available from The British Library.

Dust-jacket photograph by Phoebe Grigor.
Author's portrait by Jenny Leask.

ISBN: 978-1-7393537-2-8

Also by Mark Cousins

Imagining Reality: The Faber Book of Documentary (1996)

Scene By Scene (2002)

The Story of Film (2004)

Widescreen: Watching. Real. People. Elsewhere (2008)

The Story of Looking (2017)

Get in the action, feel the attraction.

CONTENTS

WORLD OF CINEMA

AUTHOR'S
INTRODUCTION

I'm mostly an image maker. Words don't come naturally to me, but they do come. They feel like leakage,
a run-off.

After heavy rain, bogs and soil banks seep. Sometimes you can see petrol colours in the seepage. I've
never known if that's because of farming fertilisers, or
if the land naturally produces rainbow-coloured oils
which are washed out by the rain.

What follows are my petrol colours, the things that
leach out after a downpour. Some of these writings
were commissioned and paid for by film or culture
magazines. Others were written when I was sodden.

They're my accursed share, these pieces, the things
I do when I'm not doing what I do. As you'll discover,
I'm no Joan Didion, Virginia Woolf or Walter Benjamin,
but I'm good enough not to be able to call myself useless.

In some ways I'd like to be a useless writer because then I could see myself as wildly asymmetrical – great at images and rubbish at words. Exclusively visual.

Maybe now's the time to admit that my writing isn't a poor relation to my image making and that, in fact, words have often partnered my pictures. I certainly often write to imagery, but maybe the longing that pictures have for words, and vice versa, has been a theme in my filmmaking. Or an engine.

If this is so, then the book you have in your hands is the desire not the desired. It's an espresso hit from the visual world, a world which of course you will not see as you read. The unseen is often a stimulant, isn't it? Its absence is a requirement, an appetite.

You will certainly come across appetite in what follows. I didn't realise how hungry I am for movies, cities and images until I compared myself to others. My partner once said to me "you're so interesting, you're boring", which made me (a) laugh and (b) realise that I could go through an event horizon after which passion for things becomes unrelenting, monstrous even.

If you've encountered me in this overdrive and found it too much, I apologise. As a defence, or qualification, I will say that the driver isn't ego. I don't think I have a strong sense that's keen to be seen. Oscar Wilde felt that self is a set of performances. David Bowie played with that. Art colleges and film schools around the world teach that to make art is to express yourself, that a creative person has an inner world that they should externalise.

I don't think that I have such an inner world. If I do, I try to dial it down so that its noise doesn't deafen the outer world, which is far more bizarre and intriguing. I'm Generation X, so saw the first Star Wars film aged ten. Its advice to "feel the force" electrified us and infused the Irish Catholicism in which I was marinated.

But feel the force was outwardly directed. Now I know that if I'm feeling dejected or bored I should dance or swim naked or watch a Sergei Eisenstein film or listen to Sun Ra or Donna Summer. I should tune into frequencies other than my own.

This book is the result of me tuning in, of going to Egypt or Iran, or filming in Kurdish Iraq, or taking the bus to the end of the line. The leakages, the petrol colours come from such journeys.

I'm writing this in a cramped seat on a flight from Edinburgh to New York. Before I boarded, I asked followers on Twitter to suggest music that I should listen to on the plane. I made a Spotify list of the 230 recommendations and listened to them for hours. Music from Brazil, the Arab world, trancey dance, folk ballads.

I knew few of the songs and many of them would not have been my choices, but the effect was almost hypnotic. I have long legs and am antsy, so long flights in economy are an endurance test, but the crowd-sourced Twitter soundscape really made me feel elsewhere.

I submitted to other people's musical tastes, dialled down my own and, as a result, had fun and learnt things. The key word in the last sentence isn't "fun" or "learnt", it's "submitted". I gave other people four hours of my time and said "do something with those hours". And they did. Submission is the opposite of the self-expression that the art schools teach, but rename submission as responsiveness and you get to a place when I've often lived.

It's a middle place, an equator, where I can be both invisible and aflame. Maybe that's where I'm best. Gertrude Stein was thinking of that place when she wrote that observation plus construction make imagination.

Thank you for reading this book. If you listen to music when you read, I suggest Sun Ra's *Space is the Place*.

Mark Cousins
Mid Atlantic

Screen Memoirs

— 2010 —

LOS ANGELES

For *Prospect*.

I spent chunks of my thirties in Los Angeles. I had a TV show on which I interviewed movie actors and directors, many from Hollywood's golden age. Sometimes there'd be a week between filming, say, Jack Lemmon and Janet Leigh, so, rather than fly back home to Scotland, I'd check into a cheap hotel at the beach in Venice, California, buy hippie bracelets, hire a bike and cycle the boardwalk.

I was not yet my best in those years – the late nineties – and it, the City of Angels, was way past its. We met in the middle. I couldn't drive, and didn't have a car, so felt like a Martian, or a Mexican, walking those streets. LA taught me a lot about life and living. Dennis Hopper told me how to drink martinis – Tanqueray gin, straight up, with olives. I read Mike Davis' angry, political books about the city's urbanism, its ecology, the design of its street seating – convex so homeless people can't sleep on them. I started to call Rod Steiger a friend – did I stretch the word? – and, as he told me of his depression, and as I got to know of Jack Lemmon's drink problem, I came to associate the city's smell of eucalyptus with an overwhelming sense of the parade having gone by. My dad was still alive back then, but a melancholia entered my soul, a sense of life not being endless after all. Maybe it was because endings are everywhere in LA. I went to the grave of Marilyn Monroe – the marble is pearlised, like the grotto at Lourdes, from years of touching – and almost choked at the realisation that she died aged 36. 36! The age I was as I placed a gardenia on her grave. An age at which I was still "coming up" as the song says. The age by which she had given up.

I remember realising, back then, that the movie stars in the hills were not much happier than the Mexicans in the malls. They'd swapped material problems for existential ones. Steiger and Leigh and Lemmon and the rest were lovely people at the end of their lives in a lovely city at the end of its life – or, rather, its first life as the host of the twentieth century's great bauble, Hollywood. The bauble had lost its lustre by the time I got to it but, somehow, this made me feel close to Hollywood, its receding sheen, the light from its distant star. Not physically close, but emotionally so, across the decades. And somewhere in this emotion, its objective correlative, was the silly-serious fact that LA made me feel sexy. I was youngish and prettyish and had "the especial slenderness of youth". It could be argued, of course that for twentieth-century kids like all of us, Hollywood invented young and pretty and slender. They came out of its test tubes. Maybe I had an inkling of that. Greta Garbo swam naked in the pool at the famous Chateau Marmont on Sunset Boulevard in the thirties and, so, in my thirties, did I. I wanted to spend my whole time in LA, like John Cheever's Neddy Merrill, swimming naked through swimming pools that Mike Davis so abhors and which are the sign of the crime in Roman Polanski's *Chinatown*.

———

In the decade since then, I haven't been back to LA. Not physically at least. When I drink a martini, I some-times think of the city, poured like custard over its thousand-square-mile plain (yes it's that vast). When I read in the newspapers of Steiger's death, and Lem-mon's and Leigh's, I was suddenly back in their lives, in our gentle friendships. In my work and thoughts I started travelling east rather than west; countries like Iran became my new bailiwick. I've charted this shift in cinema and me through a decade of writing in

Prospect. If you've caught some of those articles you'll have noticed that I haven't really been all that focussed on American cinema and, when I have written about it, it has been with a rather distant eye.

That all changed recently because I went back to LA for a month, to film part of a history of cinema that I'm making. It's still vast, and moving, and redolent of other things, but I'd never before been there for so long and, I think, with age (I was 45 yesterday), I can see it better and notice more. The distant star is a bit more distant now – Dennis Hopper has bone cancer, Marilyn's grave is even more pearly – and I'm rather less pretty. I've lost some of my lustre too. Maybe we've just met in the middle? Maybe we understand each other more now? When I was last there I got to know the place through its people. What people I met this time!

Where to start?

How about with Robert Towne, who wrote *Chinatown*, and restructured *Bonnie and Clyde*, and wrote the famous scene between Brando and Pacino in *The Godfather*? His house is a Surrey mansion – ranch hyphenate – big-boned and hardy handsome, in Pacific Palisades, not far from the Getty. He's so tall and thin that he almost teeters, like he's wearing stilettos. He's frailer in recent years, and still plays with his cigars like a baby plays with a rattle, but he remains the poet laureate of

LA. Unlike Mike Davis or, say, Sean Penn, Towne clearly loves the city, the way that director Federico Fellini loved Rome, aware of its iniquities, but enthralled by its mythic properties, its transformation by night. He told me that writing is like a dance in which you start by leading your partner, the story, then it starts leading you. In *Chinatown*, he had a story with two rapes – a woman by her father and the Owens Valley by the Department of Water and Power. As the dance took place he came to realise that he had to deal with the former – the more direct and personal – before the latter. He said that the best detective stories are like *Oedipus Rex* – the crime is before the investigator's eyes from the start, but she or he doesn't realise it. So it is with LA. Its crimes are there, on the surface, in the sunshine.

After talking to Towne, I felt I was wearing mythic glasses. Driving away in the car, I thought of an old interview with Agnes de Mille, the great choreographer and niece of Cecil B. DeMille, in which she recalls her first trip to LA in the early 1900s, before it was a city, before it was a movie capital. It was, she says, strewn with wildflowers; she'd walk in the hills and gather armfuls of eucalyptus and orange blossom; the air was full of mariposa. Such talk is heady, and dreamlike, in gridlock. The splendid-unreal gardens of Beverly Hills show that its denizens still buy the myth.

Still in the realm of the unreal, my producer, our fixer and I drove into the hills and climbed down the steep scrub to the back of the Hollywood sign. It's vast, there are rattlesnakes, and I was wearing a kilt so did a lot of tucking. The sign beeps because of motion detectors, and bangs as it cools when the sun sets. To try to avoid visual clichés, I filmed its rivets and bolts from the back. Even deglamourised in this way, it still has a degree of sublime. The size of the letters helps. The fact that people have killed themselves there adds tragedy. And there's the unmistakable aura of the reliquary, tacky but fascinating, the close-up presence of a legend.

Myth is an intoxicant, of course, but just when LA's perfume was getting too charged, we met the extraordinary Judy Balaban. Her father, Barney, ran Paramount Pictures from its heyday of Dietrich and von Sternberg to its partial sell-off in the sixties to former car bumper manufacturer Gulf+Western. She was engaged to Montgomery Clift, friends with Brando and Grace Kelly's bridesmaid. In Beverly Hills in the fifties, her house was party central. If her landing light was on, Frank and Sammy and Dean and Gene and Judy dropped by, and the martinis flowed. Balaban described these salad days beautifully, but when I asked her where they went, she detailed how events in Alabama, the rise of TV and the blacklist popped the mythic bubble. She and her friends raised money for Martin Luther King. Horizons widened. Fifties cinema showed the strain. The Doris Day – Rock Hudson parallel universe started to seem like Oz.

The peripheral vision of someone like Balaban shows that Hollywood was never quite the deluded citadel waiting to be stormed by truth-tellers à la Cassavetes, Scorsese and the children of the sixties, and even a short time in LA induces the kind of social vertigo that fuelled Balaban's activism. To be in the city can feel like being above it, so I asked my producer to walk with me from Echo Park in the east to Venice in the west; no big shakes in the history of epic walks, but enough to make jaws drop there.

We set out at 8:00 a.m. There were almost no white people on the streets. Mexicans queued for jobs outside garden centres. African Americans pushed shopping trolleys full of plastic and cans that they'd gathered to recycle, or the stuff of their lives. Amidst a bundle of bedding, a woman slept. I think she was white, but her face was tanned and ruddy – the mark of a life outdoors and, maybe, booze. Someone had emptied chow mein on her makeshift bed.

You have to be blind not to see this street life, but even the high life has its caste system. I was ignored in a restaurant on Sunset Boulevard, until they saw that my dining partner was Buck Henry, who wrote *The*

Graduate. Next day, in the same place, compliments about my appearance flowed. I was dressed exactly the same as the day before.

It's tempting to say that Hollywood was always thus, but was it? And has its main industry, film, always excluded the way society excludes? The film historian and author Cari Beauchamp — wisecracking, thoughtful and generous in equal measure — reminded me that half of the films made there before 1925 had women writers, directors and/or actors, people like Frances Marion, Alice Guy-Blaché, Mary Pickford and Lois Weber. Only when Wall Street noticed that there was big money in movies did men shove the women out. Paul Schrader, who wrote *Taxi Driver* and *Raging Bull*, told me that Hollywood was and is a citadel, and has almost always excluded other sensibilities. When I met African-American director Charles Burnett, who made *Killer of Sheep*, perhaps the first masterpiece made by a black American, I asked him why it took the country that co-invented cinema so long to give the means of production to its black citizens. His answer was eloquent but simple: racism. The African-American actress Juanita Moore, who was Oscar-nominated for her role, is the daring liberal weepie *Imitation of Life*, said "I spent the fifties holding open doors for white actors."

And then there's HUAC. Rod Steiger once boiled with rage when I mentioned Elia Kazan, who directed him on *On the Waterfront* and named names to the House Un-American Activities Committee. Even today, blacklistees like Abraham Polonsky, one of America's greatest filmmakers, are not on the Hollywood Walk of Fame. Nor is Frances Marion. And cinematographer Haskell Wexler, who shot *One Flew Over the Cuckoo's Nest* and *Who's Afraid of Virginia Woolf?* and many of the films of John Sayles, told me that when Kazan was nominated for an Honorary Oscar in 1999 he, Wexler, who had shot Kazan's film *America America* and who was on the nominating committee, wrote to Kazan asking if he might say a word of apology for his betrayal. Kazan wrote back "Fuck You". Hollywood is only a lifetime old, and HUAC is only half that. You can still smell the whiskey breath of those awful days.

Too many stories like this, and Los Angeles starts to become the sort of place that you wouldn't want to meet in the middle, or walk across or see yourself in. Yet talking in the car with Cari Beauchamp, we concluded that there's a lot of stuff you'd need not to be interested in – movies, books, buildings, race, Mexico, gender, ecology – to be not interested in LA. Two more people confirmed this for me.

The first was director Gus Van Sant, who's made "insider" films like *Good Will Hunting*, as well as avant-garde work like *Elephant* and *Gerry*. Somehow, about 15 minutes into my interview with him, as he lounged on his blue sofa in his house in the hills, we were talking about the Japanese master director Yasujirō Ozu, the brilliant Belgian formalist-feminist Chantal Akerman, video games and how they don't cut to get a character from one place to another – you just walk them there – and how all these things led to his walking film *Elephant*, about the Columbine shootings, and to *Last Days*, which channels Kurt Cobain. I know this sounds wanky but it wasn't. As I listened to Van Sant, and as I chatted to Buck Henry a few days later about a screenplay he wrote for Antonioni, and as I thought back to the richness of Robert Towne's talk and the insights of Beauchamp and Balaban, I suddenly realised that, as with Oedipus, the truth about the kind of sensibilities that LA houses was staring me in the face. Yes, Hollywood is a citadel of sorts, so is built to detract, but as a bauble it is built to attract, not only audiences, but talents, types, selves, classes, genres, styles and even ideas that might burnish the bauble. All the above people got in because of their own ability to shapeshift and because the citadel is like a heat shimmer. It's impressive, and more itself, from afar.

The other person who, at the end of my trip, reminded me that LA is fertile ground, was Stanley Donen, who directed *Singin' in The Rain*. He rarely gives interviews, but Buck Henry lied and said that I was worth talking to, so he did. I went to his office in

Manhattan, where I met his son – unshaven, handsome, caustic. Yet it wasn't his son. It was Donen himself. It's still a shock to realise that he was the *joymeister* of MGM, then formed a production company with Cary Grant, then went through his Hitchcock phase with comedy thrillers like *Charade*, then made great, wry films about sadness and despair like *Two for the Road* and *Bedazzled* and, after all this, 21 films, he was still only 43.

I said to him "When the French critic André Bazin talked about Hollywood he referred to 'the genius of the system'. Had the studio system any genius in it?"

Donen's reply was that it wasn't about genius. The system was simply a garden, a fertile patch of ground, on which many different things grew. Donen was one of those things.

I'd already mixed my metaphors with citadel-bauble, but here was another image, the garden. It felt right but, also, it took me back to Agnes de Mille's description of the flower strewn place that she remembered long before it became a concrete pasture.

As I flew out of New York, I wondered whether, as in a classic movie, I'd changed as a result of my adventure in LA. I think the answer is that I haven't, partly because I did a lot of my changing there the first time round, and because cities like Tehran change Europeans like me far far more. But also because, in its admixture of detraction and attraction, of pleasure and reality, of glamour and the gutter, LA is a zero-sum game. Zero-sum games change you in ways that cancel each other out.

SELF-INTERVIEW
ABOUT MEMORY

How is your memory, Mark?

Which one? I've various memories, some are hyper and some are half-dead. I am terrible at dates, years, plots of films, people's names, etc., but really good at spaces, images, painting, chemical formulae.

Has that affected your relationship with cinema?

Yes, I think so. I have made loads of films because, in an edit suite, I can remember shots, moments, etc., which speeds things up. I seldom dither or do more than one take when shooting, because I feel I know where the camera should be, what the lens needs to be, etc.

My alive-dead memory also effects how I watch films. I hardly ever see a movie twice, because I don't need to go through its spaces again. Of course, as I don't recall plots, I can watch, say, Yasujirō Ozu's *Late Spring* more than once without knowing what will happen next!

But isn't that weird? Isn't your memory then amplifying a minor aspect of a film (its spaces) and muffling its major aspect (plot)?

Maybe that's the case, but I don't care to be honest. It's the only brain I have and you work with what you've got. But, also, I'd say that (a) it's fun to rebel against the hierarchy of pleasures and (b) cinema isn't necessarily a story medium.

What?

Plot in a movie is one element, one level of instrumentation, but it's not the main melody. Movies are more about time and place than plot, I feel. The plot of, say, Sergio Leone's *Once Upon a Time in the West* waxes and wanes. It comes into and out of the foreground. But what is always in the foreground is the feeling of waiting – for change, for revenge, for the railway, for Claudia Cardinale. Think of its opening scene. It's a waiting room. Cinema is a waiting room.

But that makes it sound like cinema is always present tense.

It is in a way. Greta Garbo will always be alive. I'm always a boy, ageless, when I watch a new movie on a big screen. But I must admit that I also sometimes strongly feel my age in front of moving images. For example, I recently re-watched the TV series *Brideshead Revisited*. I first saw it in Antrim, when I was 15 – working-class, Irish, from a non-literary family etc. When I rewatched 40 years later (!) I was astonished at how much I remembered. Not the plot of course, but the languor, the lines, the atmospheres, the clothes, the elegy, the sexuality. ALL of these things affected me as I grew up. I've been using the phrases "a twitch upon a thread", "love or what you will" and "*et in arcadia ego*" all my life, and they all come from that TV plunge into a baroque, catholic, homoerotic, decadent, world. It was my other, my punk.

Did you feel sad when you rewatched it?

Yes.

Why?

Because it was a twitch upon a thread. Because I was again the boy who, despite being brought up in the

Troubles, had not yet felt strong bereavement or the pain of opprobrium.

Is there a relationship between pain and memory in cinema?

Definitely.

What is it?

Well, think of Terence Davies' *Distant Voices, Still Lives*, or Kira Muratova's *The Asthenic Syndrome* (one of my favourite films), or the idea in Ozu's films of *mono no aware*, the sadness of time passing. They are all about loss. Cinema tells the most beautiful lie, it shows us the vivacity of the ongoing moment. Its luminous here-and-nowness distracts from the fact that the clock is ticking. But I think my favourite films somehow know that. They are about the joy of the moment but also about the fact that everything is being filed away as memory. Think of Guru Dutt's *Paper Flowers*, Imamura's *The Insect Woman*, David Lean's *Summer Madness*, Orson Welles' *Macbeth*, Chantal Akerman's *From the East*, Agnès Varda's *La Pointe Courte*, Phyllida Lloyd's *Mamma Mia!*, Stanley Donen's *Two for the Road*, Jennifer Kent's *The Babadook*, Jane Campion's *An Angel at My Table*. Memory, memory, memory.

DEAR EIGHT-AND-A-HALF-YEAR-OLD SELF

Dear Eight-and-a-half-year-old Mark,

A friend of mine, Tilda Swinton, wrote a letter to her eight-and-a-half-year-old son. I was inspired by it and wanted to reply but, as I don't have a son, I'm writing to my eight-and-a-half-year-old self. You.

You're in Belfast. It's 1974. The city's at war. It's dead and locked up at night. You don't know it yet but in two years' time, a bomb will damage the house in which you live with your twin brother, mum and dad. Don't worry, you'll all be evacuated and you'll start a new life on a housing estate in a town called Antrim.

Antrim'll have no cinema. You'll see movies on TV — BBC2. You're about to fall in love with two directors — Alfred Hitchcock and Orson Welles. In Belfast in three years' time you'll see a film called *Jaws*, but it's one by

Welles — *Touch of Evil* — that will change your life. Its night-time setting, its pianola, and a scene between its actor Orson Welles and an actress, Marlene Dietrich, will make you fall in love with movies.

How will cinema change your life? It'll stop the world feeling scary. You'll discover a quietude in cinemas, in the dark, before the lights go down. In the letter to her son, who's the same age as you are, Tilda called this feeling "ecstatic removal". You'll find, as you grow up and become a man, and move to Scotland, that as well as removal, *release* is what you'll feel in cinemas, the sense that your nervous system, which is usually in the ready position, stops bracing itself.

Tilda tells her son that he'll discover "the promised land of freedom", and that's what you'll find too. You'll feel imaginative fireworks explode in your head. You'll feel the rush to tears at the beauty of Claudia Cardinale in *Once Upon a Time in the West* but then, later, you'll realise, that it was only partially her that brought those tears. It was also the exalted sweep of the scene in which the film image soars up into the air, over the railway station and further still to reveal a frontier town being born.

You'll run like a sprinter with this realisation that form moves you. You'll come to find that you need cinema, the way you need to dance, to remind you of the bodily and mental liberties that existence affords.

This dance'll become your life. And here's something you could never guess, living where you are, in working-class Belfast, a planet away from Hollywood: you'll earn your living in cinema, close to its contours. Are you shocked? I'd expect so. You'll discover that documentary films — in which the director is really co-director, with life itself — suit your sense of not wanting to be in full control, and you'll make lots. You'll write and talk about films in newspapers and on TV but you'll soon choose not to be in the mainstream. So you'll sprint some more and find that you're amongst the films of people with names like Weerasethakul, Tsuchimoto, Kiarostami, Sokurov, Dumont, Almodovar, Chahine, Farrokhzad, Mambéty, Imamura, Kötting, Bill Douglas, Jarman and Malick. By the time you realise this, you'll be miles from anywhere. You'll feel lonely there — so letters like Tilda's will mean a lot — but dead happy too, alert, paying attention, as John Sayles would say.

You'll see Mohammad Ali Talebi's *The Boot*, from Iran, and think of yourself when you see the scene where the girl wants her mum to buy her boots. And then she loses one. You'll start to write about how such simple, poetic films get squashed by multiplex ones. One day you'll count how many times a bad American film, *Pirates of the Caribbean: At World's End* is playing in the cinemas in the city in which you live, in one day.

The answer will be 54 times. In one small city in one small day. There'll be space for little else on the movie screens that day. This is minimisation of choice. It'll seem to you like bullying.

You'll go to Iran and see that it's more like Talebi's wee film than its CNN version.

But what, for now, at your age, do I wish for you? I wish the world of cinema would open up faster for you. You found your way to Iran and its cinema, the work of Ghatak and Dutt, Gerima and Muratova, all on your own. But I wish for this: something called the 8½ Foundation. A trust, based in Scotland perhaps, where Tilda and I live, which would make 20 films available for free on DVD to children around the world, on their 8½th birthday, their movie day. These films would be the best, most imaginative, movies of all time – directed by Miyazaki, Norman McLaren, Buster Keaton and Michael Powell, films with titles like *Palle Alone in the World*, *The Red Balloon*, *The Red Shoes* and *The Singing Ringing Tree*.

8½ is the perfect age to fall in love with cinema. It was the name of a great film.

You lucky thing. You're about to discover your passion.

BEAU TRAVAIL

FOR FIREFLIES

A film is like a Venus fly trap. It lures us.

I was bullied at school. The tough boys would circle, look with hatred, spit on me and humiliate. To be at the centre of such looks, such contempt, is to feel a force field.

My childhood took place in Belfast, Northern Ireland, which was at war and, so, occupied by British soldiers, who'd look at us down the barrel of their guns. Another male force field. Wheels within wheels.

A decade after I left Belfast, I saw Claire Denis' film *Beau Travail*. Early on there's a scene in which Denis Lavant and Grégoire Colin circle each other, staring, aggressive. I was fascinated, lured like a fly. I knew such circling. The fact that they are soldiers made the scene a double helix for me, a double recognition. Other soldiers surround the circle, gazing at the antagonists, as men do. Denis has the male choir from Benjamin Britten's *Billy Budd* sing as the tension builds, as the screw tightens. The choir sounds like a warning, like mourning, like wind.

Gunfights, Bruce Lee films, Sergio Leone stand-offs: we're not starved of such confrontations in movies. Usually they're in action cinema, and I switch off, but *Beau Travail* is different. It feels like recovery, like a perfection of male violence. Real fighting is fast and awkward. Denis and her team build so much stillness into the scenes, so much poise, so much control. *Beau Travail* has what the Japanese call *mu*: emptiness, the void. Denis once told me that she admires the films of Yasujirō Ozu, who has the symbol mu, and nothing else, on his gravestone. Somehow she adds the void to the soldiers' lives, their confrontations, the hot house in which they live. She removes the screech of fear and counterbalances it with the opposite – beauty, harmony, choreography. Maybe the fight is on stage? Maybe it's a dance? Maybe it's been inflected by form?

Maybe the whole of *Beau Travail* is like war refracted through a prism, and turned into light and dance?

However the film does it, it takes my childhood fears and turns them into something rare: a consolation.

— 2018 —

MARK COUSINS
ON ORSON WELLES
AND ESSAY FILMS

An interview by Janina Ciezadlo.

I would like to ask you some questions about the essay form in cinema, I see many of your films – the newest, The Eyes of Orson Welles, *and* Here Be Dragons, I Am Belfast *among others – not as documentaries, although there is certainly some connection, but as filmic essays. If you agree, can you describe what makes them essays rather than something else?*

You're right in that they aren't what's conventionally thought of as a documentary. They have little or no interviews, they aren't fly-on-the-wall observational and they don't have objective or journalistic voice overs. They are shot like documentaries, but written like letters or poems. The combination of objective image track and subjective soundtrack still excites me.

So, yes, they are more like essays in the non-scholarly sense. A fiction film is a bubble, an essay film bursts the bubble. But none of this is to say that my movies are more than or better than documentary. I'd rather say that documentary is polygeneric – not a genre but a house of genres. It contains multitudes – essay films, current affairs, experimental film, *cinéma vérité*, poetic work, etc. Aesthetically, documentary is the biggest thing in cinema.

Do you see Chris Marker, some of Chantal Akerman's work and even someone like Derek Jarman as influences on the essay film? You are a film historian, how would you place the form in the context of the history of film?

Yes, yes and yes. Chris Marker's film, especially *Sans Soleil*, taught a whole generation of us to ask the questions of a commentary – who is speaking, from where and when? It is conventionally assumed in docs that the speaker is an expert (usually male), in the present, and telling us what happened. But what if one or more of these things are untrue? That's where the magic lies. In *The Eyes of Orson Welles* film, for example, the speaker is me, but I'm talking to dead Welles. In *I Am Belfast*, the speaking is 10,000 years old. Impossible in both cases, but liberating.

It's the long, static stare in Chantal Akerman's films that I love most. She has massive confidence in an image, a moment, and lets it run as if it's sacred. She's against the glance, the impatience of fast-cut Hollywood. In real life I am fast-paced and glancy; in my movies – and those of others – I long for the opposite of that. I love quietude and contemplation rather than sensation.

Derek Jarman, whom I knew a bit, helped unblock the impasse of filmmaking. He and his collaborators showed that you didn't need 35mm and a big crew. Instead of the movie equivalent of fresco painting, he did oil painting. He was the Courbet of the movies.

In the context of film history, essay films are the most stylistically and thematically free films. You're on a bike rather than in a car when you make them.

Your The Story of Film *is global: is the essay a particularly Western form?*

No. Some of the best essay films are by Anand Pat-wardhan of India.

It is said that poetry is overheard. Would you like to comment on the connection to your work and poetry, another way to put it would be to ask you to comment on the poetics of the form in visual or filmic terms. And/or in literary terms or on the differences between the two.

I like that "overheard". It's like Agnès Varda's *The Gleaners and I*. When she makes her films she is gleaning, finding things, picking them up. Similarly, in Wim Wenders' *Alice in the Cities*, the main character, a photographer, says "I don't take pictures to speak, but to listen". The poetry is in the world. Rilke knew this, and wrote about it. You just have to keep your eyes and ears open. I love the built worlds of filmmakers like Wes Anderson, Erich von Stroheim, Vincente Minnelli and Kira Muratova, but each is a god in a sense, a creator of sets and worlds. They are dominators. Varda and Wenders can be like that, but they (and I) are also submissive to found poetry, the spark that flies when you put together two found things. In the case of my Welles film, I took a found thing – a box of his artworks – and added an imaginary thing – a letter to him. Hopefully some sparks flew.

I sense a tension or a set of polarities in your films between a very rational organisation — the sections in Eyes and Children and Film *— and a deeply subjective and emotional response to the flow and play of images and meanings. Might you on comment on this in formal terms or even talk about where these perceptions and habits of mind come from?*

Again, I think you're right. From childhood I've always loved machines, engineering, taking things apart. In every film I've done, I wanted to get the machine bit right from the start. In other words, the structure of the film, its shape, was decided very early in the planning process. Into this "hard" design, I am then free to add the "soft" elements – the emotions, observations, colours, etc. This relates to the previous answer, about dominance and submission in creativity. I want to be dominant and submissive. I want to impose a rigid structure on my Welles film, or my *Atomic* film, or my *A Story of Children and Film* and then I want to add the ghost into the machine. More practically, I can't think of the structure of a thing and its detail at the same time. I can't write a good sentence if I don't know the overall shape of the thing I'm writing. It's too confusing to me!

Your flow of images and moving camera seem to capture the flow of the mind, of visual ideas and the wondering and wandering of the voice. Would you comment on your process of collecting visual images, their arrangement, coherence and editing?

Yes, I love that flow. I often find that in a film there's too much story. I feel a bit bullied by a lot of story, as if we're breathlessly pushing onwards for the sake of pushing onwards. If I'm on a coach tour and it takes me to the Eiffel Tower, I want to get out for a bit, and not just drive on. You could call this the picaresque, the loosely structured story or string of events. It's my favourite mode, which is why I love road movies.

This is where your point about the flow of the mind comes in. Road movies often feel like mental wandering. I love the writing of Virginia Woolf, especially when she's observing, charting her own thought processes. Woolf is a fly on the wall of her own mind. Heady stuff for me. Left to their own devices, when they think no one is looking, our minds make immensely creative connections between things. Part of my job is to get out of the way of my own mind, and let it do what it does best. I shouldn't inhibit it or try to steer it too much.

Do you have any thoughts about how you came to be literate and fluid in words and images or do the films tell this story?

I was a poor reader at school, we had few books in our house, and I still read verrrrry slowly. When I read, I have to translate a sentence into an image before I can get what it's about. This means that I can't skim read, and "page turner" means nothing to me, but I suppose it does also mean that, with all that incessant translation, I've come to know the visual aspects of words, and maybe – if it doesn't sound too fancy – their feel or sculptural sense. I'm usually surprised, and pleased, if someone says that I use words well because to do so is HARD work for me!

The Eyes of Orson Welles *is all about the relationships between drawing or visual images and film: this is a huge topic, but I would like to hear a few more of your reflections on the subject.*

I love drawing (though am not great at it). I draw to stop thinking. When I'm filming a shot, I feel that I'm in a similar zone to drawing. A drawing has no soundtrack, of course. A film is a drawing with a soundtrack. I have no doubt that a great drawer like Rembrandt would have made films. Visual artists long to be musical. Musicians long to be visual. There's a mutual desire. Imagery and sound have that desire, they complete each other, and they are the one thing the other can't be. Cinema brings them together, it is their blind date.

Your use of the second person and the subjective voice is compelling and distinctive. How did you decide to take this leap away from the usual authorial / authoritative mode?

As mentioned above, a key influence was Chris Marker's *Sans Soleil*. In this film, the female commentator regularly says, in the English version, "He wrote me", yet the speaker does not exist, she's an invention of Marker. So he has imagined a correspondent who then tells the story from her point of view, thus making himself not "I" but "he". This sounds inaccessible, and some people do find *Sans Soleil* boring, but I've tried to use the impossible interlocutor in emotional ways. Their very absence adds heart. In my Mexican film, *What is This Film Called Love?*, for example, the narrator starts as myself, then I become a woman (the artist Alison Watt), and then she becomes a deer, who doesn't speak but who is subtitled. In *Stockholm, My Love*, Neneh Cherry starts her narration by talking to her father, in act two this changes to talking to an old man called Gunnar, and in act three, silent but subtitled, she talks to the city of Stockholm itself. Avoid as much as possible the object male voice in the third person. As soon as I write the word "you", a window opens.

Subjectivity, for me implies not just a poetics, but a politics of form. Could you elaborate on those implications with reference to your work?

I am political in my life, but the anger in my work is usually quite well-hidden. If there are politics in the forms of my films, they are to do with my impatience with formulaic story-telling, and fixed, authoritative world views. I want my films to feel open, moving, playful, tentative, uncertain, or ecstatic, so they have to have some looseness. I want their ends to be unforeseeable from their beginnings, just like our lives are. Back to machine words, I love the idea of "torque" or twist. A film should torque, it should transition into something else. I'm not sure if that's political. Maybe it's a basically unconservative position – change is good. In the era of trans activism and awareness, we're reminded that everything is in transition.

May I ask you the same question you asked Welles? Where does your taste for politics begin?

Margaret Thatcher. I was brought up working-class, so had some sense of class inequality and the injustices that follow, but to live in Scotland when the Poll Tax was imposed by Thatcher's government – a community charge which hit poor people far harder than rich people – was to join the barricades. Also the historic miners' strike of the 1980s: there needed to be changes in heavy industry in the UK, but under the guise of forcing that change through, the Conservative government wrecked communities and consigned at least one generation to poverty, poor physical and mental health, and reduced life expectancy. Shame on them.

One of my favorite quotes from Here Be Dragons *is about Enver Hoxha, Stalin and Mao ruining it for the rest of us. What is it that they ruined?*

They ruined the belief in alternatives to capitalism, because they were corrupt, murderous autocrats.

Again, you are an historian, and history has an implicitly narrative nature. How does narrative come into play in your work?

History has a forward structure, but I don't think it necessarily has a narrative structure. History is "then", but not always "therefore". Things succeed each other, and lots of things are caused by what went before them, but the causality is often weak, or indirect, or sideways, not forward. A historical event – take 9/11, for example – is like a cue ball in snooker or pool, smashing into a block of other balls. A chain reaction starts. And a chain reaction isn't a narrative, is it?

What kind of narratives might have a politically progressive direction?

I'm not sure. I used to believe writers like Brecht on this – that "closed" texts are conservative, and "open" texts are progressive, because they are better at change, they can incorporate history more, etc. This now sounds very naïve and even poncy to me. A simple example: I could see the homophobia in Ireland and Scotland lessen as they watched early series of the TV show *Big Brother* in which there were nice, ordinary, helpful, decent gay people. This was, as far as many homophobic people in Ireland and elsewhere were aware, the first opportunity they'd had to watch how gay people live their lives, and see that they are "just like us".

Big Brother was TV at its most popular. I would argue that its form – radical observationalism – was daring in the context of TV. Was it Brechtian? Perhaps. I think that if we are looking for progressive narrative form, one of the first places we should look is in popular media, the centre of the agora.

Can we say that I Am Belfast *and* Here Be Dragons *are organised around a geographical vision? Can you comment on that? Might they even be called psychogeographical in the Debordian sense?*

Yes, the *Belfast* film and *Here Be Dragons* could be called "listen to the city" movies – ditto *Stockholm, My Love* and *What is This Film Called Love?* I love Debord and love his idea of the *dérive*, the drift against the grain. Walk across Berlin with a map of Paris. I've walked across many cities – LA, Beijing, Berlin, Paris, London,

Mexico City, New York, Moscow, etc. – with no plan and without trying to hit the hot spots. I'm most happy, to be honest, near the bus terminus on the outside of town, where power isn't but where life is. There isn't a vision in my drifting, more a sense of getting away from the numbers, the Trip-Advisorisation of a visit. I don't want to go where people recommend, I want to go somewhere that isn't recommended, that isn't even on the recommend paradigm.

The interplay between geography and inspiration was central to your Welles film as was the filmic potential for movement in time as well as space. Would you comment on your use of space and time?

Time first: time is always sad, I think. It's always about loss and dying. I'm one of the happiest people I know, but have had quite a few bereavements over the years and, so, am always bracing myself a bit for the next one. This means that time is a kind of enemy. It's the courier of loss. It knocks on your door and delivers the parcel. As well as being sad, this makes time fascinating, unifying and humbling. You can't fight it, it is a kind of god.

Space! There's the rub. My brain is quite bad at words, but good at space. Architecture is my first love, though I've never studied it. When I walk into a building,

I adore the sense of where I am, to where I'm being led, to what extent to I feel imprisoned or liberated or narrated or moved. I love Highland glens, empty beaches at night, petrol station forecourts, shopping malls, dense forests, my own flat, abandoned swimming pools, mazes, temporary diversions, cycling fast, the miniaturisation of life in my campervan, and being constrained. Space is self-loss, the rapture of self-loss.

THE SKINNY ON ... MARK COUSINS

What's your favourite place to visit and why?

When he went to a new city, the great Soviet filmmaker Sergei Eisenstein liked to take a bus out of town, to the end of the line and explore there. I'm the same. I love city limits, transport termini, unfancy places. I walked to the edge of Minsk in Belarus at the end of last year. I knew no one, but felt totally alive and at home.

Favourite colour and why?

Yellow, by a mile. Yellow is associated with disease, jaundice, fading and – in Western societies – coward-ice, tawdry journalism and fiction ("giallo" thrillers, in Italy). But I love the yellow of gorse, my favourite architects (such as Alvar Aalto) liked yellow, and I recently died my hair yellow. I recently bought lots of yellow underpants online, but they're far too big for me.

Who was your hero growing up?

Paul Weller or Gene Kelly.

Whose work inspires you now?

The Thai filmmaker Apichatpong Weerasethakul, Jane Fonda, Cornel West, Hélène Cixous, Beyoncé, Fintan O'Toole, The Vivienne, Indian documentary filmmaker Anand Patwardhan.

What's your favourite food to cook?

I do all the cooking in our house, and run the gamut from fish finger sandwiches to Iranian khoresh (stew).

What three people would you invite to your dinner party and what are you cooking?

I hadn't heard of dinner parties until I started moving in middle-class circles. When I first went to them, I kept thinking "when does the dancing start?" I soon learnt that it doesn't, so I don't like dinner parties (and have been known to leave them and take a bus to the edge of town ...).

But, if I had to have one, I'd invite Cleopatra, the architect Eileen Gray and Catherine the Great. We'd eat in Livia's Room in Rome, then go to Cardross Seminary, where David Holmes would DJ.

What's your all-time favourite album?

Probably Bowie's *Hunky Dory*, the soundscape to my emergence from the rock pool.

What's the worst film you've ever seen?

India: The Modi Question. Not an actual film, just a horribly cinematic giallo decade of unreason.

What book would you take to a protracted period of government-enforced isolation?

Denis Diderot's *Encyclopaedia.*

Who's the worst?

Jair Messias Bolsonaro.

When did you last cry?

Yesterday, at Marcus Rashford's Twitter feed and Caroline Quentin's love of dancing on *Strictly*. I've never not cried at *DIY SOS*. I cried when I walked into the Friday Mosque in Isfahan in Iran – the most beautiful built thing I've ever seen – and when I stood in front of Leonardo's *The Last Supper* in Milan.

What are you most scared of?

The death of my partner, looking stupid, becoming poor, not being able to see, not being able to walk.

When did you last vomit and why?

I don't vomit often, but I massively did so after a lunch in Paris during which Roman Polanski made me eat oysters. I passed out on the way home, was raced to hospital and was told that if I eat oysters again I will (a) vomit a lot again and (b) die.

Tell us a secret?

When you go to the movies you get a plenary indulgence – absolution.

Which celebrity could you take in a fight?

Deadpool.

If you could be reincarnated as an animal, which animal would it be?

An Arctic tern. They live for up to 30 years and migrate from the Arctic, down the coast of Africa or the Americas, to Tasmania. They see the world every year, from on-high.

What have you most enjoyed watching on the small screen during lockdown?

Kazakh films. *Borat* sends me back to the great, humanistic, sophisticated films made in Kazakhstan.

What have you most enjoyed watching on the big screen since cinemas reopened?

François Ozon's *Summer of 85*. It's set in an un-fancy seaside resort in France, the end of a bus route perhaps.

FIRST LIFE, SECOND LIFE OR, *FIRST CASE, SECOND CASE* REVISITED

A letter to my younger self, about watching
Abbas Kiarostami's film *First Case, Second Case*.

Dear 14-year-old Mark,

I'm writing to you from the future. It's 2013 here and
1979 there, where you are, in Belfast, Northern Ireland.
I'm 48 and you're 14. You're in our first life, youth. I'm
in our second life, middle age.

I'm writing to you about a movie. You're already in
love with movies, and I'm glad to tell you that you will
remain in love with them, you lucky thing. The film I
want to tell you about is called *First Case, Second Case.*
It was made in 1979, where you are now. Maybe it is

being filmed as you read this. It was made by Abbas Kiarostami, an Iranian director, one of the world's greatest. I've filmed with him a bit.

It's December here in 2013. The wind is blowing a gale outside, but I'm cosy inside, lying on a sofa, watching the film on something called a laptop. It's nearly midnight. The world feels asleep. My Christmas tree is twinkling in the corner of the room.

I'm writing to you about the film because I haven't seen it. I know that's weird, but I want to see it and describe my reactions to you as I watch it "live". There's something, these days, called live blogging. I'd like to live blog to you back to the future, across the years. I'm also writing to you because you love *Star Wars*, *Grease*, Hitchcock movies and Orson Welles' *Touch of Evil*, films that are highly engineered, that have seductive surfaces. Films that gleam. 34 years later, I still love films that gleam, but I also love films that don't gleam. *First Case, Second Case* most certainly doesn't. It's rough to the eye. I want to write to you about gleaming and roughness, Mark, and how you – we – moved from the first to both. Gleaming is like the first case, roughness is like the second. Is your attraction to the gleaming cinema of Hollywood less mature than my attraction to the rough surfaces of Iranian cinema? I think not, young Mark. I think that your taste for gleaming is hope. You are bedazzled by life. I am too but, also, as my life has become hectic, I've come to admire quietude and stasis in movies. So let's watch *First Case, Second Case* together and see what it's like. Maybe it will be awful.

———

Wow, the sound and picture are even rougher than I expected. This is a very poor copy of the film, I fear. There's a roar and hiss on the soundtrack, and the imagery seems scratched and pixilated. The film seems so amateur, but that's no bad thing. Amateur means lover and Kiarostami's films are lovers. They express a love for life by focussing on very simple everyday events – car journeys, street encounters, conversations. He looks at such moments in great detail, as if he's unpeeling them like you'd unpeel an onion.

———

We're in a school. A teacher is at a blackboard, drawing an ear. There are many schools in Kiarostami's writing and filmmaking. He made a lovely short movie set in one, *Two Solutions for One Problem*. In the first half of it, two wee boys dislike each other, so destroy each other's jotters. In the second half, we see what could have happened if they hadn't decided to be destructive: the boys reconcile and become friends. I can already see that Kiarostami's film is very Iranian, but what a theme for Belfast in 1979, where you are now, Mark, too. Since you were born, in 1965, more than 2,000 people have been killed in the war in Northern Ireland.

I love the film's title, *Two Solutions for One Problem*. Are you and I, youth and middle-age, two solutions for one problem? The title's like that of the film we're now watching. Will it be in two halves too? Let's see.

Kiarostami has made other films about schools, too: his great film from 1986, *Where Is the Friend's House?*, is about one school friend searching for another. Schools were almost mythic places for him, like Greek fora where ideas and ideals are tried out and discussed.

It was important to try out and discuss new ideas in Iran in 1979 because, in that very year, the country was undergoing a revolution. It had just thrown out its elitist Shah of the Pahlavi dynasty, who had reigned for 38 years. His regime valued glamour and wealth and silenced dissent with great brutality. In its place came a new order which sounded, at first, as if it would be more equitable but, in a short time, became more brutal than its predecessor. *First Case, Second Case* was made right in the middle of this bloody hand over, this botched re-think.

———

When the teacher's back is turned, one of the boys makes a drumming noise on his desk. This irritates the teacher but, when he turns around to see who's doing it, the drumming stops. The film's plot seems to be getting going. This reminds me of a brilliant Iranian film that Kiarostami wrote but didn't direct, *Willow and Wind*. It is set in a classroom. A teacher is angry at the boys because one of them has broken a window. It starts to rain, which distracts them because they haven't seen rain before. *Willow and Wind* is a masterpiece because it sees poetics in each moment. The teacher starts to talk about rain, to make a kind of lesson about rain.

But back to our film. Before we get into the plot, we notice the simplicity of the close-ups. There are no camera moves, no fancy angles. We see the teacher and the boys square-on, as if they are painted by Cimabue in Italy in the fourteenth century. This is Cimabue's *The Capture of Christ*, in San Francesco in Assisi in Italy. It's so unfrivolous. Christ is seen square on, without much expression, with little depth to the image. Just like Kiarostami's lads.

And then there are shots of the boys' faces stacked, with very little perspective, like pre-Renaissance art. Is this why, for all its roughness, the film is already starting to feel sacred?

The teacher turns his back again, and the banging restarts. He tells the boys to leave the classroom and not come back until they are prepared to say. Seven of them – boys your age – walk out.

———

And then, suddenly, like they are out of the classroom, we are out of the film, Mark. We are watching it projected and a voice over asks someone – a parent – if the seven boys should name the culprit. A moral dilemma. A junction in the film's thinking. A caption tells us that the first person to answer the question is Noureddin Zarrinkelk, a filmmaker and writer of children's books. The second answer is a dad of one of the boys. The dad admires the boys' solidarity in not telling. He thinks that to do so would be to betray the guilty boy (like Judas betrays Christ by kissing him in Cimabue's image). The interviewees are taking a simple school room event and seeing principles in it, politics. The drumming is becoming a metonym, a way of naming a much bigger problem in Iranian society, in which many people have been committing acts of sabotage in the name of the revolution.

———

The debate continues, and starts to take over the film, making the school room scene something like an overture. Resisting naming names means that the students keep their integrity. But what is integrity? Keeping truth with yourself? Ali Mafakheri counters the prevailing view of the interviewees so far by saying that the kids should study. This place is a school, not a political rally. The film is now full of adults describing teenagers' thought processes, just like, in writing to you, I am imagining your thought processes.

Karim Zarrineh, a navy colonel, is next to talk. It's all men so far. Will we see any women in this film? Are these themes — solidarity, protest — gendered? And what of the men we are seeing? As the revolution curdled and turned sour, did their moralities prevent them from committing the ethical solecisms which the regime, under Ayatollah Khomeini, fall into? I have to say that, in their certainties and disregard for the teacher, some of these men are scaring me.

—

The men continue to defend their sons, Mark. Director Kiarostami's aim doesn't seem to be to solve the problem of whether the boys should inform on their friends. Rather, he seems to put on X-ray specs, to look into the bones of the problem. He does this almost gleefully. He relishes the fact that this tiny event in a school in Iran in 1979 is so layered and complex. I know from his other films that he loves the interiority of things. For him, moments in life are like Dr Who's TARDIS — small on the outside but big on the inside. Totalitarians tell us how big and noble we are, Kiarostami tells us that we are small and ignoble, and that that's good. It's easier to live up to. We want to be so small that we can dissolve into the sea or the dawn or a walk.

Talk of smallness makes me think of me, on this sofa, late at night, when the world's asleep. I feel like an atom. I take a photo of myself, but I dislike how I look in it. Vanity. So I take a second, and a third and fourth. A respite from watching this film and writing this essay to you. Taking these images feels like escaping from Kiarostami's school, his film, his ominous debate.

Here's the fifth image, the first I like. Its iris makes it look like silent cinema and captures how cocooned I feel tonight, on this sofa.

The tattoo on my arm, *Forough*, is the name of a great Iranian poet and filmmaker.

Here's what I'm scribbling to you as I watch the film:

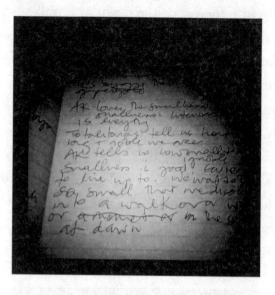

———

In the film within the film, time passes. They boys stand outside the school room all day Sunday, Monday and Tuesday. This is stretching it a bit. This wouldn't happen in real life; Kiarostami's extension of the time that they wait makes the moral deliberation bigger. The next interviewee is Kamal Kharazi, director of Kanoon, the Institute for the Intellectual Development of Children and Young Adults. What a brilliant name for an organisation, young Mark! I wish there had been a Kanoon in Belfast in 1979, as well as Tehran.

———

Then, at last, over thirteen minutes into the film, a woman appears. She's Ehteram Boroumand, Executive of Children's Programmes on Iranian TV. Someone says that "education is much more than meets the eye". This film is much more than meets the eye. And then Ezzatollah Entezami shows up! He's an art house movie star in Iran. I filmed with him once, took him back to the village where one of his most famous films, *The Cow*, was made.

Here, he disappoints me. A student has finally informed. Entezami says that, in doing so, he has "damaged the collective position". This might well be true, but it is machine talk. He's speaking of kids, young people your age, Mark. Would you like to be talked about in that way? Even as an adult, I find it hard to live up to such Marxist ideals. As I watch, I think how these adults are weighing the young people down.

And then, as if to add even more weight, a new interviewee makes this film about Freud as well as Marx. Jaleh Sarshar, Director of Educational Affairs at Kanoon, says that the boy who informed is acting against his own unconscious will. Sarshar's evidence for this is that the boy wrings his hands. Rob David Croft, religious leader of the Iranian Jewish Community, says that the informant's behaviour is right. He had to tell the truth.

———

I'm starting to hate these men, Mark. They keep talking about solidarity, but they seem like conformists. Bullies. The sort of bully boys that are in your school. As I think this, suddenly, onscreen, the person who you'd think would be the most conformist of them all says the film's best sentence so far. Ayatollah Sadegh Khalkhali, Religious Magistrate of the Revolutionary Courts, says "the child's humanity becomes a toy". Does he mean that these adults are toying with the young people, over-determining their actions? I hope so. And then this quotation, from the poet Hafez: "If you act violently for a good cause, the results will be the opposite." A very decent thing to say, but South Africa proved, for example, that this isn't always true. Is it true in Belfast in 1979? Or Tehran?

—

Around twenty-four minutes into the film, something happens, Mark, but I don't want to tell you what it is. I want to leave some things unsaid, unreported. What I can say is that the film's moral philosophy matures. Dr Ali Golzadeh Ghafouri says that, if we judge by the Islamic system of values, "it is better that a guilty man goes unpunished than an innocent suffers without reason." Better to under-, than over-, judge. Surely this is right. But then we hear "In a system based on Islamic values, there is no oppression allowed." Tell that to the thousands of Iranians imprisoned, persecuted or murdered by the country's elite since this film was made. Time has made *First Case, Second Case* seem naïve, or ironic, a fragment of evidence of the fact that things have gone badly wrong. A moral standing becomes a moral falling.

———

The film is coming to an end, Mark. Before it does so, Ayatollah Sadegh Khalkhali says, "One should approach this system in a way that values the children's souls," which is a decent stab at the truth. The truth for you, young Mark, of course, is that you are being bullied right now because you are brainy and unsporty.

The good news, my friend, is that the bullying will stop. You will escape the bullies. The bad news is that the people of Iran, some of the nicest people I've ever met, won't.

Mark Cousins

Three days later ...

I wonder if I am being naïve in writing about this film as I watch it for the first time, so I send my text to my Iranian friend, the film historian Ehsan Khoshbakht. He writes back to tell me what happened to some of the people in the film. Kharazi, the director of Kanoon, became Minister of Foreign Affairs in the 1997-2005 government of President Mohammad Khatami. The fathers have accents from different parts of Iran, to give a sense of the whole country joining in the debate, and the teacher's drawing of an ear on the blackboard is relevant because the film is about listening.

This information enriches the film for me, and I consider writing to my younger self to tell him these extra things, but then Ehsan writes:

> I think it would add a totally new layer to the film to know that Khalkhali was the notorious "hanging judge", one of the butchers of Tehran who killed many people, including teenagers. Or that one of the interviewees, Sadegh Ghotbzadeh, the director of national TV, was executed for treason by the very same Mullahs we see in the film. Or that Ebrahim Yazdi, also featured in the film, has been in and out of prison within the last 20 years ...
>
> They are all fooling us and that's why you disliked them. Your feelings haven't betrayed you

Mark. They all sound fake, and I believe that Kiarostami is quite aware of the theatricality of their talk. He acutely shows how the tone and sincerity of speeches, from ordinary people and politicians alike, change and become meaningless manifestations …

You are absolutely right, Mark, they are very scary people. And let's say that this is a film about the cruelty and absurdity of a world without poesy.

I don't want to tell my younger self these awful things. He will discover, in due course, that life can become poisonous. I don't want to scare him at the age of 14, so what is, here, in italics, is for your eyes, not his.

THE STORY OF LOOKING

Words from a film.

An autumn day.

I waken. My eyes open and my world begins. My visual world.

My eyes look outside. What's that orange light?

Seeing it reminds me of an orange dawn some years ago.

A dawn I'll never forget. How many dawns have I seen?

Back in my bedroom, my eyes see a tree.

I've seen it for 20 years. I've lived in this flat, in this city, for decades.

When I see the tree, he feels alive. When that tree is still going, growing, the world is still going, growing.

My brain isn't quite awake, but my eyes are.

Together they flash pictures in my head. A lifetime of looking.

That feather I saw on a train.

Those thermals.

My eyes saw a motorbike draw a line on a hill.

Myself in a bubble.

My eyes stared and stared at a power station near here, on the day it was to be blown up.

Decades of coal dust seemed to make a ghost.

—

After my shower, my eyes see this.

GUY ON ROOFTOP.

The scene reminds me of the power station. Of many things.

BACK TO ROOFTOP GUY.

Is the man over there OK? What can he see?

I can't take my eyes off that guy.

This shot makes me want to look. To go around his city for a day, with my eyes wide open.

To ride the thermals of looking.

I love this idea. But it's not the only reason for wanting to look, today.

Looking has been my joy, my world. But that world might be closing a bit.

Some months ago I did a DNA test ... and found that I have one of the genes for macular degeneration. The centre of my eyes might dim.

Then, a few weeks ago I found out something else. For ages I'd been trying to clean the left lens of his glasses. It was always dirty. Then I discovered … it wasn't dirty. My eye had gone cloudy.

I got a diagnosis, It's a cataract. A bad one.

I suddenly felt old. Would I stop seeing those orange dawns. That tree?

I felt sad, like the guy on the roof looked sad. Or was I exhilarated?

Both.

Today these emotions are intensified, because, tomorrow morning, someone's going to cut into my left eye, suck out the lens that I was born with, and add in a plastic one. It'll be a fixed width, so my brain won't be able to full focus from close-up to far away. And it might make the world look bluer than my right eye does.

My sight dimming and the idea of my eye being cut open is making me think about what I've seen. In the day before my operation, I'd like to tell a story of our looking lives.

The great French painter Paul Cézanne wrote in a letter the "optical experience that was *developing*" within him. Did he mean developing like a photo develops in a darkroom? So what has developed in me? How has the visual world grown in me?

And, how has it developed in you?

MORNING.

The brightness of the day, the bustle, the buzz. I feel hit by these things, by the everyday street outside in my city, Edinburgh, and by its vistas.

So much to see here.

Where do I begin to tell the story of my looking?

—

FIRST THINGS I REMEMBER? A BEACH IN DONEGAL. TALKING ABOUT BLURRING, CYCLOPS.

So where does our story start?

I started life as a baby, of course.

In real life, a baby first sees ... blurs.

When I later saw Ingmar Bergman's film *Persona*, I wondered if I ever reached out to my mum's face like this.

Did I want to touch the blur, the out-of-focus world?

But blurs are failures, aren't they? Babies see blurs because their eyes haven't developed. When I shot this in Venice, I remember wishing I could see the buildings more clearly. A blurred photo is a rubbish photo. Or is it?

I think of this Japanese painting from 1595 by Hasegawa Tōhaku. Seven of the pine trees are blurred. The image is at its best in its blurs. It's like the out-of-focus trees are ghosts of the others, a world floating around them. Italian painters called their similar blurring sfumato. Fumo means smoke. A smoke screen. Cataract art.

SUNSET BOULEVARD.

When I saw this famous movie as a kid, I remember thinking that the ending looked like a smoke screen. But it wasn't a mistake. It was expressive, an enhancement.

And then the blurs developed, like Paul Cézanne's optical experiences developed. I glanced. I saw ... a mobile world.

A lifetime of motion began.

Did we really see that?

Shimmer.

Tremble.

The relationship between motion and emotion.

Art was made to show this emotion. A man's joy, and a frame filming him which moves to echo the joy, to ride its thermals.

BACK TO THE BABY.

Often the movement I saw seemed abstract, like an insect:
Dreamlike.

My whole life as movement.

Today, the day before my eye operation, I'm so aware of movement. The number of eye movements when I cross the road. My head on a pivot, scanning for safety. A bit trickier now that I can't see well with my left eye.

Blurs then movement. What was the next visual step in my infancy?

A magnetic attraction to the eyes of others. Hundreds of thousands of years ago, on the savannah grasslands, there were about two people per square mile, but far more animals, so humans looked more into the eyes of animals.

Soviet director Andrei Tarkovsky gives us a flash of this, a solitary boy sees a goat's eyes, square on.

Are we scared by this look? Or do we feel like the animal? Included in its visual world.

In this city of Edinburgh, in which we're travelling in today, there are nearly 5,000 people per sq. mile. It's hard to avoid the electric shock of a look. In the New York Savanna there are 26,000 people per sq. mile. Eye saturation. Glances everywhere. Bring a book on the subway to avoid them.

And so, artist Marina Abramović sat for 736 hours in the Museum of Modern Art in New York, not avoiding the eye contact. She stared at people like Tarkovsky's goat, for what seemed forever. She cancelled out the avoidance, the flight from looking. It was exhausting. Tears came.

After blurs, movement, and eye contact, what did I notice next? How did my visual world advance?

Through colour.

One of the first colours I will have seen in my life, one of the biggest colours I have seen in my life. Blue.

I've been seeing blue all my life of course. My car was blue.

All those blues when I went to Niagara Falls.

But is blue everywhere? Not once are the sky or sea called blue in Homer's writings, or in the Bible.

Homer says the sea is wine-coloured or has a sheen. Maybe the sky and sea were so big, so bright, so distant, that their blueness hardly registered for ancient writers.

It certainly registered for French artist Yves Klein who, in his teens, lay on his back and signed the Mediterranean sky with his finger.

The number of times I've laid on my back and looked up at a summer sky. It's black up there, but I see blue, refracted. Hard to focus on, oblivious.

People threw meaning at blue. They played with it. I think of one of cinema's great colourists, Chinese director Zhang Yimou.

He staged a lake fight. Distant blue, then underwater, cast blue. Then their costumes. The shades of blue multiply. And the water, aquamarine. A fight for it, and a tear on her cheek.

And blue registered for Vincent van Gogh, who knew that most shadows aren't grey, they're ... blue.

And blue mattered for Leonardo da Vinci. The virgin's dress and the blue of the rocks and sky, so strong, such an affinity for each other.

This could be called a study in blue and gold.

Talk about affinity for each other. They're everywhere, blue and gold I saw them in the Imam mosque in Isfahan in Iran, the most beautiful building I've ever seen. When I walked around it, I thought of the beaches of my childhood.

Maybe that's what Paul Cézanne meant by optical development? Unlikely visual connections being made? Colours encrusting with memories.

And blue and gold occur a lot in nature.

The great writer Goethe understood such affinities of colour. Colour on opposite sides of his colour wheel long for each other.

On my walk, I think of the colours I've seen on my travels. A cherry blossom tree here in Edinburgh is the same as a shop in America.

Muted in Albania.

Grey and red in Los Angeles.

And back here in Scotland.

On a holiday a few years ago, I saw the same place in two colours, transformed.

———

When, in my visual development, in my looking life, did I first notice light? Maybe the cosy glow of a Christmas tree? Maybe in an old Hollywood melodrama on TV when I was about ten?

People unveiled, and veiled. Light made life gorgeous and shocking I began to realise that light's not one story, it's lots of stories.

In a city like this, which is dark in winter ... you look for light.

It lifts you if you're low.

Like a fresh start. I remember the lift of dawn light when I was in primary school.

Like you're docking.

Or turning into something else.

I loved those feelings. I've carried them with me.

From my bus today I see this kind of acropolis in our city, our Athens of the North, and think of the other Acropolis.

What if we think of it not as a temple or a fortress, just as something transformed by light: light that lifts, that celebrates.

And in the Middle Ages, they talked of two different types of light. The first, lux, was everyday light that you see with your eyes. The second, lumen, was spiritual light, the sort of light that took you to rapture or pain. (I know more about rapture and pain now than I did when I was 10.)

This Egyptian Pharaoh had a religious conversion about light. He became a worshipper of the Sun – Aten – and so changed his name to Akhenaten. Arrows of sunlight go out to him and his wife, Nefertiti.

Lifting, transforming, celebrating, worshipping.

Electric light brought something new again.

It meant people could work longer into the night, and often be exploited more.

Home life became brighter, more extended.

And cities?

Lightscapes. From childhood I've preferred Northern cities. The South in the summer is blinding.

In Finland, a boy, the kind of northern evening I've always loved. The lightscape behind him, the sky's gloaming. No colour, just light. Then the train's light, and water like sparks, like falling light. Sci-fi light. Dream light.

When puberty happens, when adolescence happens, you feel your world kind of smash.

Of course, in those teenage years, you start to look at yourself. And you look at your body and you think *What is this thing?*

The best thing about me is my legs. My legs walked across some of the great cities in the world.

New York, Berlin, Moscow, Los Angeles, Paris, Mumbai, Delhi, Tehran, London, Belfast, Cardiff, all those cities. Dublin.

—

I grew up. Became a teenager.

I saw myself. My visual world developed again. It became more excited and troubled.

Whatever else there is, there's always something of a shock when we look at ourselves. French painter Gustave Courbet seems shocked. What does he see? — his ego? Beauty? Neurosis? Aliveness?

He pulls his hair back and seems to say *is that really me?* He was about twenty-four.

Marie-Geneviève Bouliard saw something else when she looked at herself in the late 1700s. Was it self-satisfaction? Her head lifted and turned a bit to glimpse its shape, its setting, her setting.

Frida Kahlo was less edified by what she saw, but was compelled to look. Her self-portrait, on a plinth, on the border between Mexico and the United States. The smoke, factories and skyscrapers on the right show the America she hated. The flowers and cacti, ancient sculpture, pyramid and electric spark between sun and moon on the left are symbols of the elemental Mexico she preferred.

Or are they? Is it that simple?

Kahlo was a modernist and leftist, so she was not averse to smokestacks. It says FORD on them, and she'd just had a miscarriage at the Henry Ford clinic, so the image starts to seem as much about loss as nation. The sun, top left, has its echo in the orange heater in the bottom right.

Kahlo is like the balancing act in this nation-dream.

I feel a bit between countries too. I'm Irish, Scottish, British I suppose ... The imagery of those different places. I'm in each place. I see myself in each place.

See yourself. It's hard not to these days.

Thirty billion or so selfies are posted each year. The majority are by women.

Some people say that selfies are narcissistic. But isn't there snobbery in such denunciation?

It's OK when artists picture themselves, but when, for the first time in human history, most people can, it's called banal.

Yet look at what people mostly take selfies of. Either themselves having fun, or in famous places. Or celebrating a feeling, trying to hold on to a feeling. Pleasure, being there or the moment.

Isn't that universal? And even endearing? A love of the moment? A response to time passing?

And beyond myself in my teens, what did I see? People I liked. Other bodies. I felt the cattle prod of that.

These two teenagers are looking through the fish tank but also through their own emotions, anticipation.

I was 13 when I saw this.

The desire to run after a body. Her satin hips. His lips. He was floored by looking. The joy. The submission. There was danger ahead of those teenage years. Black against yellow. You could almost see the force field.

On the internet, now, bodies are everywhere. Too much to see, to shock, to exploit, to distort.

It's bad to look this much at bodies, isn't it?

It's always been so. So we're told. So the Irish Catholic world said when I was a teenager. A story from the ancient world tells us something about how we look at bodies. Actaeon has been hunting with his dogs. He comes across the goddess Diana, on the extreme left, and her companions. They're naked. To punish him for looking, she turns him into a stag. The antlers on his head show that the transformation has started. When complete, his dogs tear him to pieces.

Punished for looking!

Is that what we are when we look? Stags?

When I was a teenager I saw this scene in an Australian film, *Walkabout*. I wanted to be with her, but also be her. Aquatic, free, innocent, weightless.

Did that make me a stag?

I recently saw this jellyfish, and wanted to float weightless like it, so I floated near it. I loved it.

I was naked. I'm the opposite of the goddess Diana in the painting.

I don't mind being seen naked. Does that make me an exhibitionist? Or an object in your eyes? And does it make you a voyeur, a stag?

Nazi-era photographer Leni Riefenstahl, writhing in front of someone's camera lens. She sympathised with a violently racist regime, and then, as a photographer, went to the Sudan and became interested in images again. She was clothed, white, female, European and in her seventies. He was – what – 19? And naked. She had the power. He looks like a byzantine Christ icon. And she leads him like a child.

A boy called Adam. The Idomeni Refugee camp at the Greek-Macedonian border. I ask her mum if it's OK to film him. Yes, she says. They've travelled from Syria. His eyes, his looking, are taken by my camera. It keeps on recording.

Regardless.

I don't take my camera from him, because it's a toy now.

Is this without regard? Is this bad looking?

Voyeurism? It's so easy to see, now. But what do we do with this seeing?

Are we like this woman? She's from Weimar in Germany. It's the end of World War Two, and she's been taken to the concentration camp of Buchenwald, to be shown the bodies of some of the 56,000 murdered in her name.

But she turns her head away, and covers her eyes – a double refusal to look.

She should look.

But should we look when we slow down as we pass a car crash?

Or should we look at this?

Purportedly a woman being beheaded in Saudi Arabia in 2019. Do we force ourselves to face this atrocity? Does showing the footage around the world help women like her?

When I was having my shower this morning, I saw a homeless woman I know looking through our bins outside. It was very early. She didn't want to be seen. Did I violate her by seeing her?

I wanted to get to the end of my story of looking today, before nightfall, before my eye is cut open.

But October is doing its thing, warming the light, sinking the sun, hardening the ground, lengthening the shadows.

I wanted to talk about politics and adulthood today. But, instead, I'm starting to feel afraid. I don't want someone to stick a knife in my left eyeball tomorrow. I can't help thinking of a 90-year-old movie eye slice, moon slice, cow slice. A dream that Luis Buñuel had had.

I look every which way. Can you look in panic?

What images have developed in me after all these years? I try to think of the picture of my granny on my phone. Ray Charles.

THE NEXT DAY.

I can feel my heart beating, so I try to think of places I love.

They give me a sedative.

As they prepare to cut into my eye, I think of what it's seen, Cézanne's optical development.

Dr Pankaj Agarwal.

He's Bengali, from Kolkata.

A place I love.

I think of the Bengali film *Devi*.

A dream sequence I'll never forget. Three drawn eyes in the darkness, then two disappear, then Sharmila Tagore, lit from below. Her stare.

Throughout my life, movies have been my extra eyes. I think of another film, *Rien Que Les Heures*. A screen full of eyes, like cut-outs.

The film is about Paris, the eyes tell us that we look at the city in loads of ways.

Like I looked at Edinburgh yesterday?

And as the operation begins, my mind combines Sharmila's eyes and the Paris eyes, and comes up with the dream sequence from Alfred Hitchcock's *Spellbound*. Eyes like stars. Designed by Salvador Dalí.

Is the sedative making me visualise?

Even if I went blind today, I'd have those eyes, those movies, in my head. Is that what Ray Charles meant at the beginning of this film? I'd be able to play those picture games in my head.

How intimate.

Pankaj cuts through the front of my eye.

He breaks up my cataract.

He inserts a new folded-up lens. It looks like the birth of an insect.

The lens has curvy arms.

I feel like I'm underwater.

I see what looks like a cave. I draw it later.

Days afterwards, Dr Pankaj sends me pictures of paintings of what some of his other patients saw as he removed their cataracts.

I'm under the knife for 21 minutes. Long enough for your mind to wander, your inner eye to wander.

Thinking of Dr Pankaj and Sharmila Tagore, made my mind skip to another Bengali film, *The Music Room.*

It's about an old man. His life is narrowing. He stands in his music room and sees its chandelier reflected in his whisky glass.

A tiny world, a microcosm.

The scene makes me think of a dance number from the film *42nd Street.* Geometric. Like a flower. Another microcosm, another rock pool.

And from that my mind's eye goes to electron microscope images.

New types of seeing, way beyond the visible world. A microverse.

Like we're underwater. This is a marine alga covered in scales.

And the thought that this is a kind of dot, made me think of dot paintings like this.

Georges Seurat seemed to want to make his pictures out of atoms.

Writer Gertrude Stein said that "Seurat's eyes ... began to tremble at what his eyes were seeing, he began to doubt if – in looking – he could see."

My eyes are trembling.

I'm scared again. In much of the Middle East and North Africa, there's the evil eye.

In ancient Egypt, the Eye of Ra showed the destructiveness of the sun god.

Nazars bounce such bad intentions back on themselves.

And look up inside one of the world's great buildings – Hagia Sofia a mosque that was a church – and what do we see? An eye, surely.

THE OPERATION IS OVER.
MARK GETS INTO A WHEELCHAIR.

The Islamic dome makes me think of something else.

Iraq.

In the 800s, Hunayn ibn Ishaq, lived there. He wrote *Book of the Ten Treatises of the Eye*. In one drawing in the book, the eye's in the middle. The outside world is below, the inner world of the brain is above.

Hunayn said that a kind of circulatory air – he called it pneuma – travels out from the brain, down the red curving lines in the image, enters the eye from the back, then travels out, into the world, hits an object, and is reshaped by it. Then the reshaped pneuma travels back into the eye and further back to the brain. And that's how Hunayn thought we see.

One hundred and fifty years later, also in what is now Iraq, a man called Alhazen argued the opposite. He said that when we look, rays come to us not from us.

Looking is a kind of invasion, it colonises us. It is a submission to the world. We spend our lives managing that invasion.

Alhazen has a crater on the moon named after him.

And his face is on Iraqi money.

We now know that Hunayn was wrong to think that waves come out of our eyes. And yet. New studies are showing that in a way he was not far off.

Neuroscience has found that, when we look, twice as many electrical signals move from the back of our brains to the front than from the front to the back. We're projecting when we look, like Norma Desmond, we see what we know, what's in our past. It's more about us than the outside world. That's why, under the knife, I was seeing so much.

A few hours later.

My eye feels sore, like it has broken glass in it.

I want to rip this eye mask off.

What did I see yesterday and today? What is the story of looking? Just as we have our work lives, our family lives, our sex lives, we also have our looking lives.

How many sunsets have you seen? How many dead bodies?

They are inside you, those things. We add to them sometimes. And, often, we project.

MARK TAKES OFF EYE MASK.
CRIES.
NOW WE SEE HIM AS AN OLD MAN, IN WIDE SHOT.

That feels like half a lifetime ago.

I moved to Sweden in 2013 … and, no wait, before that I should tell you that the operation back then was a success. They showed me scans of my left eye before …

And after.

I could see so clearly with my new eye. The world looked fresher.

And it's still there, that plastic lens. My right eye has faded a bit, but the macular degeneration was treated and is OK.

This left eye? Thirty years after its lens was replaced?

It's seen many Swedish summers. And about ten years ago, it saw this.

WHITE MOOSE.

In Värmland.

It went into the picture book in my head.

Paul Cézanne never came here, to Sweden, so he never saw a white moose.

I just recently discovered that he wrote that phrase "the optical experience that develops in us" in the last year of his life. He was old when he realised that his looking life had developed, like I'm old. And in this old age he felt as if he'd only started looking properly, acutely! I went to his house in France and snapped off a bit of branch.

When you're old, you've seen a million things.

Ingrid Bergman aged 63, here in Sweden.

Her red eyes and lips. Warm, aged colours. She looks left, to the thing that moves her to tears.

1942. Ingrid again, 36 years earlier, over a century ago now.

Same composition, again looking left. More burnished lighting. It's almost mythic. What would older Ingrid think of when she looked back at her younger self? She'd see 36 years of looking. She might think "what those eyes have seen". She was brought up in the dark winters of Sweden but then became a movie star in California's constant sunlight-floodlight.

She'd know what that woman in 1942 wouldn't know — that the Nazis would be defeated, that she'd have four children, that she'd reject Hollywood gloss to make new, more visually realistic, movies. Perhaps only when she was older could she see herself young. The waterfall of herself. Always the same waterfall, never the same water. Perhaps she'd see calm because she'd known tumult. Perhaps she'd feel loved, because she'd been unloved. She'd see the story of her looking.

I've come to realise that late looking is often comparing. When we look at these two Bergmans, we see our own aging in them, or we see time.

They think some sharks might be over 400 years old.

Could it have started looking before Martin Luther said that the visual world was idolatrous? Before Catherine the Great tried to turn St Petersburg into a palace?

And how do we know the age of such sharks? When they died, scientists cut out the lenses of their eyes, and measured the amount of carbon-14 in them.

The memories, discoveries, fears, and shocks of looking.

SCENE FROM *CITIZEN KANE.*

Here's a shock. A grand office for a small guy in his massive chair. The camera slowly tracks in, as if drawn to a story, a memory, a visual memory.

Has a month gone past without me thinking of this guy? Maybe. But not a year.

I never saw his face. I never saw what he saw.

———

What a story we've had.

We've wondered how others saw.

GUY ON ROOF.

We've reached through time. I've imagined myself as a jellyfish, a stag. We've expanded beyond ourselves.

And when you expand, what's the limit?

When a bird sees this, they see what? An oyster shell? A falls?

A year ago, I was in Stonehaven in Scotland.

I took out my camera and filmed this:

ROCKPOOL.

I thought of my looking life. The tree reminded me of the Iranian films of Abbas Kiarostami. I wanted to plunge in and float naked like the seaweed, like a jellyfish, (but I'm too old for that).

I thought of something Virginia Woolf wrote:

> "The eye is not a miner, not a diver, not a seeker after buried treasure. It floats us smoothly down the stream ... resting, pausing ... the brain sleeps as it looks."

I thought of all the buried visual treasure in my head.

I knew it's time for me to sleep soon.

But I felt ... what's the word? Joy. Total joy at being able to see the slalom of the seaweed.

The wind came up. There was more tremble, undulation, power.

And I realised that ... Ray Charles was wrong.

He said that he feels sorry for those of us who have to put up with seeing some of the things in modern life.

But we don't put up with what we see.

I don't put up.

It isn't a burden.

It's the opposite of burden.

What's the word?

I can't think of the word.

But I can picture it.

THE END.

WHAT IS THIS FILM CALLED LOVE?

Words from a movie.

So the story began. It wasn't much of a story, to be honest. As you're about to see, it had no heroics. Or romance. Or even events. It was about a guy who's always doing something, doing nothing. It was Sunday 23 October. Two o'clock. The guy was on this airplane. He was bored. He was watching this cup. Then he looked out the window. He saw Mexico below. He'd been in Mexico for 10 days and was now flying into Mexico City.

His flight out again wasn't for three days. And he had nothing planned for those three days. Nothing. Which was rare for him.

So, what would he do in this city, the biggest city in the western world, for three days? He doesn't even speak Spanish. He didn't know it yet but he was about to have a thought about these three days. He wouldn't check emails for three days, or phone anybody, or shave. He'd just let life drift by. People watch.

He checked in to this hotel. That amateur thing? That's what he was shooting this film on. The camera lens is fixed, so he wouldn't really be able to get near people in this film. And he had no sound equipment, so he wouldn't be able to do interviews. His last film took six years to make and ran 15 hours. So this time he wanted to make a tiny film. An amateur film.

This was the very moment he had his thought. He realised that Mexico City is the place where one of his heroes, Soviet filmmaker Sergei Eisenstein, came alive.

Lying here he looked like he was thinking of nothing, but his mind was ticking over. He was remembering a cramped old apartment, not much bigger than this hotel room, that he visited in Moscow earlier that year. It was dusty and musty and full of Eisenstein's stuff. After seeing it, he re-read Eisenstein's books.

He realised he'd never seen the film, *¡Que viva México!*, that Eisenstein made here in Mexico.

So he looked online. And it was on YouTube. So, he watched it.

———

He woke. And he had an idea that morning, his first day. A few years ago, for no particular reason, he walked around the forbidden city in Beijing with a picture of an old Chinese movie star. And he felt that she was with him. So that morning he printed a picture of Eisenstein. And asked the hotel clerk what the Spanish is for "laminate". It's *enmacar*. So he *enmacared* the picture ...

At first the guy had felt a bit stupid walking along talking to a picture, but then he started to get drawn *in* to his chat with Eisenstein. He even crossed roads without looking up. In Mexico City, of all places.

———

She was one of 21 million people in this city.

———

Seeing the woman made the guy sad. It was afternoon. The guy had walked twelve miles. He'd been scribbling notes as he walked.

He stopped. Drank a beer. The beer made him happy, loved-up, like he was disappearing into the afternoon. He has friends in Mexico City. They texted him saying "let's go to a tequila bar" but he didn't. He liked being alone, looking around, filming stuff. The only person in the world who knew where he was, was the guy who just brought him a beer.

———

These thoughts made the guy scribble, in his note-book, five things to do with ecstasy and Eisenstein and Mexico and, after two beers, like a cheap gumshoe, he decided to spend the rest of the day looking for the five things. Suddenly he had a quest. Mmm. He was turning doing nothing into doing something. His friends would roll their eyes.

His imaginary quest began. He filmed the first thing to do with ecstasy from the café where he was sitting.

———

His search for what Eisenstein meant by ecstasy gave him something to look for.

———

From the protest, he walked for two more hours. North. To the Zócalo, the city centre. The Spanish paved it with stones from an Aztec temple they destroyed. Then it became a garden. 18,000 Mexicans once got naked here.

He had a song in his head, a song his mum loved, "Avenues and Alleyways" by Tony Christie.

He sang it to himself and walked to its rhythm.

After seeing the man on the bus, he sat again. Drank wine now. His legs were sore. The wine numbed the pain a bit. The bar played Elvis Presley's song "Suspicious Minds". It played it loudly.

The guy wanted to dance on the table. He always wants to dance.

He did indeed ache. And now that he was back in his hotel, he thought of Robert Frost's poem about apple-picking. A guy has been up a ladder picking them all day. He gets home and can still feel the pressure of the rung of the ladder on the instep of his foot.

And the guy had today on his body. The grime of the city mixed with sweat on his face and neck. And his hips joints were sore. If he walked for nine hours, and did two steps a second, he'd taken 64,000 steps today. But still his thoughts kept going.

He was building up to telling Sergei something.

He didn't know he'd be making this film about Eisenstein, but he wanted to say "this is how you make me feel Sergei Eisenstein".

His girlfriend Gill filmed him. Her hands were less shaky. It was totally silent. He scrambled up to a piece of turquoise rock and wrote something on it.

He's unsure about himself and about this film, for example, whether it's boring, but he's not shy about his body. When he takes his kit off, he forgets all those worries.

And yet again, that mind of his whirred. He thought of Edmund Husserl's idea of retention, how a body holds on to things it has left behind. His body remembered today. He thought that today he had probably found what Eisenstein meant by ecstasy. But tomorrow he would realise that he hadn't. He'd discover that it's something else, something simpler. He fell into a deep sleep.

———

He woke. It was Tuesday, his second day. He lay in bed and thought of his girlfriend, and from her he thought of last month when they were driving in America. He was sad that the drive was over and this sadness made him think of an essay called "Good-Bye to All That". He cried when he first read it – a bit pathetic really. Its second line is ...

"I can remember now, with a clarity that makes the nerves of my neck constrict, when New York began for me, but I cannot remember the moment it ended ... "

The memories cast their spell. He felt them and then, slowly, he saw them, and then he heard them ... the memory was as real as the bed in which he lay ... or so it seemed.

He started another bit of filming back there in America, before Mexico. He wanted to make a small film about endings. About leaving. He'd been at a film festival called Telluride, and, when he left it, he climbed up to this waterfall and realised that he wanted to make a film called *Leaving Telluride*, to thank the people there. And so he filmed the leaving ... in Asia people say that when we look at where the waterfall hits the water, we see the claws of a dragon.

His car went forward of course, but for him this was a leaving shot.

(a Frank O'Hara poem)

Have you forgotten what we were like then
when we were still first rate
and the day came fat with an apple in its mouth

it's no use worrying about Time
but we did have a few tricks up our sleeves
and turned some sharp corners ...

I wouldn't want to be faster
or greener than now if you were with me O you
were the best of all my days

They passed along here and noticed something whizz by. A yellow ribbon. He remembered that there's a painting of a yellow ribbon in Pompeii. Nowadays it means waiting for a loved one. Here in America it sometimes means that the loved one is a hostage. Or support the military.

In his memory, at night they went to Mesa Verde. The moon was out so, instead of going to a café for food, they sat under a blanket and ate potato crisp sandwiches and watched it "revealing itself like a pearl". They laughed. They drank cheap red wine.

He thought of a Norman MacCaig poem.

Let's choose a pretty word, say, *evening*,
And climb through it into the past,
Or stand on a towering If, surveying
The rosy kingdoms we have lost.

From every corner creep a thousand
Boredoms saying, *Greet us. We're life*.
Let's round the sunset up and milk it
Into a jug and drink it off.

Or in the hawthorn let us tangle
Our dreary look like gossamer
To shudder with that sparrow's chirping
And when the dew falls be on fire.

Or drag the distance home and chain it
There in the corner of the room
To charm us with its savage howling
And beg for fragments of our dream.

There's a clue somewhere. Can you find it?
Can you say over and over again
"Love", till its incantation makes us
Forget how much we are alone?

The next day, they drove to Monument Valley, where some of the great movie Westerns were shot. He expected to think of John Wayne when he was there. But he didn't.

The place was far bigger than the movies. He thought of his dad. And slim Whitman. And Frank O'Hara's line "I want to be at least as alive as the vulgar." And he was.

In his memory of that trip this looked like a painted backdrop, but it's not. The signs turned their back to him to stare at the buttes. Like they were leaving. The red car looked as if it'll fall off over the edge of the black road . . . but then the tiny white car in the distance came from where the red one was going. The buttes made a peristyle of the state.

As he lay in bed, he wanted to be here again.

They drove some more. Each mile leaving a mile of life behind. Then they stopped and got out of the car like they do in *Jurassic Park*, amazed at what they saw.

A russet place, like Saturn, called The Valley of the Gods. Totally non-indifferent, as Sergei Eisenstein said.

They thought of nothing except water and rattlesnakes and the fact that they'd remember this moment forever.

And this is where the guy got his kit off. The only sensible thing to do, he thought. A nod to Eisenstein.

He hated putting his clothes back on again.

But he did. And they drove some more. Along the Colorado River Valley.

They stopped again.

The girl sat by the river and read. The guy climbed up the river's course and found this deserted place.

And he saw this leaf. Trilling. Flickering. Because he was such a movie nut, it looked like the movies to him.

And then the leaf reminded him of something else, further back in his memories.

—

He didn't leave the leaf lying there. He picked it up and took it with him, maybe for another 22 years. From the German leaf, his memory rushed forward again and skipped an ocean, as memories do, to his recent American trip with his girlfriend. To a place called Professor Valley Road. It was so beautiful that he looked down. The dusty earth made him think of the beaches in Donegal in Ireland in his boyhood. Forty years ago. And then he raised his eyes ...

Here plunging into there. He wanted to be there, to lose himself in it, forever.

He backed away, and got into the car, and drove on.

And then, lying in bed in his second morning in Mexico City, the guy remembered what it felt like to leave those Saturn landscapes and fly to Toronto, for work.

In his memory the arrival looked like something out of the film *Metropolis*. They ate a lot in Toronto, walked in the rain and looked at the city's own brick beauty.

The guy went to a Toronto beach. Tiny people walked behind grass.

And then the girl went home. And time passed. And then the guy was in northern California. And driving over this famous bridge.

To Mill Valley. For work again. Away from home again.

Autumn had come to Northern California. Spiders spun webs on those days. The webs caught wasps, but then the wasps went.

The guy walked on, over a hill. But on the way, this caught his eye. The movies again.

He walked under a motorway and came to where the cinema was.

After work the guy walked again. It was a hot autumn day. In the distance, on the horizon, he saw San Quentin prison. Johnny Cash played there. Charles Manson was there. There's a gas chamber there for killing people. You can get a college degree there.

It dawned on him that prisons invented treadmills so that you can walk without going anywhere. And he thought of Hitler's architect Albert Speer who did a walk around the world in his prison cell, using maps and books, to imagine the journey.

It was scorching by now and he lay down. When he did he saw a line in the sky and was lying on a line, and so filmed both.

After he moved on he realised that he was walking on the San Andreas Fault line and so, where he had been lying will, one day, burst open.

And as he lay there on his second day, as morning went on, his memories came up to date. He remembered where he was before he went to Mexico City. He was in Mexico. This town. Morelia. His head was like mince, and so he could think of nothing, so, in his memories, he just looked at Morelia. Its shadows. Like de Chirico. Its colour. Its lads. Its churches. A lonely tree. A chewing gum tree.

And then crowds gathered in Morelia. The guy heard why. He could hardly believe it. The body of Pope John Paul II was being carried through the streets and was about to arrive.

———

No he didn't turn his back. He looked. And this is what he saw. Fireworks.

The body . . .

———

. . . on a catafalque. Candles.

———

He walked away. Excited and repelled. Remembering why he left religion . . . thinking that he's a Catholic is everything but faith.

Later, as he walked in Morelia, he heard that it *wasn't* the Pope's body after all. It was just a wax work of it, clutching, in its waxy hands, a phial of John Paul's real blood . . .

———

He'd walked ten miles today. He thought about the kids. He'd spent just ten minutes playing with them. As he did so he felt their age, but also like an old bloke staring at something he's left behind. He thought of what Ralph Waldo Emerson said: "Everything looks permanent until its secret is known." The kids looked permanent. He was glad he'd filmed them. They'd be permanent now. Leaving youth is hard.

In the heat of that day, he stopped again.

—

His story started about not very much, and now it's about even less, a fly ...

He walked more, then sat down beside the wheel of this truck.

He saw reflections in the shiny hub of the wheel. He didn't notice the small wheel behind the big wheel. He didn't know that when the truck drove off, he'd see what ecstasy means. Talk about a reveal.

—

That night, back in his hotel, he dreamed again.

The next day, his third in Mexico City.

—

But his story wasn't quite over. He got on his airplane and stared out the window. As he dozed off, this happened.

—

And then, to cap it all, there's something else that you should know about this story.

As the guy sat in the plane, an event occurred. It's not clear when or how. Maybe it was the wee bottles of wine. Or because he listened to Ike and Tina Turner's song "A Love Like Yours (Don't Come Knocking Every-day)". The muscles in his legs and arms spasmed. There were wild colours. Things in him reassembled. Flickered like a leaf, wafted like a sunflower. It became unclear who he was. I have no precise idea what happened in these seconds, but it was urgent, a kind of running. Thrilling. Sexual, funny.

And then he was me. He left manhood and became a woman, the woman who's been telling you this tale. Did you wonder how I knew what he did and thought? I knew because I am him.

And so, after three days of forays, not quite what I was (to say the least), I get back to the city where I live. Edinburgh. Scotland. The place looks different now. I've new pictures in my head. Don't know how long they'll last.

My friends say ... Oh! You look a bit different!

Yeah, I've been away.

Where?

Mexico. America.

What happened there?

Oh, not much. I went for a walk. Saw an old lady and a protest and the Pope. And I met some kids.

Wow, that's great! They say. Welcome back.

Thanks. Let's have a beer sometime.

I climb up to this castle and take out my mobile phone and throw it into the air and shoot it.

It splinters and looks lovely.

Virginia Woolf once wanted to go for a walk and so came up with an excuse.

She decided that she should go to buy … a pencil. The pencil wasn't the thing. The walking was. The city was.

She wrote. "As we step out of the house on a fine evening between four and six, we shed the self our friends know us by.

How beautiful a street is in winter. The eye floats us smoothly ... resting ... pausing. Let us dally a little longer ...

One catches a word in passing and, from a chance phrase, fabricates a lifetime.

... One can put on, briefly, the bodies and minds of others.

To escape is the greatest of pleasures; street haunting in winter, the greatest of adventures."

So this has been the small story of a guy who's on an airplane, and walked a lot and then became a girl. Old Virginia says that we can put on the bodies of others. And old Sergei says that ecstasy is getting out of yourself. So why don't I get out of myself again? Take leave again?

But if I turn into something else, what could it be?

— 2011 —

RUPTURE

A book begun in 2011, then abandoned.
I knew what I wanted to say in it, but not how.
Skip this section if you don't like naïve writing.

In 2008, aged 43, having been directing for nineteen years, I started to write a book about leaving the film industry. It was notes, fragments of journeys, a way of working out my future. I was physically tired and scunnered with movie conventions. My sister in-law Sandra and three close friends – Shiona, Shirley and Della – had died of cancer, and so endings were on my mind. I was starting to make the long documentary *The Story of Film: An Odyssey*, which would be a new breakthrough for me, a way out of the thicket. In what follows I'm trying to imagine it but, more than that, I'm imagining my own ending in cinema ...

I'm in Cannes, that Le Pennite former fishing village on the French Riviera that smells of dog shit but not the sea. Seaweed gives coastlines their smell and there's none here. I like to think that they comb the bay to remove it in early April, before the tourists arrive, so that the air isn't too pungent and sea-like, and so that it doesn't overwhelm the perfume of sun oil, the acid aroma of *vin rosé Provençal*, and the nose-nip of vinaigrette.

I've travelled here each May for the last sixteen years because the Cannes film festival is the movie world's annual trade fair. We, the film industry, flood the place each year like a film tsunami. Somehow, despite our exhaustion, insecurity and avarice, we find here a high tide of art cinema, the thing I love. Cannes is the anti-Oscars.

I say I travel here but that isn't exactly what I mean because to travel should be to find stuff out about places and see new things. As I've been doing this for sixteen years, as I know every sandwich shop in Cannes, the accent of every old lady who's been selling me *pan bagnat* for more than a decade, the sway of palm trees in the wind, the diesel colour of the sea before a storm, the pear-drops chemical sweetness of the local wine, and the wavy line of distant cliffs, I see nothing new here. Or, rather, I see new, often astonishing things in the cinemas each day but nothing outside the grand auditoria that touches me. Repeated looking has stopped this part of the world, at this time of the year, getting to me.

This book, I realised yesterday, is about getting got to. I was sitting on the balcony where I am now, seven floors up in an elegant sixties apartment block right on the ocean, looking out to an astonishing 180-degree view of the Med, those wavy cliffs, and seventeen liners and yachts moored at sea. My colleague Dorota and I had been talking about Cannes, travel and books. I was peering over the balcony, down to the beach below, from where the scream of kids pierced the constant roar of waves and the tinny drone of scooter engines.

The beautiful people, the vast expanse of what the Romans called *Mare Nostrum*, "our sea", the shrieks of kids, none of this was getting to me as it should, as I expected life and landscape to. Granted, I was below par from too much rosé the night before, and the wooziness of the scorching day – its apparent glories and their failure to touch me – had made me decide to have a wank to try to kick-start my sensory system, which had the opposite effect. So my non-seeing and non-feeling was mostly my own stupid fault, but it was also because I've seen this view too many times. Its turquoise and white colour scheme is too much of a Med Matisse cliché for me these days, too on the nose. The people I could see from the balcony yesterday were not going anywhere, doing anything or, it seemed to me in the misanthropy of the moment, thinking anything. They'd stopped and flopped. The kids were playing in the surf; their shrieks meant they were still close and alive. The beach below was a mirror reflecting back my lethargy. Cannes, for me, was overseen.

As I thought these things, I realised that what had happened last week – Trish and Helen, my Canadian co-producers, said they could get half the money to make the *Story of Film* project – meant that I was about to have a year or more of induced activity and promise. I was about to travel the world to meet and interview its greatest movie makers, and turn the results into three feature length documentaries that would try to tell the whole history of cinema, in narrative form. Ridiculously ambitious, I know, but that self-same ambition was inherent in my last book, *The Story of Film*. At the age of 38, I sat down for a year and wrote a whole history of world movies, growing sideburns that looked like gerbils as I went. I thought the result would be terrible, I could hear the knives being sharpened, I planned to be out of the country when the reviews came in and, yet, they were fine. Better than fine, they were the best responses I'd had to anything I'd done. Even though I sincerely expected a drubbing, the narrative ambition of the book compelled me, perhaps masochistically, to undertake the task. Now that the resulting volume seemed to have achieved something, and had been translated into loads of languages (how weird, by the way, to meet the person who spent three

months translating your 150,000 words in Mandarin
…), the real danger was that I would equate over-ambition with acclaim, so sign up for another dose of the former on the assumption that it would again result in the euphoria of the latter. Hence *The Story of Film*, the documentary? Who knows? What I do know is that it is likely that I am about to travel the world. To do so is a dream for many people. To combine it with meeting artists like Martin Scorsese, Bernardo Bertolucci, Lars von Trier, Samira Makhmalbaf and the first great African and Arab filmmaker, Youssef Chahine, whose quip "freedom of expression is not given, it is taken" still moves me, would be a double delight for movie buffs. And I am to do both.

Five years ago, when I was 37, my girlfriend Gill and I drove from Scotland's windy mediaeval capital Edinburgh, where we live, to India, in an old VW campervan. The trip changed my life. My mental geography and sense of where in the world is exciting, reconfigured. No longer was New York-Rome-Berlin-Paris the parallelogram of my cultural world. Isfahan in the centre of Iran, Ahmedabad in Western India and Istanbul excited me more. The buildings, music, people, tea, poetry, films, food, landscapes, urbanism, philosophy, humour, aesthetics, dancing, and clothes of these oriental cities get to me as much if not more, now, than those of that old Euro-American parallelogram which has incubated *isms* since the Enlightenment. Not only did they get to me more, I was angry with myself and my education because it took them so long to get to me. I studied art history yet was not told that Isfahan in the 1600s built more beautiful buildings than Rome. I adored the writings of George Steiner and Walter Benjamin (so much so that I have a tattoo of the latter's name on my leg), yet nowhere in their work did I encounter the idea that since Islamic art is largely non-figurative, it is a purer place to learn about aesthetics. Why not? I get mad even thinking about this. How much more transforming might this next trip be, as it will take me to Japan, where I've long wanted to go, and Senegal, Brazil and St Petersburg, Kolkata and Beijing? It might well shake me up, this trip, because most of these places are new to me and newness doubles the RAM in my brain, newness gives me a photographic memory, newness squirts the dirt from my eyes. And I'll be meeting movie royalty, some of whom, no doubt, I'll come to hate.

There's a book in this, I thought, as I sat on the balcony with Dorota, a book about the rapture of the open road and the art of movies, about the immersive nature of filming, how you parachute into a place and, as I will be directing the documentaries, about the need to be alert to the visual details of it, its distinctive light and colours, the shape of its buildings, the sweep of its landscapes, the things that make it it. The book will also, surely, be about how a film crew gels or doesn't for a few months, about the *déformation professionelle* that filming enacts even on nice people like me, though perhaps those are the aspects of the story to which I might be least alert. I will write character sketches of the world's greatest movie directors (not necessarily the most famous ones) and try to capture how they see and drive the medium.

Then something else occurred to me. When Gill and I set off on our big drive five years ago, I didn't quite feel that I was at the mid-point of my adult life but now, aged 42, after the death of three young friends in one year, I do. At that age I am, realistically, past the mid-point of my life but knock off the first seven years or so, when I wasn't aware of much, you get 35, the age Dante was in *The Divine Comedy*, whose first Inferno Canto begins:

> Midway along the journey of our life
> I woke to find myself in a dark wood,
> for I had wandered off from the straight path.

So let's say my sentient self is 35, the exact mid-point of life as envisaged in Psalm 89:11 and the age at which Robert Byron, who wrote one of my favourite travel books, *The Road to Oxiana*, died when his boat was torpedoed and sunk north of Cape Wrath in Scotland. Marilyn Monroe got no further in life either. It's a great age to be but, just as stories are good when they change halfway through, I have begun to wonder if my life should too. Not because I find myself in a dark wood and have "wandered off from the straight path". No. But for about a year now I have been doing little thought experiments, imagining what would happen if I stopped being a filmmaker, stopped earning a living from cinema, and drew a line in the sand after twenty years of haphazard, passionate, fulfilling writing, direct-ing and teaching. These thought experiments were not in any way born out of disaffection with cinema. On the contrary, I still love it. It is still my window on the world, my language, my drug, my place of refuge. When I was a boy, growing up in Belfast during the seventies, at a time of war, I'd go into a darkened cinema and feel my nervous system ease. The visuality of film, the expressivity of shots and cuts, seemed to me to be entrancing facsimiles of the weird machine inside my head that I was getting to know as I grew up. When I was 24, as associate director on a documentary film called *Dear Mr Gorbachev*, directed by Michael Grigsby, I spent time in the then Soviet Union and then flew from Moscow to New York, arriving on one of those October nights in Gotham when the skyscrapers dis-appear up into the clouds. This was my first time in

America. I was agog. I was working for German TV in October '89, as the Berlin wall was coming down and, continuing the *Zelig* theme, I took films to Sarajevo during its appalling siege. As a festival director then BBC TV presenter, making movie shows, I met some of the greatest figures in Western cinema – Martin Scorsese, David Lynch, Janet Leigh, Lauren Bacall, Bernardo Bertolucci, Dennis Hopper, Paul Schrader, Jeanne Moreau. Rod Steiger and Jane Russell became friends, of sorts. I spent a lot of my thirties in Los Angeles, meeting people, drinking Tanqueray martinis as the sun set, the eucalyptus trees extruding their evening perfumes, the city turning into one giant film noir. These have been unforgettable times. How could I consider giving them up?

Call it quitting when you are ahead or, as I prefer, creating a rupture precisely because there is no need to do so. Perhaps I've compressed a lifetime of film world experiences into half a lifetime so, superstitiously, like some great beauty (which I'm not), think I should call it a day before the photographers stop snapping and the limelight's gone? I'm the least superstitious person I know and the loner in me seems unlikely to have been sustained all these years by the attention. Whatever. There's time to work these things out. For now the point I want to make is that when I imagined being someone else – an architect, a gardener, a maths lecturer, a Tennessee Williams-esque male escort, a painter, a novelist, a furniture remover – most of which I am ill-equipped to do – I found the thought ... exciting. The air I breathed in those imagined new lives was clean and clear. This is grass-is-greener territory, and universal. I'd stay with Gill of course (if she'd stay with me), at least until the world notices that I don't deserve her and because, after twenty years, I don't have a sense that when I write "I" or "she" I mean only me or her. But everything else could be transformed. No more Cannes, no more broadcasting, no more going to parties where people come up to me and tell me their favourite films. I say again, I love some of these things and in no way have they become stale, but if I took them out of my life, for what would they leave room?

After a year of these thought experiments, as I sat on the balcony yesterday, as Dorota popped open another bottle of rosé wine, I realised that if I was to draw that line in the sand of my life, the time to do so would be after we made the three documentaries telling the story of film. What better way to bid a lachrymose adieu to working in cinema than to tell its zigzag history, as I see it? I have a low boredom threshold so what could I do as a filmmaker that could top the excitement of making these three films?

This, then, is what this book is really about. Should a man in what he hopes is only the middle of his life who, inside, feels about 29, who is happy and fulfilled, suddenly and without cause, in order to open his eyes, to see even more, change it? If life, despite its iniquities and tragedies and whose absurdity dawns slowly, is nonetheless as good as I suspect it might be, then shouldn't I force a rupture in its pattern, in order to make the most of its second half, if indeed I have a second half? If the lesson from my non-seeing from this balcony in Cannes is that familiarity can lead to dullness, maybe I should make a pre-emptive strike on my own life? In the next year or more, as I travel the world and meet the big movie cheeses, I'll ask these questions. Sometimes I'll forget to do so, no doubt, because of wanderlust, exhaustion and because filming doesn't leave much room for thought (which is one of its problems). Even so, a background noise in this book, which should remain audible even in the cacophonous city to which we are about to depart, will be an interrogative note, in a minor key. I have no idea what my final response to it will be, but last year, before I even realised I was asking questions, I took my first steps to answering them, on the polluted, pot-holed, swarming streets of Cairo.

1. Cairo in Chahine's Mirror

In Cairo life is triple-distilled. Everything you see looks and feels like it lived before, then was boiled down to its essence, then lived a second time then reduced that time too. The street scene is clammier, louder and grittier than in the cities where I've spent most of my life – Belfast, Edinburgh, London, Glasgow, New York, Paris and Berlin. Run your car for ten minutes then open the bonnet, put your face up close to the engine and breath a lung-full – that's what the air's like. Smoke the sheesha pipe there, on the terrace of a café, on the hills, as the sun sets and, through the grey-orange air, as your head reels from the tobacco-oxygen hit, you'll see on the horizon, barely visible, a group of chevrons like a campsite of the gods.

I first visited them, the pyramids at Giza, with my friend Simon, a young Scottish filmmaker who somehow attached himself to me in Cannes three years ago and who I've been unable to shake off since. He'll get the sarcasm. Simon had written a screenplay about Iraq, I'd started travelling in the Arab world, our friendship was based on excessive drinking and adventures and so (or perhaps not so) we decided to go to Cairo. The city was too hot for milquetoast Celts. We brought and wore shorts until we read in a guidebook that wearing them in Egypt is like going out in your underpants in Europe, and we got the runs after three days. All this notwithstanding, it immediately became clear to me that if you are into buildings, the languor of afternoons, the surrealism of camels in rush hour traffic, the possibility that human beings are innately hospitable, or the humiliated nobility of Arabism, Cairo is the bees knees.

I don't know why I didn't know that I'd get to go inside the Great Pyramid of Khufu (Cheops), the only one of the seven wonders of the ancient world to survive, but I didn't. Simon and I went to the massive Giza platform on the edge of Cairo to see the pyramids – man-made mountains, exquisite works of abstract sculpture, god toys, "idle and foolish exhibitions of royal wealth" (Pliny the Elder), proofs that people have always glorified the supernatural. We climbed about ten massive limestone steps, to the opening of the labyrinth that leads to the centre of the pyramid and, as cameras are forbidden inside, left mine with a custodian who put it under his kaftan as if, it seemed to me at that moment, the camera was a new-born chick that needed protecting from the scorching, pearlised, white-out sun. The warnings in the guidebook, which we read after we got to Giza, quickened my heart. Those with a tendency to claustrophobia, or fear of the dark, should not proceed. I have both, but we decided to go in anyway. Within seconds we were in a shaft half our height, that smelt of armpits and was so humid that my pores seeped. My T-shirt and shorts became glued to my body. The shaft, which did dogleg turns sideways, then shot upwards, was lit in fluorescent green. To climb and crouch at the same time is back breaking and to try to think, as well, about the fact that you are inside the Cheops pyramid – perhaps to keep the claustrophobia at bay – is almost too much. Faced with this overload, all I could do was climb and suck from the air any oxygen molecules that had been hanging in it. After about ten minutes, we arrived at the most thought-provoking place I've ever been. If you've seen the sepulchral red-black paintings of Mark Rothko, or the films of Alexander Sokurov, or you've worn sunglasses at nighttime, you'll know how visually dim the central burial chamber is in the great pyramid. A vast, rectangular room clad in dark red granite, a marble sarcophagus sits in one corner as if here was the spot where the fourth-dynasty Pharaoh Khufu came to bathe rather than lie, mummified, for all eternity (he thought), whilst empires rose and fell, and deities were invented and slain. I don't know when his remains were discovered, but is it the eight-year-old Indiana Jones in me that finds the idea of being there, on that day when whoever it was broke into the chamber, undisturbed for millennia and, by flickering torchlight, found an ancient tomb, the most exciting thing imaginable?

Tourists came, took photographs (how did they get their cameras in?) and talked. I was glad they weren't speaking a language I knew, because whatever they were saying – "This is sublime", "That was some climb", "Imagine the history" – it would have dented my awe, which I was trying to turn into words. The sentence that did form in the humid gloom (of my head and the chamber) was "Everything I've ever known or heard of took place as that man lay in that sarcophagus." Later it struck me that the big bang and the formation of the solar system pre-date that remarkable room, but as I sat there, I thought of Leonardo da Vinci, of Julius Caesar, of Paul Weller's The Jam, which was my life as a teenager, of Agnès Varda, the Iranian poet Forough, the Mahābhārata, of the Aztecs, of Gladys Knight, Orson Welles, and of my two decades with Gill, and imagined them all being born or formed, evolving or becoming famous, dying, disappearing or becoming permanent whilst in this room, in funereal stillness, a body lay and air molecules hung (or do they somehow die or go stale or get used up or polluted by the putrefaction of the embalming fluids?) I wondered whether a scarab beetle might have scuttled in here, down some air shaft or cosmic vent, and I looked up to see if there were any such openings in the ceiling. This place had been oblivious to everything. I sat in the semi-dark, sweating, and cried.

Which is just about as far away from the present tense medium of film as you can get. A year later I went back. My Scottish producer on *The Story of Film*, John, a friend for years who'd been head of arts at BBC Scotland, had got money from Europe for us to shoot a section of the project and I'd decided we'd do so in Cairo. Los Angeles or Paris might have been a more obvious choice, as each plays a crucial role in movie history, but from the start I wanted *The Story of Film* to be properly, boldly global. I wanted it to feel not only different from, but opposed to, the Euro-American account of movie history, which is the inventors' account and which is blinded by self-regard. Years earlier I'd noticed that American, Chinese, Indian and European cinema had often been great at lush, chromatic, excessive melodramas in the 1950s. Then I realised, as many had done before, that in Cairo, a filmmaker emerged in the 1950s who was a great melodramatist too. As in Eisenhower America, China and India, so in Egypt in that decade, social attitudes were conservative. Sexual, artistic and gender freedoms were limited. The Dionysianism of youth and the expected liberties of middle age were unacknowledged and repressed. These countries – most countries – were like social pressure cookers in the fifties, and movies were a way to let off steam.

And so they did. That's what melodrama is, I think, a hot, intense, sometimes Freudian release of pent-up feeling and, in the fifties, it was everywhere. Think of James Dean in *Rebel Without a Cause*, think of that Douglas Sirk movie *All That Heaven Allows*, which skewers suburban America's disapproval when a middle-aged widow starts a relationship with her younger gardener.

In Egypt in the 1950s, Youssef Chahine made such a pressure cooker film. *Cairo Station* pre-dated Alfred Hitchcock's *Psycho* by four years in that it, too, was about an emotionally immature man who, by repressing his sexual desires, ends up killing women. Like Norman Bates in *Psycho*, as the man, a disabled newspaper seller, could not express his erotic impulses, he turned them into misogynistic resentment and disgust. *Cairo Station* was a fantastic illustration of the festering of imprisoned, resentful desire but if I wanted to tell the story of film in the fifties, was it enough to justify doing so from Egypt? Should we not film instead in America, where melodrama was more widespread and whose Eisenhowerian conformism is not only well acknowledged but, you could argue, the signature of the mid-twentieth century? I don't think so. America at the time was oppressive and tried to magic eros away behind nice drapes and Doris Day melodies. But Egyptian society did the equivalent, even more so. Women and men were not allowed to have relationships before marriage. Sex was sacred or procreative, not fun.

Little wonder that Chahine's film was so deeply felt and caustic an illustration of how the form of melodrama was *the* cinematic form of its time.

Yet another reason for telling the story of fifties cinema from Egypt was my interest in origins. Chahine was one of the first great Arab directors and one of the first great African directors. Europe and America invented movies and, afterwards, other countries borrowed them tell their stories. Here was a young man – Chahine was twenty-four when he made his first film and thirty when he hit his stride with *Cairo Station* – doing it from scratch, in Africa. I am so interested in how such greatness emerges. I am gripped by where creative people who have few forerunners, find the confidence to make work that, like *Cairo Station*, becomes a state of the nation film and a landmark in a culture's self-awareness. Musicians, businesspeople, writers and pioneers in any field have to have the courage to introduce a mode of work or set of ideas that force those methods and ideas that are already there (musical comedies, theatre, epic poetry, etc., in the case of Egypt) to shift their chairs to make room for them a little, or a lot. Someone once said that a nation without its own cinema is like a house without mirrors. I believe this, so to look at the first great films of Chahine is to see Africa and the Arab world begin to see itself in the movie mirror.

The mirror that Chahine held showed warts and all. Why? On the plane to Cairo producer John and I talked about him. Chahine was born in Alexandria, the most European of Egyptian cities. One of his parents was Christian. In his teens he realised he was bisexual. He studied film in Pasadena. As a boy he loved Gene Kelly musicals. In his films, which are often about Nasserian Arab socialism, he manages to weave in the odd musical number, a song and dance routine performed by some pretty Arab actor. This not only counterbalances the politics, it provides utopian interludes. For years I'd been intrigued by this hybridity in his life and movies, his miscegenation of truth and hope, his insistence that his culture is noble yet his lambasting of it as oppressive and macho, his high seriousness and moral authority, which is laced with camp. So outspoken has Chahine been over the years that he was banned from appearing live on Egyptian TV. His new film, *Chaos*, is a portrait of the disorder he sees when he looks at the window at twenty-first-century Egypt. For all these reasons, Chahine was a hero of mine and, on that plane, I was going to meet him.

John and I arrive at Cairo airport. We get a taxi to our hotel. On the way I watch the tiny black cabs weave from lane to lane along the city's snarled motor-ways. When you direct documentaries, you're always looking for ways to film people that are other than conventional, sit-down interviews. As we snake our way along the hot freeways, I notice that, just as our taxi weaves, so others do too. They pull into and out of my view. They are dancing around each other. I think to myself – what if we put Chahine in one car (I have no idea at this point how mobile or otherwise the eighty-year-old is) and we film from another, trying to keep pace with his, but inevitably falling behind at times and getting ahead at others? If I combined such a shot with a commentary that said, "one of the first great Arab and African filmmakers was … this man" as his car emerged from the traffic, it would be a visual way of capturing the chaos of Cairo, and him amongst it.

John and I arrive at our hotel, and meet Rose Issa, who has set up the shoot for us, who is a curator of Middle Eastern art and film and with whom we previously worked in Tehran. Rose's ebullience, her passion for the Middle East, and her eccentricity (she is in late middle age but professes to like only young people), fuel my love of Iran and Egypt.

Next day we take a taxi to Chahine's office. A handsome Nubian guy in splendid robes is the doorman. We ride up in an ancient cage elevator and get to Chahine's office, which is labyrinthine and plain, but has stained glass windows. His assistants, niece and another man are there, drinking tea, welcoming us. I recognise the other man, then someone whispers to me that he is Seif Abdelrahman, the actor from Chahine's greatest film *The Sparrow*. The actor is clearly not there because we are so I conclude, perhaps wrongly, that Chahine created such a scene around him in his heyday, such an engaging world that, like Warhol's Factory, made stars who might only fit into that world and not the real one, that his collaborators have found little since as appealing, so stayed.

"He's not here yet", someone says, his name not needing to be mentioned, and there's an air of expectation, even anxiety. Rose, John and I wait, drink tea and sit under a large photograph from the ending of *Cairo Station*, where the newspaper seller (played, brilliantly, by Chahine himself) has gone mad. Our crew arrives and we start to get to know our cameraperson, sound recordist and fixer. Then a commotion. Youssef is in the building. He shuffles in, red cashmere sweater draped around his shoulders like Sebastian Flyte. He's smiling, smoking and greeting people to his left and right, like royalty. He's wrinkled, but still so recognisable from his photographs and performances. I've met so many movie stars in my life that I am seldom star-struck but here, in this corridor, with sweet tea in my hand, I've come face to face with one of the inventors of Arab and African cinema, a maverick phrase maker, an iconographer and a sexual crusader, and I quake.

People say I have to SPEAK LOUDLY because Youssef can't hear well. I introduce myself. We go into his office and chat. After some preamble, we start the interview. He says, "We are the first world. We've been around for thousands of years." He talks of the chaos of modern Egypt. He remembers *Cairo Station*'s world premiere, almost fifty years ago, after which he was spat upon because people hated what they saw of Egyptian life in his mirror. Afterwards, we take photographs and he does the strangest thing. He stands in front of me, his back to me, leans backwards and reaches his left arm around my neck, as if he's Leda's swan or Marlene Dietrich. He holds the pose as cameras click and, in the resulting photographs, he looks meltingly feminine. I look silly and nervous. We tell him the shot I'd like to do – him in a car, us in another. He says fine, as long as he can smoke. Then we are out onto the street and people stop and stare. He's famous in Cairo. He gets into his car, the cameraperson, sound recordist, John and I squash into a taxi (me on the floor out of shot, the cameraperson on top of me) and we head off. For an hour or so we feel like we're making a Steve McQueen movie, racing on the motorway, phoning between cars, trying to keep up with each other, almost getting the shot I want, of Chahine's car pulling up beside ours, pausing, then heading off again, into the mid-afternoon heat shimmer. I love this stuff, making imagery, getting to know a city, working with a team of people, all focused on the same idea. That night in the hotel, we eat Persian food and drink beer. I go to bed and think about Chahine and filming Cairo. I feel alive and unable to sleep.

And so I lie there and think about topics which would, a year later, become the mood music to this book: how to assess life at its halfway point, whether to create a rupture in it, merely for the sake of doing so. I think of Chahine's career. A groundbreaker in the fifties. In the seventies he made his masterworks about Nasserian Egypt and the loss of the Sinai to Israel in the Six-Day War. History gave him great subjects and he turned them into remarkable melodramas, emotional parables about his country and its times. But then, you could argue, the parade moved on and, perhaps, he wasn't able to follow it. As late as 1996 he made *Destiny*, a daring picture about the Islamic philosopher Averroes, who was a modernist but who was denounced by fundamentalists. Four decades after *Cairo Station*, he was taking Islam head-on. *Destiny* notwithstanding, however, through the eighties and nineties, his films lost bite. Their Gene Kelly softness began to outweigh their grit. At their worst they felt like telenovelas. What could Chahine have done about this? Gone and lived in Reaganite America to find new stories to tell? Become a novelist? A politician? As I lie in bed in my hotel I wonder if he "lost it" somehow, somewhat, somewhere, around the mid-eighties. He got the fiftieth Anniversary Prize in Cannes in 1997, which was culmination and recognition, but by then his cinema was no longer quite on the boil. Judging by what I saw today, his life most certainly still is. So, surely, he should have had a rupture? Shouldn't he have re-directed his energy elsewhere, outside cinema, or done so many new things that he could come back to cinema re-charged with experience? This seems unarguable to me. Round one to rupture.

I wake up the next morning and all thoughts of Chahine, his career and the insights it might afford go right out the window because Cairo is right out the window. If you are into buildings, Egypt's capital is as big a treat as Rome, except for one difference. In Rome or in Florence, the great palazzos, the Borromini churches and the soaring Baroque cathedrals are national monuments and, therefore, guarded. Visits to them are limited to approved walkways. It would be unthinkable, for example, to get to prowl amongst the rafters of these places, looking at mosaics or frescoes as closely as their creators did. Yet go to the vast, impoverished, architecturally astonishing City of the Dead on Cairo's eastern flank, where kids sleep amongst the graves and you come across, for example, in its northern section, the funerary complex of Sultan Qaytbay, which was built at the same time as the Italian Renaissance, the 1470s, but is seldom mentioned in histories of architecture written in the West. The complex is a sublime combination of mosque, madrasa and mausoleum comprising a gorgeous pineapple dome, honeycombing, iwans, latticing, corridors built to channel cool air, rooftop vistas, a triple-layered minaret, and remarkable elevations from every angle, all in serene grey-brown stone and brickwork. It creates expectation, provides glimpses of what's to come, builds to second act climaxes, pays off and grace notes. Yet when Simon and I went there, a kaftaned old man, its security guard, was sitting alone on his charpoy in the shade of the Mosque entrance and offered to take us up into its domes, through the windows of which, shafts of light shone and were made magical by the dust in the necropolis' heavy air. We accepted the offer of course and to see the honeycombing, the tile work, the weight dispersal and construction methods up close was like getting to poke around Florence's Baptistery on a grand tour in the 1600s, long before Italy was Italy and its state registry of national monuments made it out of bounds for plebs like me. If too many people get to see the Sultan Qaytbay complex in the way we saw it – too close with too much free reign – then it might be damaged beyond repair but, for now, as I write this, the memory of it is so precious. That afternoon, in the smelly, heartbreaking necropolis, I saw buildings and beauty like I've never seen buildings and beauty. I crawled around one of the greatest things in the world and felt pure joy.

On that trip and on the subsequent one to meet Chahine I felt, too, the informal, proud generosity of the Egyptian Arabs. Even if you don't love buildings, the people who sell you tea in Cairo, or re-light your apple sheesha pipe, make it hard not to want to be there more, learn more, and get to be part of their – as Chahine says – first world, ancient, cultured ways. The people we meet assume we are American and so have money and so might buy something from them but, they give before they take – tea usually but also baklava or nuts or bread. Though the Security Police are everywhere and there are metal detectors in most hotel lobbies and holes in the pavement, Cairenes have something that we in the West mostly don't have and that makes me jealous of them – a gift economy – the impulse to give and an understanding of the spiritual fillip of doing so.

I fucking love the place.

2. Hiatus and, so, the West of Ireland

I get back to Glasgow, we edit the fifties/Cairo melo-drama section and somehow, I think, it works to go from Egypt to James Dean to Rock Hudson to *Tokyo Story* to India's *Pather Panchali*. The result runs 20 minutes and is dense – films, names and connections come at you thick and fast. Which, if I'm making an accessible history of cinema, is a no-no. But the piece has to be ideasy and passionate and new as well as accessible. What I hate about it is, as usual, my voice. It sounds flat and fake to me. What I hate even more is recording the commentary. I've always been a slow reader and detested reading out loud in school. My face went bright red when I did so. I stumbled over words. Sentences looked shapeless, daunting and full of potholes, like the streets of Cairo. They tripped me up. I fell into every one. Now I have to read into microphones when I make documentaries with commentaries (which is seldom), so I panic and spend hours beforehand under-lining the *stress*es in every *sen*tence to help me read *na*turally *when*, in *fact*, *few* things come *less* naturally to me than reading *na*turally.

Anyway, months pass. I am back in my life of cof-fee-fuelled 6:00 a.m. starts and long days writing, film-ing and talking movies. I spend these days on my own mostly. I get up, drink coffee, shower or don't, don't get dressed and sit naked at my computer writing articles or book chapters or ideas for films. I can't sit still when I think so I'm always jumping up from my chair, pacing my flat, walking into my kitchen, putting on the kettle then forgetting that I have done so. If I don't get dressed, if the phone doesn't go, if I don't speak to anyone, I can slip from sleep into the penumbra of the waking day. In not going out onto the street, in not chatting as I buy a newspaper, I can make believe that the voices in my head are the only ones in the world. I get so much written this way and then, perhaps at 3:00 p.m., when I do go outside onto the street and life crackles and pops around me, I realise how much more exciting it is than I am. The fug of the day has snapped into focus. A hundred things are suddenly happening.

Producer John hears that the BBC doesn't want to co-fund *The Story of Film* because "we're already doing a history of film". What? After decades of no history of cinema on TV, there might suddenly two? Then we hear that what they are making is a history of *British* cinema – rather less ambitious. When this is pointed out to them they say something along the lines of *well yes, but, still, it's film and history so that's enough for us for the time being.* I feel disdain, but there's a less expected partial knock back from Channel 4. Their lovely commissioning editor for arts is finding it hard to get money to support us, either. Arts series are out of favour, she says.

Would *The Story of Film* work instead as a single 90-minute film? My mind flicks to a *Macbeth* in 15 minutes I saw at the Edinburgh Fringe years ago. How could I tell the history of world cinema in an hour-and-a-half? I don't say no, and decide to set aside three days to try to write it up, to see if I can find a voice to do that kind of overview without it skating the surface or being an over-compression. Will this project fall apart because we can't raise finance in the UK, the idea's home patch? If it does, if I don't travel around the world, then this book dies too, a cutting thought.

Writing this is the most enjoyable thing I'm doing at the moment. Can I continue if the trip doesn't happen? A travel book about not travelling? Hitler's architect Albert Speer did a "walk around the world" whilst imprisoned in Spandau. He got maps, plotted a route that would take him decades, then walked the route in his head, reading travel guides, books on geography, history and urbanism, and the literature of each place he traversed. I heard about this from the artist Ian Hamilton Finlay, who similarly didn't leave his house and garden in Dunsyre in Scotland for nearly two decades. Maybe I could complete this book by travelling only in my head? If I did, perhaps I should excise this paragraph and not fess up to you, the reader, that I didn't undertake the journey? In which case, would the book be a novel?

I enjoy this train of thought. It spins the disappointment of Channel 4's apparent knock back into something more positive and fizzy, but I'm so busy at the moment that I don't have much time to pursue the idea. Three big projects suddenly loom large: the Scottish government has asked me to tour a festival of Scottish films around China – which I'd love to do – but the dates are October, and it's now June. This is tight. My pal Catherine has convinced the film funding agency Scottish Screen to give us money towards the financing of the feature film *The Man Who Walks*, to be written and directed by *Trainspotting* author Irvine Welsh, an adaptation of a great novel by Alan Warner. And my next book, *Watching Real People Elsewhere*, has to be edited and delivered by the end of September. The latter is a collection of my essays for a magazine called *Prospect* and, luckily, a former student of mine, a brainy guy called Guy, has agreed to shape it for me. Which leaves China and *TMWW*, both of which could eclipse my autumn. I've been freelance for exactly twenty years now. In that time, the dread of clashing commitments, of having to do two things at once – a documentary and a festival, or a book and a series of lectures – has become a beast that comes out of the forest, stares and slavers. The coincidence of China and *TMWW* calls that beast forth, and my stomach churns.

So I decide to go on holiday, which sounds like avoidance I know, but isn't. After I've selected the films for China, they need to be submitted to the Chinese censors for approval, which will take time. And Catherine is on a bit of a holiday, so we can't work together on *TMWW*. If life is going to be at fifth gear in a month's time, and for the foreseeable future, now is the only chance for holiday. So Gill and I book our clapped-out campervan on a boat to Belfast, from where we will drive west into gorse-covered Sligo and Galway, which I haven't explored properly in 25 years. As we make the booking I realise that this revisit to the beaches and slate mountain passes of my youth might awaken in me memories from the start of my life, when everything lay ahead as in a vast glaciated valley on Dingle Peninsula, where sky-, land-, and seascapes combine in panoramas. If this book is about my future, where better to go next than to my past?

We take the boat, see my family in Belfast, then drive west, towards the border between Northern Ireland and the Republic. In the seventies, when I last travelled here, that border marked an abrupt, heavily policed, change from British road signs, straight roads, tamed countryside and Victorian, colonial, Protestant architecture to windier roads with rougher surfacing, cowering cottages which looked like a less rational place.

Nowadays North and South blur into each other. The Celtic Tiger economy and the rush of European money into the Republic of Ireland have blinged that country up. The roads get better once you cross from the North. The cowering cottages are still there but beside them, and making them look like servants' accommodation, are showy second houses for Dubliners that sprawl like Texan ranches, have faux Georgian windows, balustrades and plastic Doric columns appearing to hold up the pendentives of porches.

Beneath all this newness in Ireland is the question of confidence. As we drive through the pouring rain, our van leaking because it's so old, we hear a news story about the increased suicide rates amongst the young Irish. An expert says economic booms raise social expectation. Those who don't have broadband at home or an Xbox, a six-pack where a flabby belly was once perfectly OK, or a Jennifer Aniston haircut, or who don't know who the Arctic Monkeys are, can feel left behind in ways that are more hurtful than slower, more forgiving, social change could envisage. Hours after we hear this report, we drive up a lane to the thatched cottage where Pádraig Pearse lived in the early 1910s. Pearse was an educationalist, poet and revolutionary. Here's "The Proclamation of Irish Independence", which Pearse wrote at a tiny wooden dresser in the cottage we are about to visit and which he himself read from the steps of the General Post Office in Dublin on Easter Monday 1916, a matter of weeks before the Revolution failed and Pearse himself was executed by the British (during the night so no crowd could gather):

POBLACHT NA H EIREANN.
THE PROVISIONAL GOVERNMENT OF THE
IRISH REPUBLIC TO THE PEOPLE OF IRELAND.

IRISHMEN AND IRISHWOMEN: In the name of God and of the dead generations from which she receives her old tradition of nationhood, Ireland, through us, summons her children to her flag and strikes for her freedom ... she strikes in full confidence of victory.

We declare the right of the people of Ireland to the ownership of Ireland, and to the unfettered control of Irish destinies, to be sovereign and indefeasible ... Standing on that fundamental right and again asserting it in arms in the face of the world, we hereby proclaim the Irish Republic as a Sovereign Independent State, and we pledge our lives and the lives of our comrades-in-arms to the cause of its freedom, of its welfare, and of its exaltation among the nations ... The Republic guarantees religious and civil liberty, equal rights and equal opportunities to all its citizens ... Until our arms

have brought the opportune moment for the estab-
lishment of a permanent National Government,
representative of the whole people of Ireland and
elected by the suffrages of all her men and women,
the Provisional Government, hereby constituted,
will administer the civil and military affairs of the
Republic in trust for the people … we pray that
no one who serves that cause will dishonour it by
cowardice, inhumanity, or rapine. In this supreme
hour the Irish nation must, by its valour and disci-
pline and by the readiness of its children to sacrifice
themselves for the common good, prove itself worthy
of the august destiny to which it is called.

"Rapine", a great word for plunder, and there's that word confidence near the start.

Pearse's declaration moves me as much as Mary McAleese's comment, when she became Ireland's first female President, that the women of Ireland, Mná na hÉireann, have stopped rocking the cradle and started to rock the system. It is an essay in confidence, a map of modernity that doesn't so much show the pathway there but declares that we are *already* modern. The new and the post-colonial, the equal and the fair, the confident, are here in our lives, and have been for some time, and all we must do is lift them out from the backwardness of aspects of Irishness, imposed and innate.

At the cottage in Galway – three sparse rooms, white walls, wooden beds with patchwork quilts – a guide, Donal, tells us about Pearse's life there, his fury at Britain's ongoing prohibition of the study of the Irish language or culture and the forced anglicisation of Irish life. The Defence of the Realm Act prohibited Irish people to meet in public. The windows in the cottage are so small because Britain taxed them. The cottage feels like a hiding place; the Irish who opposed British rule had a need to hide, from the brutality of the colonisers. Gill and I listen. She's English. We live in Scotland. Donal assumes we are both British. It's hard not to feel uncomfortable. I tell him I went to an Irish-speaking Gaeltacht for a bit, as a boy. "Have you kept it up?", he asks. Suddenly, for the first time in my life, I'm ashamed that I didn't try harder to maintain what little Irish I learnt at school. We were force-fed grammar rather than the vitality of the language (I still remember that the irregular verbs are *come, go, give, get, say, do, hear, see, eat, catch, carry* and the verb *to be*, for example). As Donal speaks, I think to myself that the story of modern Irish confidence, the same confidence that you can see (or don't see) in the fancy houses of recent years, starts in this room.

Three things strike me now as I write about Pearse. Donal told us that he, Pearse, went to Belgium to study its bilingual education system, hoping to learn how to establish a duoglot equivalent in Ireland. I love both the internationalism of this and its hybridity. Pearse didn't want to boot the English language out (his father was English), but preferred instead to create a linguistically hyphenated country, which enjoyed the best of both worlds. Secondly, Pearse was gay. The previous day, in Lissadell House in Sligo, where W. B. Yeats used to visit the revolutionary Countess Markievicz and the Gore-Booth family, a generation before Pearse's revolutionary activity, I read about Markievicz's elder sister Eva. Eva was a poet and suffragette, yet another Anglo-Irish wild child who railed against the iniquities of Britain and patriarchy in the misty green landscapes in which we were now holidaying. She was also lesbian, but the L-word is not mentioned at Lissadell just as the G-word is not mentioned about Pearse. Surely these homosexualities are not only not inconvenient anomalies in otherwise impeccable revolutionary lives, but central to the process whereby Ireland didn't so much set sail for modernity but declare itself already there. Add in the fact that bang in between Eva Gore-Booth and Pearse came Oscar Wilde, and it's hard not to conclude that the discovery of modern Ireland was fuelled by hyphenated national and sexual identities. If the European modern movement was in part created by Jews and gays, then surely we can say something similar about Éire? I look back at Pearse's declaration, above. Socialist James Connolly was at his side when he announced that the *"Republic guarantees religious and civil liberty, equal rights and equal opportunities to all its citizens,"* so Connolly's politics probably steered Pearse's rudder somewhat, but surely the author's own, anguished sense of being disapproved of because of his sexuality has flavoured this too.

The third thing that strikes me is the stirring irony of all those new conservatories I've been moaning about. If the British taxed the life out of the Irish for the very windows they had in their cottages, and so those windows were few and tiny, why not, in the twenty-first century, have big, vulgar, fuck-off feature windows in every wall, to enjoy the landscape for yourself but, also, in memory of your forbears who were forbidden to do so because of London's punitive exchequer? Irish glazing firms are surely minting it, the country has leap-frogged Britain by entering the Eurozone, and has plonked itself on a Parker Knoll recliner, with a plasma screen dead centre and a glass wall behind, looking out onto the mysterious Benbulbin, beloved of Yeats. These buildings are vulgar but they are, I realise, funny and stirring too. The great Senegalese filmmaker Ousmane Sembène said that in post-colonial countries people tell stories not for revenge but to find their place in the world. These big showy houses have a hint of revenge in them, but assert, confidently, a new kind of Irish self.

As our days go on, as it pisses with rain, as we listen to Bourgie Bourgie on tape, or Irish phone-ins on the radio, as beautiful rocky vistas come and go in the mist and rain, the unexpected conjoining of old and new becomes the holiday's signature. On our first night we spy on the map a bit of Sligo sticking out into the sea that looks like it won't have many tourists on it. At its tip is Mullaghmore. We arrive there, the clouds part, the sun comes out, and raspberry-coloured clover flowers sway in the sea breezes. The weather's mild here, palm trees dot the bay. Lots of 4x4s are parked at the water's edge and families wearing multicoloured crocs queue for scuba diving trips around the lough. We are tired and damp so decide to stay in a B&B rather than sleep in the van, so we see if we could afford the village's main hotel, The Beach, right on the harbour with what looks like great views over to the Donegal hills.

I am dressed in scrubby shorts, boots, an old T-shirt and a woolly hat. I haven't shaved. The woman at reception is welcoming and funny. Our room does indeed look over to the hills. The sun comes out. We drink wine we bought from Lissadell House, and Mullaghmore seems perfect.

It was here, in August 1979, in this loch edged by clover flowers swaying in the breeze, that Lord Louis

Mountbatten (uncle of Queen Elizabeth II's husband, mentor of Prince Charles, bungler of Britain's withdrawal from India, friend of Charles Chaplin, bisexual) and three others were killed by a fifty pound IRA bomb attached to their thirty-foot pleasure boat, the *Shadow V*. One of the other three was an Anglo-Irish aristocrat, the Dowager Baroness Brabourne. The other two were boys in their early teens, one an aristocrat (The Hon. Nicholas Knatchbull), the other a 15-year-old Protestant crew member (Paul Maxwell). I know these details because I've just looked them up, but I remember the TV news footage of Irish police in wetsuits diving for, I presume, bits of the boat or the bodies. Now people in wetsuits dive for fun. I wonder what lives the boys might have led had they not been murdered by the IRA. I wonder how Pearse might have lived had he not been murdered by the British. And the hundreds of other Sligo people who were killed. I think about the film *The Wind that Shakes the Barley*, written by Paul Laverty and directed by Ken Loach, that depicts the guerrilla war waged for independence in Ireland. The film was made in 2006 and set from 1920 onwards, four years after Pearse's death but very much in the spirit of his declaration. The most moving scene for me comes after the Irish men have attacked some British soldiers. They are right to have done so, their cause is right; the oppression of their people is appalling. Yet a small line of dialogue tells us that the men they've just killed are not long back from the Somme. Life bounces these men from one war of unimaginable human cost, to another in which they sacrifice their lives for an ignoble cause. As we drive out of Mullaghmore, as I think these things, it is raining, the sky seems only half-lit, and the landscape has lost most of its colour, all of which seems appropriate. The last thing we see is a vast gothic pile sitting like Thunderbird One on a hill, lording it over the area, expressive of power and architectural vulgarity (that again). Mountbatten lived there.

We get to Drumcliff, where W. B. Yeats' grave sits in a Protestant churchyard, swarmed by coach loads of tourists. The sky has brightened a bit again, and I lean against the gravestone. I was snapped in the same spot by my dad when I was perhaps 14, the age of one of the boys killed with Mountbatten. If I was that age, it would have been summer '79, when their boat was blown up. In the old picture, as I recall, I'm a bit bigger than the grave, leaning against it, wearing a fake leather blouson jacket, a black shirt and one of my dad's skinny yellow ties. I look as if I'm making a statement, trying to be what I thought French might be, or at least not Irish. I could recite scarcely a word of Yeats back then, but I'd read enough about him, and enough of his poems, to have felt the intense heat of his writing and life. That I dragged my Mum, Dad and brother to his grave must have meant that I liked that heat. In the new picture I'm far bigger than the grave. Though I'm 42, I'm wearing paint spattered skinny jeans and Converse trainers, as if I want to be an art student. I've no gel in my hair, which is rare, and I dislike the bulging of what I suspect will soon be jowls. Do I really look like this? Are those skinny arms and that big nose mine? If anything is the sign of me for me, it's the look of this computer screen, at which I stare each day, on which my self appears, bit by bit, as I type these words. I would like to find the picture of that 1979 guy with the yellow tie at the grave. What was he about? All I really can feel about him now is that he was inward, like me, and that he saw clothes as a way of showing that inwardness and saying *no he is not at all like you, so please don't assume he is.*

I pile back into the van and we're off, to Knock. In 1879, exactly a century before the Mullaghmore bomb, Jesus' mother Mary is said to have appeared, with St Joseph and St John as a divine apparition on the gable wall of the chapel in the village, which I'm sure was charming then, but now, after more than a century of Mariology, an avalanche of holy tea-towels, the administration of the Catholic Church, plastic bottles in which you screw off Mary's head in order to fill her body with water, plaster casts of major and minor deities and separation of ailing pilgrims from their savings it is bleak. People fly from all over the world to Knock, but I'm not sure why we went. I was navigating and took us there, perhaps assuming that since the weather was miserable, we might as well wallow in it.

Before we are even out of the van, we are arguing (about where we parked). I am desperate for the toilet so go to the one by the basilica. The village is empty like a seaside resort in winter is empty. We go into a café to shelter from the rain. Its door is wedged open. A freezing wind blows. Gill's teeth chatter. We share a scone. We go back into the cavernous, ugly church. The Pope visited it in 1979. As we get back in the van, I see a cemetery plaque: "In Loving Memory of a Beautiful Baby Girl – A Tiny Flower, Lent Not Given, to Bud on Earth and Bloom in Heaven." €39.99.

We drive to Killary Harbour, where *The Field* was filmed and near which Ludwig Wittgenstein wrote some of his book *Philosophical Investigations*, in 1948. Wittgenstein stayed in Rosco, a cottage up the hill from the harbour, which had been used in the IRA in the 1920s to hide prisoners. Wittgenstein argues that the stuff I'm using now, language, goes on a holiday when it stops being used in the context of real life and tries to move into the frictionless territory of metaphysics. Language doesn't belong in that territory, it has no bearings and no purchase there. It works in the everyday world, as jokes do. Language makes sense to us (it paints a picture, to use Wittgenstein's words), because we get its context. Does it make sense that he went to such a remote place (Rosco is ten miles uphill) to write about language's inability to deal with the heights of metaphysics? The cottage had just two rooms. It was full of wood lice, which the fastidious philosopher hated. He was depressed whilst there, and wrote in his diary, on June 29,

> Don't let grief vex you. You should let it into your heart. Nor should you be afraid of madness. It comes to you perhaps as a friend, not as an enemy, and the only thing that is bad is your resistance. Let grief into your heart. Don't lock the door on it. Standing outside the door, in the mind, it is frightening, but in the *heart* it is not.

Wittgenstein had had a breakdown before he went to Killary. The fright he mentions in this diary entry sounds like a scare that has just waned. The deaths of my dad and others caused me grief but in my case it started in the heart and, over time, migrated into my mind and became something I could understand. Joseph Campbell writes about the "revelatory shock" of myth, and I'd describe my bereavements as revelatory shocks. For me these shocks move from feeling to understanding, in that direction. Judging by this small entry in Wittgenstein's diaries, it was the other way for him. How could he think grief and contain it in his mind and keep the door closed to it, before he felt it in his heart? I wish now that I'd scrambled up the hill to find the cottage.

And then we get to Dingle Peninsula. Clouds look like the Hagia Sophia cathedral-mosque. The fuchsia of Connemara and Mayo share space, down here, with straw yellow honeysuckle. Privet flowers the colour of clotted cream are so perfumed that they saturate the air with their narcotic sweetness; bramble flowers nestle beside their hard green fruit. Our van chugs up the road to the Conor Pass and we stop at a scramble to a corrie which I suddenly remember as a boy.

Dingle has the tease of beauty. It draws a cloudy veil across itself until nothing can be seen but mist and a distant crescent of sand. Then the clouds part and a beam of El Greco light traces a path along a valley, a chromatic revelation.

In campervans you are higher than the hedgerows, so see into fields more. Your centre of gravity is high so you roll on bends. We roll down to the Gallarus Oratory, a small, intact stone church built between the sixth and ninth centuries, CE. In Diyarbakır in

Kurdish Eastern Turkey I saw churches from the 400s, but I love this tiny little one in Dingle because it has no markings, altar or crosses. It is like a beehive from the front, and has thick walls that lean into each other and meet at the top in a corbelled arch. A dry stone lean-to which has stood strong for 1,100 years. Each chosen stone slopes downwards away from the centre of the building, repelling rain. It's mobbed by tourists.

We stay at a campsite a few hundred yards away. I lie on the grass in the hot sun and feel the woozy self-loss moment when a holiday starts to become a holiday. A tame robin, which looks like the mechanical one at the end of *Blue Velvet*, bobs up to me, looking for bread, then hops into the van and searches for food. The sun gets low in the sky. The ring of mountains around us glows. The windows in a distant cottage on one of them reflect this light back in beams the colour of buttercups. The flowers at the top of the hedgerows, particularly the honeysuckle, gleam and spark in the embers of the day. I cast a shadow the length of Cú Chulainn onto the road, whose lustre is wondrous in these minutes.

We wake up in the van to blinding light. It's not yet 7:00 a.m. We decide to go back to Gallarus.

We walk down an avenue of fuchsia, flies buzzing us. Spiders have spun silken ties across the path. We get to the Oratory. At this hour the sun is behind it, so a shaft of light falls from its window. The Dingle Peninsula was no backwater in the 600s. When the Emperor Justinian closed the schools of pagan (classical) learning in Athens, the wisdom of antiquity was preserved by the Moors of Spain who sailed to, amongst other places, western Ireland. Abbot Ailerán of Clonard quoted Hellenistic sources Philo and Augustine in 660. In 820, Abbot Sedulius of Kildare corrected a translation from Greek to Latin. In this morning light it's hard not to see the Oratory's simplicity as a classical virtue as well as the product of Celtic modesty, or taste or fear of persecution. It is forbearer of Pádraig Pearse's ideas.

We head off from the campsite early. The roads are empty, the skies blue, the landscape brilliant. Clouds boil off the tops of mountains. We arrive at Reask Monastery. How glorious is the world today?

Reask was founded in the same period as the Gallarus Oratory, but its oratory, and all the other buildings, have long fallen down. Its standing stone has an early Christian cross carved at the top, as if drawn by a kid with a crayon, spiralling lines along most of its length, very like the drawings of the splayed genitals of men in Monte Albán, near Oaxaca in Mexico last year. On the left side of the stone, again in kid's crayon line, are the letters D N E, *Domine, O Lord*.

The secular buildings – the beehive clocháns where the monks slept, etc. – are separated from the religious buildings – the oratory, the place for relics and the like – by an s-shaped wall. Knock is a mess because religion, recreation and commerce coincide and so cheapen each other. Many of modern America's early thinkers did not see civil life in religious terms (Benjamin Franklin said "Lighthouses are more useful than churches" and Thomas Jefferson wrote "To say that the human soul, angels, god, are immaterial, is to say they are nothings, or that there is no god, no angels, no soul. I cannot reason otherwise …").

We drive on and Dingle gets even more Mediterranean. I expect to see bougainvillea. We pass a sign for the Blasket Islands. We stop at the Islands' modernist visitor centre, these words on a wall:

> *Then I went to Ireland. The conversation of those ragged peasants, as soon as I learnt to follow it, electrified me. It was as though Homer had come alive. Its vitality was inexhaustible, yet it was rhythmical, alliterative, formal, artificial, always on the point of bursting into poetry.*

> *George Thomson*
> The Prehistoric Aegean (1954)

On the Blaskets, the Irish language, vocabulary and speech rhythms were protected from gradual or enforced anglicisation. J. M. Synge visited them in 1905. In the 1920s and 1930s, Norwegian, English, Swedish, French and Irish linguists turned up too, and encouraged the residents to write. Many could not do so, so dictated their stories, but soon three acclaimed books – Tomás Ó Croimhthain's *The Islandman*, Muiris Ó Súilleabháin's *Twenty Years A-Growing* (complete with E. M. Forster encomium) and Peig Sayers' *Peig* – emerged and from an island of a few hundred people, more than forty books were published. I read a line from Sayers' book, "I sat down on a bank beside the beach where I had a splendid view all around me. Dead indeed is the heart from which the balmy air of the sea cannot banish sorrow and grief." Wittgenstein does not mention the landscape but was, of course, writing within it. The sophisticated Austro-Hungarian philosopher and the islander both are concerned with the interaction between land and sorrow.

We spend ages in the visitor centre. The last islanders abandoned the Blaskets in 1953. Many of the descendants live in Springfield, Massachusetts. Of the emigrations, Muiris Ó Súilleabháin wrote,

> *I looked West at the edge of the sky where America should be lying, and I slipped back on the paths of thought. It seemed to me that the New Island [Manhattan] was before me with its fine streets*

and great high houses, some of them so tall that
they scratched the sky; gold and silver out on the
ditches and nothing to do but gather it. I see
the boys and girls who were once my companions
walking the street, laughing brightly and well
contented … the tears were rising in my eyes but
I did not shed them.

Twenty Years A-Growing (1933)

The Empire State Building was being built as he penned
these lines. I love the word "lying" in the first sentence,
and that thought is made up of paths. When I drove to
India, a song that seemed to go with road and the roll
of the van was "Gentle on My Mind", sung by Bobbie
Gentry and Glen Campbell. Its lyrics, by John Hartford,
talk of "the back roads, by the rivers of my memory,"
exactly what Ó Súilleabháin had in mind.

The plenitude of Dingle had made our trip soar.
Our sense that we are living seemed to lift us off the
ground, and then, caught by sea breezes we soared.
When you make films, you are looking for the mood
and feel created by light. In our final days in south west
Ireland, a crisp light made things hopeful. The camshaft
in my head stopped whirring. I forgot myself.

Back on the boat to Scotland, it started spinning
again. The demeaned country I knew as a child was

strutting now. Confidence can be a performance or, in excess, revolting and I think we saw a touch of both.

But the real reason that the previous ten days had enlivened us is to be found in Pearse, Blasket and Wittgenstein. For the first time in ages I felt the excitement of words and talking. If I have come to like writing, and if it seems to suit the solitary way I spend a day, then perhaps I should indeed stop working in film and try to get good at writing? Round two to rupture?

My next trip is to a country whose language I don't speak and whose culture is new to me. I know it through cinema. It is on the opposite side of the world. Let's see if the scales continue to tip onto the side of rupture, of life-change, of abandoning film when I take the next step on my *via curioso e felice* – to China.

3.

It's autumn now, and what an autumn. The sky today is a field of such uninterrupted, powder blue that even birds seem not to be in flight. The blue isn't Dingle blue, it's lighter than that – like bluebells rather than Dorothy Vallens' eye shadow. The rowans around my flat seem to be dying from the trunk outwards, so their centres are umber. Further along the branches there are bracken-coloured leaves, then rust-toned, then copper ones, then marmalade and then, as if the rowans are singing a Liza Minnelli song, there's pizzazz at the leaf tips. Cherry red and lime green zing amidst the alert oranges of the season. Today, outside, there are no young colours.

The Taiwanese director Tsai Ming-liang is coming to Edinburgh to discuss a retrospective of his work. I am asked to interview him. I don't really do interviews anymore, but he is a master.

I first heard of him in the early 1990s. I got a copy of Tsai's film *The River* and saw … what? An almost wordless movie about a young man, played by Lee Kang-sheng, who has a sore neck, who lives in an apartment that is turning into a river, who is lusted after by his mother. The young man seemed lost in life. And the story seemed lost in the mysterious geometry of the film. Key bits of information – where scenes were set, how people were related to one another – were revealed belatedly, or in the background of an image, or in a room glimpsed through another room, like a Vermeer painting. Not since *Blue Velvet* had I seen such a dreamlike film.

It was the second Tsai film that I saw, *Vive l'amour*, which hooked me. Again Lee Kang-sheng, this time as a small-time salesman of funerary wares. Somehow he is connected to a sad and beautiful young woman who sells empty apartments in Taiwan. And somehow each of them interacts with a third character, a man with whom the woman starts a casual relationship. Their lives criss-cross in one of her apartments. At one point Lee hides under a bed and masturbates as the other two make love. Then he sneaks out and kisses the man. *Vive l'amour* was like Billy Wilder's brilliant film *The Apartment* remade by Michelangelo Antonioni.

Tsai's characters drifted like the gorgeous Monica Vitti in *L'Eclisse*, *L'Avventura* and *The Red Desert*. They were searching for love. Tsai seemed drawn to old cinemas, petrol stations, half-constructed underpasses. At the ending of *Vive l'amour*, the woman sits on a park bench, smokes, feels the sun on her face and for five-and-a-half minutes, without a cut, sobs, then stops. The sun comes out, her breathing calms, she lights a cigarette, the wave of grief seems to have passed but, then, another one comes and she's almost hyperventilating again. I cried too and became obsessed with this scene. For a long time I had been interested in the question *Where is the time in a film?* In old-fashioned Hollywood entertainment cinema, it is in the story itself. The story sets the pace of events then allows them to unfold at an appropriate rate. In more modernist films, like Nicolas Roeg's *Don't Look Now*, for example, the ticking clock is in the central character's head. The events are organised according to Donald Sutherland's character's consciousness. If he remembers something, we see it. If he foresees an event, we do too. In most recent films time is a structured as a combination of the two – story time and psychological time.

Beginning perhaps with the Italian neo-realist films made after World War Two, a third temporal dimension entered cinema. In these films we'd watch people sweep a kitchen floor or walk down a street and the event would take as long as it would take in the real world. There was no attempt to relegate the duration of the action to its narrative significance (Alfred Hitchcock's "life with the dull bits left out"), or to make us feel it as the sweeper or walker's consciousness felt it. It simply was what it was. The clock, the timekeeper, was in the real world.

In Tsai's last shot of the weeping woman in *Vive l'amour*, time was most definitely in the real world. You could see this because an unfakable, real-life event – clouds clearing and the sun shining for a moment – came to bear upon the rhythm of an actress's breathing to the extent that it calmed her temporarily. I don't know exactly what Tsai told his actress to do in the scene but I'd wager that part of his instruction was take your time, let the emotions flow naturally, there's no need to rush this scene. After five minutes of real time ebbing and flowing of half mysterious sadness, Tsai audaciously ends his film with his own signature, as if he was signing the world the way Cézanne might sign a painting of Mont Sainte-Victoire.

I turned up at Filmhouse at 5:00 p.m. Tsai and I were due to introduce his movie at six and I would chair the question-and-answer session afterwards. I am always jittery at such times. Tsai had come all the way from Taipei. At 5:05 p.m. the Taiwanese consul arrived and with her a small, smiling, shaved-headed man in a designer jacket, jeans, black slippers and, despite it being a cold Scottish afternoon, no socks. We shook hands. I told him how welcome he was, how honoured we were. I was wearing a kilt and he immediately commented on it. We sat down. He was tactile, giggly and friendly. He touched my leg, which would have seemed intrusive from anyone else but that Tsai – for whom touch in movies is something craved but, often, a disappointing or even destructive event from which we recoil – that he would be so at ease with touch, fascinated me.

I introduce him to a sell-out screening of his new film *I Don't Want to Sleep Alone*. He says that often his films open with only five people in the audience. Sometimes he himself takes tickets out onto the street to sell them. Thunderous applause. The film starts. Actor Lee again, this time in two roles – a man in a coma being washed and a guest worker who's been beaten up, being nursed back to help by a Bangladeshi man. In one scene the Bangladeshi man washes him gently, removes his underpants then scrubs them clean, as if they were sacred. Later Tsai says that these are his favourite scenes in the film. The magnificence lies in the unexpected ellipses and emphases. We do not see the guest worker being beaten up. We see a minor character in big close-up but the Bangladeshi, the emotional centre of the film, only in wide shot, from behind or from the side, until a key scene near the end of the film. An abandoned concrete building becomes a theatre. It has half-filled with water, a haunted well of loneliness and fecundity.

I Don't Want to Sleep Alone is a return to the rain-drenched austerity of Tsai's best work. It contains all his brilliant elements – a fascination with architecture, the sadness of time passing, almost no dialogue, almost no cutting within scenes, night-time settings and the nocturnal lives of cities, shots angled at 45% to the action, and enigmatic storytelling that gradually comes together. More than ever, though, his drifting souls perform real acts of kindness. For fifteen years now, Tsai has shown how rapid urban growth takes its toll on people; how urban modernity outruns human subjec-tivity, leaving it confused and lost. Migrant workers in Tsai films become foreigners in Taipei and the effort to get their bearings is almost too much for them. This is his great theme. This is what makes his films universal and timely. The human tenderness in *I Don't Want to Sleep Alone*, the endless, kind, transgressive touching, suggest that despite all this upheaval, there's hope. Its very last shot, which comes long after the film seems to have ended, is one of the slowest and most daring in movie history. I ask Tsai if he is interested in Buster Keaton, Laurel and Hardy or silent American comedy – there are scenes in the new movie where guys carry a mattress around Kuala Lumpur which remind me of Laurel and Hardy carrying a piano. He says he loves Keaton and that the music in the last scene is from a Charlie Chaplin film!

After the screening five of us go out for dinner. We play a game: each of us has to name their two favourite Eastern and Western movies. I mention Fei Mu's *Spring in a Small Town* as my favourite Eastern one. Tsai says the same. He adds Mikio Naruse's *Floating Clouds*. His Western choices are *The Night of the Hunter* and Robert Bresson's *Mouchette*. I interview him next day. I want to film him lying in bed or in the bath – many of his films are about bodies in bathrooms and beds – but am too shy to ask. Some filmmaker I am. I should chuck this medium.

4. The Lost Object of Chinese Cinema

But I don't. I keep meaning to leave cinema, but then am rejuvenated by someone like Tsai. I keep coming back for more film, like a moth to a flame, thinking up ideas for films. It's as if the manic guy who does all that stuff doesn't know about me, typing away inside his head, writing this book of detours and dithers. He's like a Blasket islander. He is the doer and I am the considerer. He is the gas pedal and I am the brake.

As if to prove this point, he got on a plane to China recently, filmed famous movie directors, did crane shots on the Great Wall and is now in seat 48e, on a flight over eastern China, heading north, towards the great Mongolian plain. I look at him. There he sits in a Fred Perry T-shirt, scribbling where most other people are dozing. Here's what he scribbles:

I'm in seat 48e of an Air China flight from Shanghai to Beijing. It's 8:30 p.m. in the evening. To my right, an old Chinese lady, dressed in turquoise, is dozing. To my left, producer John is reading a novel called The Big Clock. *We've had a long day. Shanghai was rainy and grey. The clouds were so low that the tops of the city's forest of turquoise skyscrapers were lost in them.*

My brain is so tired that I want to play solitaire on the screen in front of me but my handset doesn't work, so I'm forced to write this to pass the time. Doing so means trying to work out what I think of the behemoth of the country that lies below, that I've been in for eight days now, eight days that have coincided with the worst civil unrest in China since the Tian'anmen trauma. Up to a hundred protesters have been killed in Tibet. We've been filming almost non-stop, but in the early mornings I've been flicking between BBC World, CNN and China's state TV news in English, CCTV9. The BBC is measured; CNN is mythic — when the Chinese state censor doesn't pull the plug halfway through a sentence. CCTV's counter-myth is that protestors are murdering people and that the noble state authorities are intervening to prevent bloodshed. The woman in turquoise is watching Gong Li looking sultry in the Curse of the Golden Flower. *I'd rather watch Gong than think of China but I'll have to do the latter at some point, so why not now?*

We've still got two days in Beijing to go and, so, China is still all around me. I am so busy feeling and reacting; to try to think at the same time is hard. I can start, though, with this: in these last few days I've become more used to Chinese faces than my own. Mine, in the mirror in the morning, is battered from jet lag and too little sleep, and foreign to me. I feel I've been eating pak-choi and suckling pig all my life. And the world has become more pictorial for me in the last week than it has ever been. It always is to an exaggerated degree when you are filming — you're always hunting for shots. But in China, shots come galloping at you in a stampede.

So industrious are many Chinese people that I no longer think of myself as a hard worker. But these are small and obvious things to say. I have as yet no broader sense of what I've been caught up in and, so, to make up for this absence and to get the wheels turning, I'll tell you what I did today.

Zoe and Yifan, our Chinese production manager and DP, met John and me at our Shanghai Radisson hotel, which is surmounted by a revolving restaurant a quarter of a kilometre above the city. Shanghai this morning was as rapacious and capitalist as any other morning so far. Han and non-Han Chinese and foreigners walked along, or hung around on, the Nanjing Road. The rain and the flat light killed what sometimes in Shanghai you might call a dazzle.

But we weren't subject to the city's mood this morning because we had our own. We were going to meet and interview the legendary filmmaker Xie Jin, who was like the Vincente Minnelli or Mervyn LeRoy of Chinese film in the sixties, was re-educated during the seventies by cleaning the toilets of the film studios whose panoply was once at his command, whose parents both committed suicide because of authoritarian pressure and who, in the eighties and nineties, made state of the nation movies – such as Hibiscus Town – through which mainstream China began to face the wounds of its recent history.

I saw Xie's Two Stage Sisters (1965) about a decade ago and scribbled notes about its visual dynamism, its packed compositions, its acid colours and the sodden weight of ideology that makes its second half slump. Xie has since rejected this third act preachiness (and suggested that he was leaned on), but the first half's art direction is as dreamily lovely as Black Narcissus, as well composed as Touch of Evil, as compositionally precise as Meet Me in St Louis. His best scenes were wee solar systems of staging, where everything moved around everything else. Add to that the fact that he rode some of the biggest historical waves in twentieth-century history (revolution, the purge of the Cultural Revolution), that his personal life underwent reversals that would seem implausible to the most ardent Hollywood melodramatist, and you have a man I'd like to meet more than almost any other.

So I'm on my way to do so. I'm nervous. I've heard that Xie – who's 85 – joined the Communist Party recently. Am I about to meet one of those robotic apparatchiks that have busts of Mao on their desks and conformism in their eyes? This would be so disappointing to me but John and I are also taking Zoe and Yifan to meet him. I'm worried that I'm forcing them to spend an hour with the kind of party waxwork that I see every morning as I flick Chinese TV.

So we get to Xie's building. A young woman in a CP uniform sits in its lobby. Workers arrive and shake the rain from their brollies. We're early. John does emails. Zoe and Yifan smoke. I pace. An old man turns up. Is it Xie? He doesn't look like his photographs. Xie's assistant phones. She's waiting on him. Ten minutes pass. More ciggies, more pacing. Then another call. He's there. It must have been the old guy.

We take the lift — which smells of the rain — to the sixteenth floor. When the doors open, each of us holds back. No one wants to be the first into Xie's office. I ask Zoe to go ahead as she's been speaking to him.

We go in. Tangles of film cables. Lights. Messy desks. DVDs on shelves (including Borat ...). Yellowing curtains screen out the daylight. Posters of Two Stage Sisters, Hibiscus Town, The Red Detachment of Women, etc. And two photos of Xie with Deng Xiaoping.

But then a tall, gangly, smiling man with died black hair and two hearing aids arrives. He's wearing three fleeces and a scarf over his shirt, baggy trousers and trainers. Big man handshakes. He asks where we'd like to film him — his office or the front office? I mumble that it's an honour to meet him. I want to show him how thankful we are but, also, scout the rooms to see which will look best on camera. His own office is nicotine-stained, lined with books and awards, and has its curtains drawn too. His desk is a heap of papers but feels personal. It's the place to film. I have no common language with Yifan, so have been using lots of sign language with him. He and John get the cameras out. Xie is cracking jokes and making us feel at home. He points out a brass plaque congratulating him on 60 years of filming. It's from the State Administration of Radio, Film and Television, the government organisation that issues permits and therefore controls everything that happens in film in China except the underground. Xie laughs. Like many older Chinese men, he has a comb-over. Zoe has clearly been taken by him but whispers that his hearing is bad and he isn't making total sense. "We should start now", she says.

As we go to, John realises that the sound isn't set up properly. To do so takes five long minutes. I get flustered. John fixes the problem. We begin. I ask Xie about growing up in Shanghai in the thirties, China's first movie golden age; why most of his main characters are women, his use of strong colour; whether he was influenced by Western directors; the impact of the Cultural Revolution on him; whether he sees film as a commercial industry driven by money; if cinema had never been invented, whether the world would be any different. To keep things moving, I ask Zoe not to translate unless she thinks Xie needs a subsidiary question. She speaks loudly. I can hear her repeating the same question several times. Paraphrasing, skipping questions. I have no idea what Xie's answers are but his face and hands are animated and I can hear him mention John Ford and Zhang Yimou.

We shoot for 30 minutes or so. We pull back Xie's office curtains to film him writing his name on the window overlooking Shanghai. The light floods in for what feels like the first time in years. He signs one book to "Mark Cowsins". We take photographs of ourselves with him. We say our goodbyes and ride down in the lift. Yifan mimes a sign for crazy, or senile. Zoe says he was adorable but couldn't answer any *of the questions. He did, however, say nice things about a thirties movie star called Ruan Lingyu.*

———

That's as far as I got in writing on the plane. The flight was short so my time in seat 48e was not long enough to describe the rest of the Xie Jin day. A few days later, I write again. I am in Beijing now. After the interview with him, which was exhilarating and disappointing, we had a celebratory lunch – also a relief lunch – and drove a couple of hours out of Shanghai, past women planting pak choi, past massive coal-fired factories, to a traditional Chinese garden where Brotherhood of Man's "Save Your Kisses for Me" was piped from tannoys, where wooden pagodas rise into the smoky air and where the remains of Ruan Lingyu lie.

Or perhaps they lie there. Ruan is sometimes called the Chinese Greta Garbo. Born in Shanghai in 1910 into dire poverty, she was servant girl in her teens but wangled her way into movies aged 17. By 1930 she was a star and within a year or two her name was on soap bars and billboards. Ruan's films of the 1930s, especially *The Goddess*, show how great she was onscreen. The realism of her acting predated Marlon Brando's by decades. But she killed herself before her twenty-fifth birthday after being hounded about her boyfriends by the sordid tabloids. Her funeral was three miles long. 100,000 people attended it. Women and men committed suicide. Yet the tabloids had so poisoned the air that she was given an ignoble gravestone. Though her funeral was on the front page of *The New York Times*, she has never had her dues in the West, and appears in few film encyclopaedias. In China, as the decades wore on, she was remembered by those – mostly poor women – for whom her realism was a shocking affirmation, but then came the Cultural Revolution which considered her singularity to be rightist, so her grave was destroyed. Then, in the nineties, the patch of ground where her skeleton is thought to lie was overlaid with a new (ugly) life-size sculpture of her lolling in white stone.

More even than Xie Jin, Ruan is the reason I am in China. Her body language in her silent films is so weary that, seventy years after they were made, you can still see the world on her shoulders. But then she smiles her unexpected, luminous smile. Not until Maggie Cheung in Wong Kar-wai's film *In the Mood for Love* did anyone wear a cheongsam (the high-necked, side-buttoned silk dress) as Ruan did. Roland Barthes argues, to paraphrase, that a photograph of a long gone thing touches him like the delayed rays of an exploded star. These thirties movies of Ruan are also beams of light from a long-expired supernova. The writer

Bérénice Reynaud once called Ruan the "lost object par excellence of Chinese cinema".

You'll be surprised to hear, therefore, that she is with me now, as I write. Not bodily, but today, 19 March 2008, 73 years and 11 days after she died, with all our filming over and on a drowsy day in Beijing, when the sun looks as if it has a soft filter clipped to its front, I've gone to the forbidden city and taken a picture of Ruan with me.

Outside, with tourists thronging and young Chinese soldiers standing tall and aligned along the city's astonishing two-mile-long superstructure which plunges to a vanishing point, I held up the picture against the vast painting of Mao that's stuck to the front of the Forbidden city like a belt buckle. Ruan lived long enough to know about Communism and Mao, of course, but not to see that his attempt to redress the centuries-old inequalities of Chinese feudalism would, due to his iniquity, power-worship and sometimes sincere wrongheadedness, result in the appalling deaths of a proportion of her fellow Chinese. I don't know whether she was ever here in the Forbidden City and, if so, whether she sat on these steps southeast of the Gate of Supreme Harmony, pale sunshine warming one half of her face, cold wind on the other, and, if so, what she thought. But her picture is here today. Has anyone ever taken a picture of

Ruan around this vast, tranquil, conceited, insolent place before?

We walk on and I am overwhelmed. The buildings in this cascading megastructure, this procession of palatial gates surmounted by tiled and gold-leafed roofs with a touch of coquetry in their upturned edges, are named harmony, peace, tranquillity, heaven.

Ruan and I walk north, through more courtyards, gardens and gates, for another forty minutes. Like most imperial architecture, it tries to belittle. It wants to blast me with its opulence, its awe-story. It is telling me how unpolished, un-thought out I am. The Topkapı Palace in Istanbul does this, as does St Peter's in Rome, and Versailles, the federal buildings in Washington, D.C. and the like. They present for me to survey – because it is theirs and not mine – a domain. But because the Qing dynasty was Buddhist, the bits of this city that they in particular built also do something like the opposite. The open spaces, Zen planting, the balance and relative emptiness in the Qing sections are calming and even enlarging. I feel little and large here – in awe at the city's immensity, but becalmed by its gentleness.

Yesterday I went to the Great Wall of China so, in two days, I've seen two wonders of the feudal world. Plus I've absorbed a skinful of ordinary Chinese life, all against the mood music of whatever is happening in Tibet. Am I able to make any kind of sense of all this? At breakfast this morning, eating sausages and steamed dumplings and drinking haw juice, I realised that I've been dreaming in China far more than I dream at home. Anxiety about filming? Yes, but I get that on any shoot. Then it clicked. China, particularly at the time of this Tibet fighting, is Freudian. It has a surface – just, proud, mindful of its minorities, modern – but under the surface is uncensored energy. You can feel that energy everywhere.

Suddenly the double vision I see here, is comparable to something from my world that I understand: the split between conscious and unconscious life. The former is audible but limited, the latter is wild but can't quite be heard. In China as you walk down the street you feel that what you see around you is whispering about what you don't see. The country, in my very limited experience, double-solicits. Its *prima facie* street tangle does so but so does that which it disavows.

Then I realise that this isn't the first time I've had this thought. My Chinese publisher took me for a meal in Shanghai recently with a playwright, a filmmaker and some academics. They decided that there should be a serious theme for our table talk. It would be "the difference between above and below the table culture." At fancy dinners I am usually the joker in the pack, but here I had to be serious. A silence fell across the circular table and everyone looked at me. I'm sure I reddened. I didn't really know what they meant. But I started to talk, saying that maybe there's what we profess and genuinely think we believe, and the forces of what we really are. This didn't lead the discussion very far and the brainy people around the table could see me toiling, but I was talking about how their vast country feels to me after three visits.

—

That's what I wrote in and about China, some months ago now. As I reread it I find the writer strange, all gas and no brake. As I type, an email appears in my inbox from *Screen International*. XIE JIN IS DEAD. I click on Chinadaily.com. He was found in a hotel room in his hometown of Shangyu on 18 October 2008. He was there to celebrate the 110th birthday of his old university. The article says that his 58-year-old son, who had cancer, predeceased him by just a few months. I discover that his two other sons had learning difficulties. The Chinese reports don't mention that his parents committed suicide.

And I haven't mentioned that Egypt's Youssef Chahine has died too. Of a brain haemorrhage, in July. Both lovely men. I click through my photos of each. Since I've started making *The Story of Film*, Ingmar Bergman,

Michelangelo Antonioni and Ousmane Sembène have died too. Five more lost objects who, from now on, will only touch us by the delayed rays of their movies.

5. Iraq. Talk about the Gas Pedal

The truth is catching up on me. As I've been writing these pages about leaving the film industry, about putting my put on the brake, I've put my foot on the accelerator. The rupture is no more. Starting filming *The Story of Film* seems have allowed me to shake off my doubts. Until now I've always worked with cinematographers, but in recent years cameras have become simpler to use and so, in China, I started shooting myself and discovered that the new intimacy with my imagery excited me. I could go out at dawn, on my own, and frame shots. Film sequences. A distance had been closed.

When I started writing this book I didn't know where it would go. If I'd made a list of all the places I didn't know I'd go, near the top would be Kurdish Iraq, during its war. And so that's where I'm heading as I write. The foot is on the gas pedal once more.

I'm on a plane flying to Istanbul with Gill Parry, a film producer. We've both travelled in Kurdistan – she in Iraqi and Turkish Kurdistan, me in the Iranian and Turkish bits. We both felt buzzed by the vitality of the

Kurds, the way they slalom around things they're not allowed to say, their ideas, politics, gleaming eyes, their angry songs. Aspects of what I saw reminded me of my own childhood growing up Catholic in the Troubles in Ireland.

So we wanted to make some kind of film with them, to hand cameras over to them, point a camera at their life force and in doing so reflect on my own. I've become interested in kids' imaginations and have always loved the Scheherazade stories in *One Thousand and One Nights*, so suggested making what I called a magic realist film with kids who can fly or are invisible, about dogs that talk, about trees that sing, the sort of thing I imagined during the Troubles. As such, as well as the usual film equipment you need for such a doc, Gill and I have brought lots of cameras to give to the kids, a bag full of toys, including a wind-up turtle and a wide-eyed alien that keeps making bleeping noises because I don't know how to turn it off.

Given the fact that we are trying to combine magic, fun, dreams, war, fantasy and childhood, and the fact that the kids and I will be filming without a DP, we are nervous. I stare out the airplane window. I read Scheherazade. Her stories get me thinking. What if I try to film in Iraq using the technique that the surrealists called "exquisite corpse"? What if one child starts a story – about chickens, the moon, whatever – then another continues it, then a third and fourth do so too, in relay fashion? Would that work?

We arrive at Istanbul, late. I go to a hammam at 11 p.m. It's $60. I hover. Could it be seedy? Especially at this time of night? Çemberlitaş Hamamı was built by Sinan in 1584. The changing area is all wooded slats. The towels are seventies colours and hard – no fabric softener. I get soap and a bracelet for my key. I go into the baths. The room is a dimly lit, misty Ottoman octahedron, with stars cut in the roof and niches, washing stalls and rooms off. I lie on the huge central heated stone. The heat is pressing on my chest. I breathe in fast, but out slowly. The sound of this, the bellows of my life. I am in a Scheherazade story. Do I wake or sleep?

Wallop. A huge guy hits me hard. I stare at him. His jaunty smile tells me that I did nothing wrong. He just wanted to tell me that it was my turn to be washed.

I remember what happened next. He held an inflated bag, like a huge balloon, above my head, and burst it. From it came a cloud of foam that smelled like the powdered soap that my mum used to do her hand washing with. That cloud covered me. I was eight again. The guy went to work. He moved my loin towel around expertly. He washed my ears and it was heaven. He was gentle with my neck, but then seemed unaware that I might need it once he had finished with it. He seemed unconcerned about my shoulder socketry. As I change, two guys from London recognise me. They say they go to hammams regularly, "because our bodies are worth it".

My body has seen nothing like it. I walk back to the hotel, drifting with cleanness. Hundreds of birds are lit by the sodium lights of the vast Blue Mosque that always looks like a power station to me.

Our flight onwards to Iraq is delayed by ten hours. We meet a posh British man dressed in linen. He smells of cognac and talks about the micropolitics of the Kurdistan. He's like someone in a Graham Greene story, in security, working with the guys who used to guard him. Six, seven, eight o'clock come and go, and my eyes are burning. We get onto the flight to Erbil. I fall down into the well of sleep, then surface to see desert below.

We clear customs at Erbil airport, and then push our trolleys out into the oven heat glare. People stand in line in the long thin shadows thrown by flagpoles. Shade is like money here. Inexplicably, Graham Greene man-phones ahead to Gharib our fixer translator, arranging where we might meet him. He does not consult us.

We meet Gharib, who I take to at once, and Sami, our boy racer driver. They take us to our hotel. Sami's car blasts warm air con. It's like standing behind the engines of our plane.

It's – what – noon now? Breakfast of tinned spaghetti and cardamom coffee. Barbra Streisand sings "Woman in Love". I go to my room. The sink's broken. Seventies furniture. The thick navy curtains are pulled closed to mask the blinding scorching heat. I thought that I'd be able to think of nothing but tiredness but in fact the heat is more compelling. It roars at us, in our faces. A chink in the curtains lets in a beam of sunlight, searing like a laser. I sleep …

Minutes or days later, I put on a suit and white shirt, and factor 50 sun cream, and meet the others in the lobby. We drive to the Kurdistan Regional Government (KRG) and its culture and film ministries. Our two security guys, Farhad and Abdullah, follow in their car. They are a condition of us getting insurance. Their walkie-talkies beep constantly. They offer us bullet-proof vests.

We get to the ministries. Though they are KRG, they are guarded by Arab soldiers whom we greet in Arabic rather than Kurdish. We meet the Culture Minister. Handshakes, greetings, tea. We sit politely, straight-backed, on sofas like my mum had in the early eighties. The minister is nice to us. He approves our mission and gives us our filming permits on government headed paper. We do five such meetings. My bright, friendly face masks exhaustion. I want to curl up on the sofas and sleep. Producer Gill is better at these formalities.

I get irritated. I want to start filming, or eat or drink wine, but we go to meet yet more officials. The favourite films of the Culture Minister's son are *Rush Hour 1* and *2*. I try to turn this into a conversation, but my brain is dead. The film minister's ringtone is Lionel Richie's "Hello". It rings again and again. Somehow the minister is answering his phone, handwriting permission letters and auditioning on camera for a Danish film producer, all at once.

Our filming starts. Days pass. The temperature rises to the high thirties and low forties. The heat feels as if it is between me and the world around me. I'm locked in. All I can smell is factor 50. We drive in Sami's wind tunnel, then I jump out, climb a ridge, set up the camera, line up a shot, film a landscape that looks Koranic or Talmudic, then jump back in the car. I'm wearing white – including a white woolly hat – but am cooking ...

———

Looking back, fourteen years after I wrote these things, fourteen years after I went to Kurdish Iraq to make what would become my first feature length film – *The First Movie* – I can see that what I was looking for was, simply, inspiration. *The First Movie* gave me it. By filming it myself, I stepped across an invisible line into a more creative period in my working life. I started to think of my films as lyric prose. I read a line by Gertrude Stein – "observation plus construction make imagination" – and thought and underlined it. It took me some time to realise that it sums up my approach to filmmaking precisely. As I wrote the above, a shift in me took place. I find many of my sentences about sunlight on hedgerows in Ireland irritating now, and I search in vain in these words from 2008 for a real understanding of the change that was happening in me. But that's because it was happening under the table.

Arthur Rimbaud gave up poetry and became a quarry man and then a circus cashier. Was I ever likely to undergo a similar rupture, or was I always going to return to cinema?

Dear Directors

— 2016 —

DEAR ORSON WELLES,

Can we go around the world together? You're dead, of course, but that doesn't stop me imagining us as a gruesome twosome, on the road. Maybe you will accept my offer because you were a mendicant friar. When Hollywood didn't know what to do with you, you set off and out to Spain and France, Yugoslavia and Morocco, to ply your trade, to set up your baroque stall in souks and courts and on stages, between rages.

From where I'm sitting – about which, more in a moment – it looks like you couldn't stop making films, Orson, from *Citizen Kane* onwards. You had a will to cinema, a longing for it, or maybe not quite a longing because that implies that it was outside you, far away, something to be reached for when, in fact, it's better to say that it was inside you. You embodied movies. It's hard to write to you and not use the word embody, Orson. Your body was like an echo-chamber, like the belly of Ahab's whale; it produced that voice of yours that rumbled, and all those kings you played.

So can we go on this travelogue, Orson? We could see it, also, as an epilogue. An epilogue to your life, which was so baroque that it is begging for one. I wish this letter could be a dialogue, Orson. For me it is a kind of dialogue. Shall we make it a decalogue? Shall we visit ten places around the world, with cinema on our mind the way Diego Rivera had Frida on his mind, in that great picture he did of himself? To mention Frida and Diego is to think of Mexico, of course. Can we travel the world together without going to Mexico? Without thinking of Sergei Eisenstein's time there? Without nodding our caps now to the fact that part of the reason for travelling, the compulsion to travel, the propulsion of travel, is what Eisenstein called "ex-sta-sis": the desire to get out of yourself, the rapture of self-loss, the hope that, if we are fleet of foot, we might be able to outwit ourselves, leave them behind, reverse the polarity of self and other?

Indulge me, Orson. Let's strike out together on this travelogue, epilogue, dialogue, Decalogue. Let's travel the world and, as we do, ask a simple question. What are the movies? Years ago, when I was in my twenties (and as close to handsome as I was ever going to get), I went to Naples to film a grand lady in her sixties, Flora Pinto d'Albavilla Mariata Capaldo. As her name suggests, she was from aristocratic stock. Just as the years of Garibaldi were long gone, so was her money but, somehow, she managed to ignore this fact and live in a small apartment gussied up with chandeliers and French furniture. One evening, after filming, she told me that she'd like to take me to "le plus beau balcon du monde." We drove for an hour in her fancy car, arrived in Ravello, from where she took me to a balcony overlooking the bay of Naples, the Costiera Amalfitana. The moon was full and twinned with its reflection in the sea. As we stood on the balcony, Flora told me that Greta Garbo took Leopold Stokowski there. It was indeed, for me, a working-class Belfast boy, the most beautiful balcony in the world. As we stood there, she said to me:

> Travel the world with me. I have not long to go, but we could visit the great art galleries together. I would pay for everything. All I'd ask for in return is your company and, occasionally, for you to wear swimming trunks.

Did Tennessee Williams write her lines that night? Did he write this scene, Orson? Did you? I mention it here, of course, because her invitation – "travel the world with me" – seemed to me then, and still does, one of the most risky and beautiful things that one person can say to another. And so I say it to you, Orson.

1.

Can we start our journey here, where I am now? I'm in Cannes, France. I'm sitting in a cheap restaurant called La Frigate. It's lunchtime. The sky is grey – the Matisse colours are only here in the sunshine, as you well know – and, just to further dispel the glamour, I can tell you that I smell of sweat (I've been schlepping around town today) and *vin blanc provençal*. I'm away from the numbers, as someone called Paul Weller once wrote, beyond the Cannes film festival bubble; it's where I want to be. There's a quietude in this small restaurant. Nobody's talking about the film business.

I don't need to describe Cannes to you, of course, because you were here often. In 1948, you lived in the exclusive Eden Roc hotel at the Cap d'Antibes, near here, didn't you? And in that year Rita Hayworth visited you at the Cap, to try to reconcile your relationship. Two years later, you took a taxi from Italy to the hotel, at a cost of $500, to try to convince producer Darryl Zanuck to fund your film of Shakespeare's *Othello*. You dropped to your knees and begged him. The place went silent. Perhaps to bring the moment to an end, and out of embarrassment, he offered you $100,000 to play a part in *Prince of Foxes*. You accepted. The money helped fund your film. You charged him for the taxi. Two years later, in 1952, *Othello* won the Palme d'Or here. And, then, in 1966, you were given a prize here for your contribution to world cinema. Jean Cocteau's lover Jean Marais made the announcement. Raquel Welch, whose beauty then brought tears to our eyes, took you to the stage. Behind you stood Mademoiselle Présidente du Jury, Sophia Loren, who was from Naples and who, therefore, had probably stood on *le plus beau balcon du monde*. So I don't need to tell you about this place. Unlike me, you've seen its inner sanctum, its upper echelons, its holiest of holies, its tracking shots, its foleys.

But what does Cannes tell us about the movies, Orson? As I sit in this restaurant, ten metres from the sea, with scooters buzzing by like wasps, I notice what I've always noticed about this place. There's no smell of the sea. I've heard, several times – can this be true? – that before the Cannes Film Festival starts, they comb the sea to remove the seaweed. If they do do this, why? To make the water look cleaner, clearer? Seaweed gives the sea its smell so, removing it, makes the water more like an ideal but, also, more distant, because it isn't confirmed by smell. Is it the wine that makes me see, in this, a metaphor for the movies? What we see in a film is there and not there, isn't it Orson? Just like you're here and not here now. Movies are over-available to some senses and completely unavailable to others.

2.

To think of the lack of smell here, and then the lack in film, is to start with the bad news. So let's get it out of the way, Orson. Let's fly to Krakow in Poland, then take a train to Oświęcim, a place the world knows better as Auschwitz. Let's go there in autumn, when the trees are copper. Those trees make Oświęcim a lovable place, or would do so if it wasn't so hateful. Did you go there, Orson? I know your film *The Stranger* is about a Nazi and you said that Kafka's *The Trial* is "pre-Auschwitz" – which is why you changed its ending in your film of the book. Auschwitz is the mother of all elisions, isn't it? A place where people were so de-imagined that an unimaginable factory system was perfectly imaginable.

So why go here, why make this the second of our decalogue, after Cannes? To acknowledge what movies are crap at, that's why, and to cede initial ground to the cinephobes. The homicidal gas chambers of Auschwitz-Birkenau were amongst the worst things we made in the twentieth century, Orson. And yet we didn't film them. There's almost no footage of them. We stand here in front of where they once were and look at the place where film cameras of the time did not look. Of course the Nazis didn't want their unholiest of unholies, these crematoria, to be filmed, so it's perhaps not cinema's fault that it didn't do so. But it has to accept joint responsibility, I think, because, in the mid-forties, cameras were too big to smuggle in here to record this as evidence of the attempted extermination of the Jews and, of course, cinema was still too redolent of entertainment in those years to look into such a heart of darkness. It was morally serious sometimes, in some places, but such times and places were the exceptions Orson, weren't they? Did you know this when you were making *Citizen Kane*, before the gas chambers here started murdering people? When did it dawn on you that movies were a bit trivial? Or did it? Or are they? Or aren't they? Claude Lanzmann released a film, *Shoah*, in the year that you died, Orson. I wonder did you manage to see it? Its nine-and-a-half hours are Lanzmann's attempt to make something big enough and serious enough and detailed enough and evidential enough to begin to undo cinema's solecism in not filming these gas chambers, whose foundations lie before us.

3.

So that's the worst bit done, Orson. In our road movie to find out what movies are, or why they matter, we've started with their fatal flaw. Can we go now to our third place, Yugoslavia, where you met your beloved Oja Kodar? Let's go by train and, as we do, can I tell you that Yugoslavia is no more? It broke apart in the mid-nineties, a decade after you died. The Soviet Union collapsed and, so, its satellites did too. The break-up of Yugoslavia was the worst European war since the time of Auschwitz. The town of Sarajevo was besieged, and 11,000 people died, Orson. I mention this because I was in Sarajevo during that siege and, whilst I was there, discovered why cinema matters. I was invited, by Obala Art Center, to bring films to show underground, to local people, in defiance of the siege. I did so and was amazed that, during a war and at great risk to themselves, those people came out at night, during the shelling, to see films. Why? Because, I realised, cinema and art aren't the icing on the cake, they are the cake. Movies make us feel alive, connected. Cinema makes moments seem more than they were, as big as the sphinx, as available for inspection, as gnomic, as here and not here as life, as sensuous and intoxicating.

Do you agree Orson? I think you do. You spent so much time in Hollywood, in a world where cinema was thought of as the icing, and yet you ended your film of Kafka's *The Trial* with the mushroom cloud of an atomic bomb, and *The Magnificent Ambersons* and *Citizen Kane* are about hubris. You seem certain in your work that the movies aren't *Loin de Vietnam*.

4.

Can we pack our bags now and fly again, to the place where I live, Edinburgh in Scotland. You came here in 1953, Orson. You went to the Cameo cinema, where we are now, and made a state of cinema speech. Do you remember? I wish I had been there. Here are the newspaper reports about it. Look at the headline, it says that you "Limp into the Festival with a 'Moan'". You'd sprained your ankle. On the stage of the Cameo – let's climb up onto it now and stand in front of its champagne curtain – you said "The new artist goes out to Hollywood or Rome or London ... and, until they catch on to him, he does something coming out of himself, something original ..." Then, you argued, the industry diverts the filmmaker from such personal filmmaking to something more mainstream and formulaic because "films take too long to make, they cost too much and go out to too large an audience." You said that by having to appeal to an audience of 60,000,000, rather than, say, 3,000,000, the art gets blunt and bland. The result of this is that cinema is "dead, dead, dead".

Guess what, Orson? Are you ready for a good surprise, a surprise which opened up the movies? Four decades after you said these words, on this stage, in this spotlight, the medium of film started to be digitised; equipment miniaturised, processes speeded up, budgets dropped and, so a new artistic-business model emerged in which films with strong aesthetics could be seen by far smaller audiences and not be called failures. Your dream came true. Film stopped becoming an autocratic art, an art that needed a patron the way Italian fresco painters needed the Vatican. It became like oil painting on canvas – intimate, for self-starters. Here in the Cameo, you recommended "a world congress to discuss the economics of the film industry." That didn't quite happen but technical change did and, as Le Corbusier said, the technology created the poetics.

I wish, wish, wish that we could see the films you would make with such poetics and your will to form. There's a film called *Festen*, Orson, made in Denmark by Thomas Vinterberg, and it was shot by tiny cameras planted all over the set. The imagery was rough and almost fell apart, like the paintings of Seurat, but films like it removed the inertia from the movies, its lumbering, slothfulness. What your friend Gene Kelly could have done with such techniques! If you had made your film of Cervantes' *Don Quixote* with such cameras, you could have finished it in a few months.

5.

Talking of *Festen* makes me want to take you to our fifth place, Orson: Copenhagen. Let's go to its outskirts, to a production company called Zentropa, housed on an old army barracks, with a tank at its entrance, an outdoor, unheated swimming pool in which to swim naked at lunchtime, and garden gnomes on which to piss. The people at Zentropa – Vinterberg, a director called Lars von Trier and others – would have applauded your speech in the Cameo and, also, probably heckled you. In the mid-nineties, like latter-day surrealists, they published a manifesto called Dogme, which was a vow of chastity and simplicity which repudiated the complexity of filmmaking, its aesthetic gloss and Hollywood lustre. They would look for a new directness in film. Their ideas energised the movies.

So, whilst we're here in Copenhagen, shall we come up with our own manifesto, Orson, our own ten commandments for cinema today, based on your Cameo ideas, and the chutzpah of Dogme? Let's. To get our blood going, let's swim naked in Lars' chilly pool. No? You don't like the swim bit? Ok, I'll be back in a moment. Here goes …

The Edinburgh Movie Manifesto

1.

Try to show that which, without you,
might never have been seen.
— Robert Bresson

2.

Make films about what you don't know.
— Kossakovsky

3.

Always remember Garbo's face.

4.

Watch films like a child.

5.

Never make a film whose end is
foreseeable from its beginning.

6.

Movie stardom should be like presidential
terms — no longer than four years.

7.

No clichés, reverse angles, three-point
lighting or well-made scripts.

8.

No advertising in cinemas – there's none in churches.

9.

Death to the Oscars.

10.

Shoot sex scenes with as much energy as car chases.

11.

More sound design, shooting silent, pauses.

12.

Put on screen lives that have
never been there before.

13.

Film fights the way Ozu shoots kettles.

14.

Understand the full tenderness, tragedy,
and rapture of the movies.

15.

Remember the z-axis.

16.

A movie is a love letter. Poetry, not prose.

That was fun, wasn't it Orson? Let's print it up on a poster. Let's hang it on walls, and paste it on multiplexes. Let's spray paint it on the Hollywood sign. Let's write it in the sky, let's get it tattooed – I'm game if you are.

6.

Our trip's starting to feel like a manifesto, a pub crawl. Shall we drink something? Brandy's your thing, I think. Let's drink some at the sixth stop on our world tour of the movies, the Hollywood sign itself. From the hill behind it, let's climb down to it at dusk. There are rattlesnakes here. The sign bangs as it cools, like there's someone trapped inside it, trying to get out. Buster Keaton, maybe? Or your ex-wife Rita Hayworth? People whom Hollywood destroyed. Those crushed by the wheels of industry. How did Hollywood destroy people, Orson? How and why did it try to destroy you? By commodifying them? By sating every material need imaginable and, at the same time, starving their exis-tential needs? By glorifying beauty and youth – beauty and youth came out of its test tubes – and then gagging when people get old? By being repelled by the very egos that were its vast, unburyable waste product? By feeding stars and directors on the desire to be desired so that they slaver for it like Pavlov's dogs and, then, standing back and watching the adulation wane, the heat go out of the day, the selfhoods begin to bang as they cooled, just like this sign?

7.

As we think these things, shall we go to and leave a gardenia on Marilyn's grave in Westwood Memorial Park? Our seventh of the Decalogue in this travelogue? Let's. Look at it. You told Peter Bogdanovich that you met her at a party when she was a starlet. A man pulled down the front of her dress to reveal her breasts. And she just laughed. Is that right?

The marble on her grave here's pearly smooth with all those years of touching, like it is in the grotto of Lourdes. Every time I come here I'm stopped in my thoughts by the realisation that she was 36 when she died. I was only getting going when I was 36, but she was already gone with the wind, a lesson unlearnt, nuclear waste. Just as Auschwitz-Birkenau was unfilmed, Marilyn Monroe was over-filmed, over-filmable, the definition of *photogénie*. The camera loved her, as it loved India but, in both cases, it failed to show us that the tragedy should not be passed over. We bought our movie ticket to see Marilyn, and became tourists in her beauty and sadness, visitors for a day who, then, upped and left, leaving her to face the mess that was mostly not of her making.

Let's leave this memorial garden, Orson. There's Joseph von Sternberg's wall crypt to our left, tiny, at ground level. You and he shared Marlene Dietrich didn't you? You each loved her; you each filmed her smoking, and saw eros in that smoking.

8.

Let's jump on a plane and fly 11,500 kilometres from this place, which many think of as the centre of the movie world, to our eighth place, which in some ways is the centre – a centre – of the film world. Let's fly east to find out something else about the movies. Let's go to the city of Ouagadougou in Burkina Faso.

Not the first place that comes to mind when you think of the centre of the movie world, I know. But walk with me in this heat, Orson, across this red soil, to the centre of the city and look ahead of us. That big sculpture in the middle of the road there, that tiered thing stacked with discs, is a monument to ... filmmakers. In no other city in the world is the central space, the ground zero, dedicated to film. Why is it here? Firstly, because in 1969, when Africa was trying to organise its movie industry, the Ouagadougou film festival FESPACO was established here as a pan-African, bi-annual colloque and congress. But there are film festivals all around the world; what makes Ouagadougou different? Its opening night is the biggest film event I've ever been to. It takes place in the national Stade du 4-Août, and feels like an Olympic event. The reason it's so big explains why film is so central to Burkinabe life. Literacy levels in this country's 15-24-year-olds are 33 percent now and were 6.6 percent when FESPACO was founded. Burkina Faso is, therefore, a visual and oral culture rather than a literate one like Scotland (which, because of Protestantism, had amongst the highest literacy levels in the world in the 1800s). As you know, countries that value the word highly often see imagery as redolent of surface, fashion, unreason or even decadence. Hence the iconoclasm of Protestant and Islamic fundamentalism at the time of the Reformation and the destruction, in 2001, of the Buddhas of Bamiyan in Afghanistan, which had been carved in the sixth century CE.

Film, then, was a key part of how Burkinabe people were entertained and socialised. It helped this, and other Francophone West African countries like Senegal, find their place in the world, share ideas and do moral and aesthetic thinking. This reminds us, I think, of the fact that cinema is as close to a universal language as we can get. It clearly transcends linguistic barriers. It also works inter-culturally as well as intra-culturally. I can learn a lot about Bengali life from the movies of Satyajit Ray, and of Japanese life from the movies of Yasujirō Ozu and his onetime assistant Shōhei Imamura. Cinema acts like an empathy machine.

9.

We're getting towards the end of our trip, Orson. I've been thinking about our manifesto and your talk in the Cameo in which you envisaged that a new smallness of scale in filmmaking would, paradoxically, open it up and make it creatively bigger. At the time I thought of Manila in the Philippines, and wanted to bring you there, but I wasn't sure that you would be game. Now I can see your wanderlust, I think we should go there. I've never been. Shall we go together?

Here we are. It's as humid as I expected. More tragic, external. Have you ever been somewhere where you can see everything in the streets, in the fields? In golden days the glimpse of stocking was thought of as something shocking … You never needed to be optimistic about people did you? Or did you? The New Deal shaped you, which was progressive, which knew that people would grow if they were fertilised. That's what we are seeing here.

But in filmmaking terms, why are we here? Because the filmmakers are leading the way. They don't have a fancy film school, or film magazine, or great films on TV or large budgets but, nonetheless, directors like Khavn De La Cruz and Lav Diaz are rethinking the movies. De La Cruz makes manic montage mash-up movies, at least one a year, and sometimes one a week – like your old hero John Ford did in America in the early days. He – De La Cruz – shoots on video, mocks religion and gender, uses kitsch, pop, porn, camp, punk, melodrama, news, violence, graphics and elegy to create shanty town cinema that feels poor, vibrant, desperate and compelling. As his movies cost little, and grab our attention, they make money. This way of working is what you hoped for.

Lav Diaz's films are as slow as De La Cruz's are fast. Some shots last 10 minutes. The movies run many hours. They are numinous, modernist, symphonic, mysterious frescoes of great sadness and stillness. They could fill a cathedral.

When I say the word cathedral, I always think of the last shot of Andrei Tarkovsky's *Nostalghia*. Did you ever see it? It was made two years before you died. The shot starts on a man and a dog, who are outside a small country cottage that we have seen several times in the film. Then it pulls back to reveal that the whole landscape is inside a cathedral. It's as if the whole world is sacred. And then it starts to snow in the cathedral.

10.

It's been quite a trip Orson. We've been kings of the road, the Don and Sancho Panza maybe. Where should our last place, be? There's a col in the west of Scotland, called the Rest and be Thankful; at first I thought we could stop there, but then I realised that it's good to end on a grace note, isn't it? A small thing. I have a tattoo on my arm which says "the oar and winnowing fan". You probably know the story. It comes from Homer. Ulysses has been travelling by boat (the kingdom of the oar) then walks away from the sea, carrying the oar, until he comes to an agricultural place where they no longer recognise the oar as an oar, and think, instead, that it is a winnowing fan for cutting down crops.

I love this parable of misrecognition. It celebrates in-between places, nowhere places, exactly the kind of places where talent comes from, and begins to apprehend the world. Such places, with their lack of expectation or hubris, have perfect sight lines. On a clear day you can see forever from them. Shall we end our Decalogue-epilogue-travelogue to try to see what cinema is today, three decades after one of cinema's greatest thinkers – you – died, in such an in-between place?

I spin the globe, as it spins at the start of RKO movies, which distributed *Citizen Kane*, and then stop it at Traverse City, Michigan, 292 miles from where you were born. They're showing *Chimes at Midnight* and *Citizen Kane* at their film festival.

Orson, you gave me the movies, and they took me in their arms. Thank you.

Mark Cousins

DEAR CHRIS MARKER,

He Wrote Me: King's Cross Station,
London, 7 March 2013, 9:51 a.m.

You don't know me, but I'm on a train and thought of
you and wanted to write. It's raining outside. In four
hours and 45 minutes I'll be back home in Scotland.
Between me and that lie 500 miles, misty fields, an
England trying to work out how to deal with what it
thinks is foreign, and a Scotland wondering whether it
should secede from the UK. Motion, emotion, attachment and its opposite.

Once before, when you were still alive, when I was
director of the Edinburgh International Film Festival,
I wrote to you. I was doing a season of films called
Great Moments in Documentary History. I asked you
for suggestions of great documentaries. You replied
gnomically, as I recall, and suggested that I show your
film *Slon Tango*, in which an elephant dances. We did so.

I thought of you this morning because of Mexico. I made a film there, *What is This Film Called Love?*, which was influenced by you. The film is narrated by a woman who, we discover in the end, is me. I had the idea of writing as a woman because of your film *Sans Soleil*: in particular, the commentary in that film, in which a female voice, referring to you, regularly says "He wrote me". I loved that you imagined a woman who had received letters from you. And so, because of your three words "he wrote me", I am writing to you.

I'd love to know how you decided to use the "he wrote me" frame.

Yours,
Mark Cousins

Cher Monsieur Cousins,

Thank you for writing about "he wrote me". If your train is on the move, look out the window. What you will see is why I wrote those words. Are London's suburbs drifting by like clouds? Are fields whizzing past your window so quickly that, in the foreground, they blur? If so, that's all you need to know about the commentaries in my films, especially the one in *Sans Soleil*. As I travelled around the world, filming, I always felt an immediate blur and detachment between the image and what it recorded. A relative velocity. A moment after I'd filmed the boat, the cat, the face, the cityscape, the bullet train, the beach, the cemetery, it had changed, moved on, so my image of it was an image of what it once was, even if that once was just a moment ago. To accept this, that all images are the light from a star which might no longer exist, is to realise that the words that accompany such images (if indeed they are combined with words, a commentary) must acknowledge such a detachment. Do you remember the TV and film footage of rockets blasting into space? After a certain ascent, their fuel cylinders and boosters detach and begin to fall from the sky, leaving the smaller rocket to continue into space (and time). An image is like those fuel cylinders and boosters. It detaches and is left behind. So, *Sans Soleil* is what's left behind from my filming in Japan and elsewhere. It falls from the sky like the burning magnesium from a firework. My commentary takes the form of "he wrote me" to capture the past-tenseness of this, its elegy, its threnody, its beautiful decay.

There is a multiple detachment in the commentary of *Sans Soleil*. I did not write any letters; therefore no woman exists who received them; therefore she could not be reading them now, in some present tense, after she received them, because they don't exist and neither does she ... A Möbius strip of sorts. I made the strip not just for fun, for the game, but because its contours, its distance, allowed me to take (and invoke and depict) the distance I feel whilst sitting in an edit, a place out of the world, looking at images of the world. "He wrote me" allowed me to put sadness into my film, and metaphor, and doubt, and hope, and thought and a numinous quality. It allowed me to question films and filming, and to worship, fetishise filming. In the edit suite, looking at my footage, I was like James Stewart looking at Kim Novak in Hitchcock's *Vertigo* – not sure if the footage is alive or dead, aware of me or insensate, awake or dreaming, acting or being, *eros* or *thanatos*.

"He wrote me" are three words against flatness, affectlessness, inertia, silence, thinness, meaninglessness. They are, I hope, a singing, ringing tree. Make of them what you will. Take your distance from them. They are already a threnody, a prayer for the dead. Me.

Yours,
Chris Marker

DEAR PAUL SCHRADER,

We've met a few times. We got drunk once, an exciting event in my life but not in yours, I'm sure. I remember more of what you said to me on those two occasions than almost any other encounters I've had with a film-maker. Until I met you, I thought I'd thought about things like religion, story, metaphors and bodies, but you ran rings around me. Billy Wilder had the words "What Would Lubitsch Do?" in a frame on his office wall. Since those two meetings, I've sometimes asked myself "What Would Schrader Think?"

I've been asking that a lot recently, probably because your new film *The Canyons* is coming. It sounds as if it takes you to a different part of the taste map, the sex map, the filmmaking map. It sounds as if you are thinking aloud with *The Canyons*, trying to keep ahead, perhaps, or keep your head perhaps?

I'm on the top deck of a bus in Edinburgh as I write this. Front seat. As the bus drives forwards, its cinemascope window, like a movie phantom ride, makes me think of *Taxi Driver*'s windscreen. But the cityscape today isn't moving in slo-mo, isn't scored to Bernard Herrmann's sliding minor chords, isn't coloured like Uccello. And as I'm not driving, the film of yours that this bus ride is closer to for me is *Light Sleeper*. I imagine myself as Willem Dafoe in that film, staring out the passenger window of cars, at the passing scene. Everything for him is a passing scene. Life slides past him like Herrmann's chords, like a drug comedown, like Cyd Charisse.

As my bus makes its winding way from the housing estates on the outskirts of Edinburgh, Paul, towards the stately, centre of this capital city, from the local to the national to the international, it strikes me how much your work so far has been a tracking shot, a phantom ride, a rear-view mirror. You said recently that you had to write your book *Transcendental Style in Film: Ozu, Bresson and Dreyer* when you were young, when the experiences of your Calvinist upbringing were still fresh in your mind, because you could sense them slipping away. You were probably glad to see them in the rear-view mirror, receding, releasing you, and yet you got a book out of them before they went, before they were a dot on the horizon. Granton, a part of Edinburgh that's working-class, where I got on this number 16 bus twenty minutes ago, is a dot on my horizon. I was brought up in a place like Granton, but now I live in a fancy flat, with arty people. My own private slippage. We're slipping now, on this bus, between worlds. Can you hear the social glissando, Paul? Could you hear it in the early seventies, when you were suddenly free and yet, to use your word, festering?

The bus is climbing, now, up Leith Walk, towards the posh centre of Edinburgh. The street scene is getting fancier, the people here are whiter. Travis Bickle and Dafoe's John LeTour, taking his tour, would have noticed, their eyes darting, seeing the change as their change.

And at the end of youth, what did you turn into? American cinema's existentialist in chief. *Taxi Driver*, *Hardcore*, *American Gigolo*, *Raging Bull*, *Mishima*, *Light Sleeper*, *Affliction* were films about men in a godless world, in which the tide has gone out. They're obsessed by bodies, their own bodies – interfaces, prison houses. Did you read Merleau-Ponty, Paul, or did you end up making films about bodies as pale proxies for souls because of that fruity phrase of Freud's "the representation of a thing by its opposite"? However you got there, such existentialism was your heyday, wasn't it? Your bailiwick. Your city centre. I'm in the centre of Edinburgh now. Solid buildings, certitude.

But then came the mid-nineties, Paul, and your certitude went out the window. Is it true that, when you were watching *Pulp Fiction*, you turned to the person you were with and said something like "it's over"? I hope so. I love that you could see, instantly, in its postmodern cut up, its iridescent serious-and-not-at-the-same-time, that your seriousness was suddenly in American cinema's rear-view mirror. Did films like *Pulp Fiction* dethrone you? It and *Barton Fink* and *The Big Lebowski* and, even, your compadre Martin Scorsese's *Goodfellas* were post-existential, weren't they? They weren't asking why we exist and *is this body, this anxiety, it?* – they were burnished Möbius strips of story and other movies.

So you found yourself outside the citadel again. Or, rather, you stayed put and the citadel moved. Digital changed the map of cinema, which became a multi-verse when, of course, you made universes, films about lonely men in cars, boxing rings etc. As well as the city shifting under your feet, you were shifting too of course – having kids, losing friends, getting older, and so you shifted your central peeping character. Travis Bickle in the front of the car, who morphed into John LaTour in the back, became Woody Harrelson's Carter Page III in *The Walker*. Page was on a grand tour too, though life was more a performance for him than Travis and the rest. My bus is going through Tollcross now, a mixed-up place – African cafés, posh and not, a small multiverse.

What shows how alive you are, Paul, is the way you've have tracked the changes. In media interviews and festival appearances, it's clear that your thinking has shapeshifted, kept up and, more than most (more than me) looked ahead. You've talked about the end of Empire, of cinema, of movie-going, yet instead of saying goodbye to all that and becoming a painter like Soderbergh, or of making funerary art, you've made *The Canyons*, which has a new type of business plan, and Twitter-era teasing. In Lindsay Lohan, you've gone for Warholian casting and, when you could be aloof and grand, played the legend, dissolved into movie history or hidden behind your canonical films you have, instead, thought yourself out into the era of online porn by casting James Deen.

The trailer of *The Canyons*, with its closed cinemas and undressing people, makes it look like Bogdanovich's *The Last Picture Show* meets *American Gigolo*. Such a film would be great but, also, safe in a way, and tasteful and deep. I suspect that there's more surface to *The Canyons*, more of that disco tinny-ness that Giorgio Moroder's score gave to *Gigolo*. I'm glad I'm writing to you before I've seen it, because it's fun to imagine how you've taken your fascination with bodies further than ever before; how you've checked-in your pride or dignity to make a film on favours; how you've seen, in Lohan, elements of Marilyn Monroe; how you've not done an

Ozu on us; how you've kept driving your taxi. You're a centrifuge, Paul. Outwardly directed.

Have you seen the new documentary *Leviathan*, Paul? Or Lav Diaz's recent films from the Philippines? You'd love them I think, and you'd understand them more than most.

I have to get off my bus, now. To be honest, I'd no need to be on it. I just wanted to write this on the move. One last thing: could your next film be five hours long and have twenty shots? And could it be about Bradley Manning?

Thanks,
Mark Cousins

DEAR PIER PAOLO PASOLINI,

It's forty years since, aged 53, you were murdered. Forty years since the Italian – and world – press treated your death at the hands of a rent boy, or rent boys, or your enemies on the political far right, or closer enemies of the left, as a piece of grand opera, or a bloody climax from a play by Aeschylus.

There's something called the internet now, which is an instant access library of every image in the world. I press a button on it and see photographs of your dead body, forty years ago, lying broken like roadkill in the sand. The red of the blood from your smashed brain and the black of your hair together look like a painting by Rouault, or Francis Bacon. The photographs are terrible and beautiful, like your late films. As you know, because of their political turmoil, the 1970s in Italy were called the *anni di piombo*, the years of lead. In the photos of you dead, you look like you've been bludgeoned by lead. You look like a stained-glass window. Your blood looks sticky, like jam. Stickiness was your thing. In your life and work, Catholicism stuck to Marxism stuck to gayness, when they more usually repel each other.

The comet of your fame long since left the sky, Pier Paolo, but there are other celebrity comets now. People with names like Julian Assange, Ai Weiwei and Chelsea Manning rail against the modern world, as you did against the 1970s. They are dangerous and, in some cases, endangered, and ventriloquise themselves, as you did, but there are few like you, Pier Paolo. Your passion, anger, absolutism, hedonism, sex and drive place you in a line that goes through Caravaggio, Rilke, van Gogh, Eisenstein, von Stroheim, Schiele and Johnny Rotten, but that line buckles with you. The line has been drawn by scores of books about your vision or abjection, and by films too, including a new biopic starring a great American actor, Willem Dafoe, and directed by Abel Ferrara, but none of those quite answer what I'm burning to know as I write this letter. A cheap question, a sleazy question: what was it like to be you?

———

Let's cut the small talk, Pier Paolo. Did you believe in paradise? I think you did. You were brought up in

Casarsa, loved the grand and misty Po Valley and the learnt to speak the Friulian dialect. Despite the iniquities of fascism, which we will come to, it seems that the land, its timeless ways, its sublime, was *terroir* for you. It was your food and flavour. Your early films, like *Accattone*, and your novel *Ragazzi di vita* show youth as violent but full of hope. Your famous film *The Gospel According to St Matthew*, despite telling the story of a tragic life (Jesus Christ's), is exultant and earthy, not wan like most god flicks. You had your non-professional actors in it filmed square on, and often close-up, as if in awe of their life force. Your poems, especially "Diary", often use the word "stupendo", stupendous, as if more qualified adjectives under-imagine what it is like to be alive. I can't help seeing the ideas of Jean-Jacques Rousseau in all this rapture, Pier Paolo, in your love of the rural and timeless, the unadorned and unsophisticated. And the problem with Rousseau is that he's a collision course, but I'm getting ahead of myself.

Your mytho-poetics (sorry for such a clanger of a word) amount to more than your early over-estimation of people, of course. Your very Catholic love of imagery – and total rejection, at the start in any case, of the Protestant idea that imagery is redolent of surface – is so moving. It's what makes you a movie man. Remember how you had your mother seem to levitate in the sky, above the building in your film *Teorema*? More austere or sceptical imaginations would call that a far too literal way of depicting grace, but you were uninhibited at showing the metaphysical directly. You were as visually unabashed as the Italian painters of the thirteen and fourteen hundreds – Cimabue, Giotto, Duccio, etc. In their paintings, we see the words of angels, and heaven and earth interact, as if both are on the same visual plane. Like them, you show faith in the visible. I think of that amazing image in your film *The Decameron*, where you recreate, with all its flattening and gold, the Final Judgement fresco by Giotto in the Scrovegni Chapel in Padua. Imagery was your creed. For me, for any of us who work in visual culture, that's paradise.

———

From paradise, did your life seem to move on to limbo, Pier Paolo, or purgatory? An in-between place? As I write this I'm drinking wine in a place called Carlisle, in England near the Scottish border, where trains split and people wait for other trains. I'm thinking of when you moved to Rome, aged 27, and soon found yourself drawn to that city's outer edges, the *borgata*, where the poor people lived. The *dolce vita* lights of the Via Veneto didn't reach there. The beautiful people stayed away, but you went there because your sense of beauty was not theirs. Your film *Mamma Roma*, filmed in the *borgata*, is so harsh, so black and white, that it's like a wood cut. You spent your days filming in the margins, and your nights in them too. Margin, for many people, would mean not quite here or there, half-alive in a way, but you turned this on your head. You seemed to be more alive in these places, where there are not required ways of behaving, or bourgeois identity routes.

There's a word in English, psychogeography, which describes how places can free your mind, how they can be read against the grain. Boy did you read the places of Italy against the grain, Pier Paolo. Psychogeography has affinities with another modern idea, queer: both say that identity is fluid, a kind of limbo. Queer says that sexuality is drifting, uncontrollable. You thought that didn't you, Pier Paolo? That bodies are bodies, and desire is desire, and it is uncontrollable and that the Christian Right is wrong in proscribing what we do with our touch, our genitals? If that was true for Italy in your day, Pier Paolo, you should see America now. But let's not go there …

There's a fuzzy picture of you on the internet that I hadn't seen until last week. It's one of the last pictures ever taken of you. You are naked, it's black and white, you're in a stone-clad bedroom, reading a book. The photographer is Dino Pedriali. What's striking is how toned your body is. In middle age, Italian men and women often pile on the pounds, your generation even more so: after the privations of World War Two, curviness (look at Sophia Loren) became a beauty ideal. The naked picture of you, which was taken in 1975, has no curvature. Your belly is drum tight. It might surprise you to hear that, here in the twenty-first century, an image we see all the time in our newsagents, is men with drum-tight bellies. In your day, in those *borgata*, in the gay economy, you stayed ageless by staying thin. Now, magazines like *Men's Health*, show that all men are part of the gay economy. Capitalism is cruising.

———

Which of course brings us to paradise lost. If you felt hope in your youth and then were in limbo, on the edge, when you grew up a bit, Pier Paolo, you later felt the flames of hell, didn't you? Consumerism came to Italy, and everything was up for sale, and nothing just was anymore, and Rousseau's chickens came home to roost, and TV made us passive, and we glared at its hairstyles and advertised appliances, and the *anni di piombo* came, and Antonio Gramsci's writings about hegemony and alienation seemed spot-on, and you couldn't celebrate life anymore, and a switch flicked in you, and the sacred died. The music died.

We can see this everywhere in your work. The bourgeois Milanese family in *Teorema* are all so caught up in money and power, so dead to life, that it takes an angel, in the guise of Terence Stamp, to make them feel life and love again. Your unfinished novel *Petrolio* rages so much against modern life, the vulgarisation of everything (including blow jobs) that it made me feel dirty. And in your film *Salò*, you returned to the afore-mentioned fascism of your youth to depict it not only as repellent, feral and coprophagic but, worse, unsee-able, unavoidable. Everything in that film is touched by fascism and sadism, even you. It sounds as if you were nasty during its making, Pier Paolo, as if you had given up trying to be decent. Did you conclude that because Italy had changed forever, and that hell was no longer a threat of what *could* be but that its flames were *already* licking at your heels, then you might as well throw in the towel? If it's true that people had a horrible time working with you on that film, then you should be ashamed of yourself. But, to be fair, your predictions of apocalypse were not far off. Until recently, your country was governed by a man called Berlusconi, the details of whose crassness I will not trouble you with here. Italy in the twenty-first century has much to be ashamed of – much of its media, its corruption and political parties like Forza Italia.

———

It's dark now, Pier Paolo, and I have no more wine. It's easy to write about hell – English and Italian have many words to describe it. But I wonder, as my train hurtles through the night, to what extent your sense of hell came from inside as from without. Yes, Italy cheapened in the 1970s, but did you also, personally, run out of hope, of life? Did you burn yourself out? Did you see too many cities, parties, cocks? Did you stop discovering? Did you become incurious?

I think so. You were murdered – that bloody, sticky, leady image of you came into the world – at a time of despair, when it was dawning on you that there was no going back to the Rousseau world.

And yet. I read again your poem "Diary", that I mentioned earlier (actually I don't read it, I simply remember it because I committed it to memory 20 years ago when I realised that it was as good as your best films):

> Grown up? Never – never – ! Like existence itself
> which never matures – staying always green
> from splendid day to splendid day –
> I can only stay true
> to the stupendous monotony of the mystery.
> That's why I've never abandoned happiness,
> that's why in the anxiety of my sins
> I've never been touched by real remorse.

Equal, always equal, to the inexpressible
at the very source of what I am.

The stupendous monotony of the mystery? In the anxiety of your sins, you've never been touched by real remorse? Splendid day to splendid day? Is this the answer to my question of what it was like to be you? In this poem, and in your best films, you seem to acknowledge that, no matter how shit life is, hell won't quite happen – you'll never be touched by real remorse. But, also, no matter how great life is – the glories of Friuli, or the *borgata* – you'll never "abandon" yourself to happiness.

There's a rebalancing in this poem, a paradise regained, Pier Paolo. Or, rather, it is put on the scales, on which hell is on the other side, and, suddenly, rapture and despair are in equilibrium. The result is a "splendid ... monotonous ... mystery."

If you had lived, might this balance, this accommodation, this resignation to the valley of tears and the mountain top, become your theme? It would have required a dissipation of your rage and lust, which might have lessened our fascination with you, but your films might, as a result, have become more ... Eastern. Your poem "Diary" reminds me, in the end, of certain Asian philosophies about being in the moment, accepting the flow, the indifference of the world. Riding its wave. If you had lived on, and not been burnt up by the fires of despair or cynicism, then you'd have needed to glimpse the resigned wisdom in your "Diary" poem.

I'm not sure I like the idea of a tamed Pasolini. I'm not sure anyone would. You see, we like our heroes to burn brightly, and do our raging, for us. You do the raging, we do the aging. That's the deal, Pier Paolo. A shoddy deal from your point of view.

In the end, I like to imagine that you could have had a paradise regained. You knew that there were times when you had to rage against the dying of the light but, also, that there were other lights that weren't dying. Not all of Italy was despoiled. Bodies weren't entirely ruined by commoditisation. And there are always new beauties.

Thanks for listening, Pier Paolo. Thanks for doing our living for us. And, most of all, thanks for *Teorema* and "Diary".

Mark Cousins

A LETTER TO THE DIRECTOR OF *SINGIN' IN THE RAIN*

Dear Stanley Donen,

Finally, you've gone. To be honest, it was remarkable that you were still here, in 2019, because you were so connected to a golden age in Hollywood, and, through *Singin' in the Rain*'s rear-view mirror look at silent cinema, even further back. You once said that, when you got into film in the early 1940s, it felt that silent cinema had not long ended.

Should we stop all the clocks as a result of your death, put crepe bows round the white necks of the public doves and let the traffic policemen wear black cotton gloves? No, though your movies rank as highly as William Wyler's or Michael Curtiz's, you were too much fun for such mourning, and too hard-hearted.

When you died I thought of a not well known number – "The Leg of Mutton Dance" – in *Deep in My Heart*. You won't remember, but you and I argued about this movie. I said it was one of your best. You said that you only did it because of producer Roger Edens. It's about Viennese composer Sigmund Romberg, of course, and the clash between his sophisticated European music, and the hotsy-totsy entertainments of Broadway. The dance is silly, feels improvised, and is one of the most entertaining things I've seen on film. It captures a momentary joy. Its characters are not thinking, they're having fun.

Is that the central theme in your work – the fun of Eden, the joy before the fall? Can we talk through your films to see if that's true?

Your childhood in South Carolina wasn't Eden. You were bullied and bored, and Hollywood was a continent away, but you got there and did *On the Town*. It was already about the moment – a day in the life of sailors and their girls. It was European in a way, like a René Clair or Ernst Lubitsch movie, and what was noticeable was how libidinous the women were. Betty Garrett, particularly in the "Come Up to My Place" number, was sexually voracious, a pre-echo of Ingrid Bergman's "I need a man, tonight, here, right now" in *Indiscreet*. You said later that *On the Town* is about "how much juice there is in life".

There was a lot of juice in *Singin' in the Rain*. It brought new tones to your emerging voice as a film-maker. At its centre was a threesome – Gene Kelly, Donald O'Connor and Debbie Reynolds – and this repeated throughout your movies, especially *Lucky Lady*. In the latter, the Gene Hackman, Liza Minnelli and Burt Reynolds triangle become more sexually explicit, and didn't you plan an ending in which the three would be seen as old people, in bed together? Friendship was a key element in your Eden.

But there was more to *Singin' in the Rain*, of course. It had the same clash between high art and popular entertainment – between the intellect and the body – as *Deep In My Heart*. Reynolds thinks that the stage is superior to mere movies. Did the fact that you didn't go to college help you choose films about this subject? *Funny Face* is more explicitly about that theme, and errs (I feel) on the side of anti-intellectualism. Then of course there were the split screens in *Singin' in the Rain*. "Yes, I used split screens a lot", you said to Bertrand Tavernier and Daniel Palas in 1973, and there they are in *Funny Face*, *Royal Wedding*, *Damn Yankees* and that famous split phone call between Cary Grant and Bergman in *Indiscreet*. If you are into threesomes or more, then it makes sense to split the screen, but they are, also, about the moment. A flashback shows the same people at different times, but a split screen shows different people at the same time.

And as I mentioned flashbacks, can we touch on the time structures in your films? You and your great screenwriters – Betty Comden and Adolph Green on *Singin' in the Rain*, Frederic Raphael on *Two for the Road*, Peter Cook and Dudley Moore for *Bedazzled* – seemed to like complex story backbones. *Singin' in the Rain* has that big flashback in the first half, then the "flash to" *pas de deux* in the second half. *Two for the Road*'s present tense hardly advances at all, so chambered it is with time shifts. And *Bedazzled* jumps seven times from its present tense to Dudley Moore's wishes, which are all bound to fail.

This raises the question of what happened when your own timeline advanced, when you got older. *It's Always Fair Weather* was an unofficial sequel to *On the Town*, wasn't it? It's ten years later. TV is atomising American life. You said that it was "subtle and scathing at the same time," that "everything is derision in the film ... even its title is satiric."

What had happened? You were only 30 when you made it, but had done nine films, were already divorced from Jeanne Coyne, would divorce Marion Marshall a few years later and were undergoing the painful split from Gene Kelly. You were losing your optimism, and squeezing out the juice of life. The H Bomb was being built and the Korean War had started. You had more to remember and more to fear. It was harder to sing in the rain or do The Leg of Mutton Dance.

And so you played it safe for a while, adapting musicals and plays into films. *The Pajama Game* again had strong female perspectives, and was the best thing Doris Day ever did. You must be proud of the "There Once Was A Woman" and "Hernando's Hideaway" numbers, are you? And "Once A Year Day", which you choreographed with Bob Fosse, was one of your last Edenic moments. Those camera moves! How did you learn to plan them so well? I'm thinking also of the ones in the Thames night-time walk following Cary Grant and Ingrid Bergman in *Indiscreet*, made the next year. Every time I walk the Thames Embankment I think of them, their grace, their elegy.

For a filmmaker interested in Eden, it's no surprise that there are devils in your work. In *Damn Yankees*, also 1958 (were you not exhausted? This was your fourteenth film and you were only 34!) Ray Walston is a kind of Faust, and Peter Cook is another one in *Bedazzled*. Of course, your screenwriters scripted these stories, but you chose them and, of *Bedazzled*, you said "It's a very personal film in that I said a great deal about what I think is important in life … [it's] the one of mine that has more to say." Dudley Moore's character finds it impossible to stay in the moment, to sing in the rain, and Peter Cook's line

"Adam and Eve were happy because they were pig ignorant" seems to pull the carpet out from under the hotsy-totsy naïvetés of "Leg of Mutton". *Lucky Lady*, which came in 1975, seems to have been equally personal. Minnelli-Hackman-(Burt) Reynolds are escaping the kind of drudgery that you felt in your childhood in South Carolina. They are the offspring of Kelly-O'Connor-(Debbie) Reynolds, but with a new tone. The wheel has spun, their highs are more pastiched, and their lows? Maybe they don't even realise that they're unhappy, that Eden is far away.

And the imagery in your films show that. Your Metro-Goldwyn-Mayer movies are so polished, so visually sure, so controlled. Their moments are perfected, but the shots in *Staircase*, starring Richard Burton and Rex Harrison, and *Two for the Road*, both filmed by Chris Challis? There's a new roughness and plainness. We get zooms, hand-held shots, and what seem like unplanned moments. The images have absorbed the new social uncertainties about sexuality and the future. People no longer live happily ever after, and so the moment is more fleeting than ever. The key line in *Two for the Road*, I think, is "The world is changing beyond recognition. There is no such thing as permanence any more. And we should be glad."

Let's not stop the clocks, Stanley. They aren't stoppable, as *Two for the Road* shows. We're all aging, and we're further away than ever from the MGM Eden. That's fine.

When we did the retrospective of your movies at the 1995 Edinburgh International Film Festival, we learnt The Leg of Mutton Dance. I can still do some of it. We remember the dances of our youth.

Let's do it again, now, but wearing black cotton gloves.

Mark Cousins

DEAR LARISA SHEPITKO,

I'm an Irish-Scottish filmmaker. I saw your film *Wings* years ago, at the beginning of the twenty-first century and loved it. The solitude of the retired pilot, the way you show her memories, her self-doubt. I wanted to know more about you.

Decades later, though I've met people like Lynda Myles who knew you, I still want to know more. I'm sitting in an airport in Belfast in the North of Ireland, waiting for a flight. I always think of you and *Wings* and loneliness in airports. I usually travel alone, and so my mind wanders, or wonders. It's wandering now. Can I kill some time by writing to you? (My Ukrainian friend Polya Moshenska tells me that you have exactly the same "killing" time phrase in your language.)

Where to start? Maybe with the ending of your war movie *The Ascent*? I'm not sure I've seen many things like it in the whole history of cinema. I show it often and each time I cry. As you know, Boris Plot-nikov's Soviet soldier has been captured by the Nazis and – it slowly dawns on us – is to be murdered by hanging. Snowy Belarus, and your shots gradually, and with dread, zoom in to the faces of the onlookers, the Nazis, to Boris as he starts to look more haunted, more Christ-like. Alfred Schnittke's music builds like *Das Rheingold*, layering the horror, the crawl to the atrocity. A boy cries, Boris seems to be transfigured, like a Guido Reni painting.

The scene's a gale of feeling, and I'm sure you're proud of it, but as I picture it here in this airport on a Thursday afternoon, can I tell you some things? The Soviet Union was dissolved on 26 December 1991, Russia invaded the Crimea on 20 February 2014, and the East of your home country on 24 February 2022.

These things happened decades after you died in your car accident, but I'm guessing that, as a Ukrainian who believed in the Soviet Union to a certain degree, but whose work was censored by it, these invasions would split you in two? Your earliest memories are of World War Two, and the Red Army at its best did indeed help defeat Nazism, but I know that by the time you made your first student film in 1956, Stalin had died, Khrushchev had asked questions about the barbarism of the previous years and the cautious Soviet introspection that ensued allowed you to begin to make cinema.

Seventy years later, it's hard to see Russian intro-spection. Many of its citizens support the invasions. My question to you – to myself – is how such changes would have affected your filmmaking. Most of the people in Ukraine have found common purpose in their hatred of Russia's violent land-grab. They are decolonising. This would chime with you in some ways because your movies are often about detached people – the retired pilot in *Wings* seems outside her times, the soldiers in *The Ascent* are part of an army but alone too, the doctor in *You and Me* (one of your greatest films) has out of body experiences. You weren't a natural joiner-upper were you? You were a lone wolf, and such people are sceptics away-from-the-numbers. That's where I want to be.

I've been appalled by Russia's murderous inva-sion of your country and I've seen how Ukraine has responded. Statues of Pushkin are being taken down because, he has been used to tell a story of Russian exceptionalism. Such stories debase. The great soul of Mother Russia is grating now. Maybe it grated for you decades ago.

So the detachment is right, and the detachment in your films is looking mature in new ways. I wish you were here in this airport, however, to help me understand where the detachment might go. Ukraine further disconnects from the control of its invader, and here in Ireland, in a more minor way, we had to take some distance from the colonial story told by the British State. We are not an outcrop, simply grateful for the influence of a superior culture. But a friend of mine recently told me that some of his friends think Catherine the Great was as bad as Hitler.

The fog of war, the fury of killing, etc., but this is surely wrong. If we detach so completely, then don't we under-imagine our own humanity? There are Soviet scenes in your films, but it looks to me like you were neither naïve nor cynical. As you travelled internationally (our mutual friend in Berkeley, Tom Luddy, told me a lot about you, and I think was in love with you), you saw that it was harder for women in capitalist countries to make a career as a filmmaker.

So how far do we detach Larisa? How much does Ukraine rid itself of Russian culture? How much does the North of Ireland emphasise its non-British-ness? When a country like Scotland rightly objects to un-democratic impositions from the UK's London government, where might that lead?

One of your tutors was your fellow Ukrainian Alexander Dovzhenko. He, too, leant his shoulder to the Soviet wheel. In your years with him, I wonder were there ever moments when you distinguished between your Ukrainian and Soviet selves? Or is that not even a good question? His films *Zvenigora*, *Arsenal* and *Earth*, which came at the end of the silent era in cinema, are as great as yours, and also interested in poetics and loss. What did you talk about in bars in Moscow in the 1950s, when he was past your best, when you were approaching yours?

Did you have a sense of the baton passing from him to you, the baton of detachment?

My flight is delayed, Larisa. I might film something to kill time. Lynda Myles says that many people who met you fell in love with you. I suspect that I would have been one of the many.

After your tragic death, your husband made a lovely short tribute to you. It's on something called "YouTube".

You are remembered.

Mark Cousins

Thoughts On Form

DOCUMENTARY IS …
ME, MY CAMERA
AND THE UNEXPECTED

When you film a documentary, life comes barrelling at you like a wild bear, so the filmic equivalent of the fight or flight mechanism takes over. Things happen and you try to frame them visually, capture the key words (if there are words), think ethically, and keep one eye open, beyond the camera, all at once. You're submitting to events, people, tensions, ch-ch-changes. When you're making a doc, you try to be your best self. You are caring on the hoof, judging what matters and what's moving, and – always, somewhere, if you're good – keeping the plate of form spinning.

Of course, most of that could be said of John Cassavetes or Chantal Akerman's fictions, but the zone doesn't have clear demarcations. The zone is just making scenes that are new and true, sincere or hopeful, a kind of *darshan*. When you make a documentary, you need to submit, to be humble about how little you know and how much you want to know. Documentary makes you feel young, un-jaded, alive, hungry.

The greatest films are documentaries.

DOCUMENTARY

For *Empire*.

You never know with what you'll fall in love.

When I was a kid I couldn't care less about documentary films. I'm not sure I'd even heard the term. I knew that *Star Wars*, *Grease*, the horror films I was watching on VHS and the Hitchcock movies I saw on the TV were directed – they had mood and tone. But I think I assumed that non-fiction was undirected, that it just flowed onto the small screen like a river flows into the sea. To me that seemed too everyday, too impersonal too boring.

Now, I absolutely adore documentary. It makes me feel alive and alert. How did I fall head over heels? What has happened to non-fiction cinema in these last 40 years?

I started directing docs in 1988. I was in my early twenties, had an idea, sent the idea to Channel 4, and found myself at the helm. I poured my heart into those early short docs but when I looked at my rushes in the editing suite, I thought *it's not really there.* They were missing something. I didn't quite see reality in them, or cinema.

A sobering realisation. I'd never been cocky, so I hadn't presumed that I'd make *any* films, never mind good ones, but when I watched my first rushes it dawned on me that documentary isn't an easy flow, like a river. And not only that. I also realised that I didn't really fit into how the industry worked. My crew was quite big; on the equipment and technology side it was all men. They were mostly nice, but there was a boys-with-toys feel that scared me. I felt crushed.

When you're crushed, you can close down, or open up. I opened up. I got to be associate director on a doc about Mikhail Gorbachev, directed by the great British filmmaker Mike Grigsby. Grigsby had a distinctive filmic voice or style – long takes, no interviews, soundtrack crackling with radio broadcasts, etc. It was beautiful, like the famously poetic British films of Humphrey Jennings. What a voice. But not my voice.

Then I saw the Japanese documentary *The Emperor's Naked Army Marches On*, and it was a like a creative earthquake. Where Jennings and Grigsby were detached, associative, gentle, this one was about a soldier beating up old men because they, or people they knew, had killed and eaten his fellow soldiers at the end of World

War Two. I loved the film's impoliteness, its rage, its moral authority and ambiguity, and so I had an idea. Together with another young director, Mark Forrest, I directed *Another Journey By Train*, a film about Holocaust denial in which we took young neo-Nazis to Auschwitz-Birkenau to show them the homicidal gas chambers. It had an impact, was on posters around the UK before it was on Channel 4, and created a stink.

I liked the controversy, the stink, but I also liked the Jennings poetics. Maybe my filmic voice could be a stinky poetics?

Around this time I got to explore this question more, because the filmmaker Kevin Macdonald and I got to edit *Imagining Reality: The Faber Book of Documentary*. We didn't focus on any of the usual theory stuff about non-fiction cinema. As burgeoning filmmakers, we used the book to ask creative questions – how do you tell a documentary story, what are the great techniques? Soon afterwards, I became director of the Edinburgh International Film Festival and, in its fiftieth year, decided that our retrospective should be Great Moments in Documentary History. Humphrey Jennings was in that season, and of course *The Emperor's Naked Army Marches On*. I think we had only one female filmmaker in our retrospective, Barbara Kopple, who won her first Oscar for *Harlan County, USA*. Realising that made me, from 1997 onwards, seek out women directors.

Then came another documentary landmark for me, another stage in my falling in love. It happened when I saw Scottish director Margaret Tait's short film *Portrait of Ga*, a five-minute 8mm portrait of her mother. It had no raging Japanese soldier, no neo-Nazis, yet it seemed so pure to me, so perfect. We see Tait's mother outdoors, windswept in Orkney, wearing a sturdy coat and shoes, eating a boiled sweet. And Tait had filmed it herself. No crew, no schedule, no guys fetishising the equipment. Just her.

Wow. Filmmaking could be a solitary thing. I could shoot my films myself. For a shy person like me, a bit of a lone wolf, *Portrait of Ga* made me feel free, and creative. And, I realised, it is about love. Many of the great docs are attacks on society, and – having experienced three wars – I have seen some of the problems in the world. I love those attacking docs, and have made a few, but Tait's film was an artisanal act of worship, a kind of love letter to everydayness.

A love letter to everydayness: that idea stayed with me. It was in the back of my mind as the new millennium came, as twin tracks opened up, one in the big world of documentary filmmaking, the other in the small world of my own evolving voice.

The big story was that documentary, which had always been a poor relation to the more lucrative world of fiction cinema, started to ring the box office bell from the 1990s. Films like Wim Wenders' *Buena Vista Social Club*, Alek Keshishian's *In Bed with Madonna* and Michael Moore's *Bowling for Columbine* and *Fahrenheit 9/11* mainstreamed the ne'er-do-well art form. Many of us benefited from this rising tide.

My smaller, personal, story is that I became my own cinematographer. I filmed in Iraq for *The First Movie* and around the world for *The Story of Film: An Odyssey* and loved doing both, loved framing and choosing lenses. And as I fell deeper in love, so I cast my net wider. I swooned at the docs of Aleksander Sokurov and Pirjo Honkasalo's *The 3 Rooms of Melancholia*, about kids affected by the war in Chechnya. I was guest programmer at the Sheffield Doc/Fest where, over three years, I showed the classic Japanese docs of the sixties, seventies and eighties. With each of these, my knowledge grew, my sense of the cinematic aspects of documentary grew.

Like a tree, love can take years to grow and branch. The more I travelled, the more I realised that docs were not only my travelling companions, but part of the reason why I was on the road in the first place. I drove from Scotland to India and, looking back, the impulse was a documentary impulse – centrifugal, restless, and hungry.

The mainstreaming of documentary, my evolving voice (stinky-poetic, mendicant) and my increasing visibility as a filmmaker meant that the Cannes Film Festival started taking my films (*A Story of Children and Film*, *The Eyes of Orson Welles*), and Venice, Toronto, Berlin and many of the others too. That was a confidence boost, and gave me some power, which I've tried to use wisely.

For example, a decade ago, I would not have got to make a 14-hour doc about the many female filmmakers who have been written out of movie history. Even now it is tough. My newest movie, *Women Make Film: A New Road Movie Through Cinema* was made with no funding from TV or film bodies. If it had been shorter, or about the filmmakers we've heard of, like Jane Campion, Kathryn Bigelow or Agnès Varda, there might have been some financing, but its idea was to show us what we don't know. The resulting film is a bit like Margaret Tait's *Portrait of Ga*: a low-fi act of love. Making it, I've learnt so much, discovered so much: films like Swedish director Marianne Ahrne's doc about aging, *Walking in the Land of the Old* and Canadian filmmaker Anne Claire Poirier's *Les Filles du Roy*. Previously unknown to me, they are now part of why I love docs.

Women Make Film is being shown around the world, and I'm hearing from film fans across the globe. My love of documentary is shared by many. What started for me as indifference has now become the way a shy boy is less shy, more open.

And of course, when you open up to other people, places and stories, you are changed by them. I love not being what I once was. Documentary has taught me that there's no essence of me, that I'm excited by, inflected by, distracted by other people's lives. I've also realised that, as a filmmaker, it's good to search for my voice, but as I get older that voice is changing. I used to hate commentary and then I loved it. At first I only used tripods and wide shots, and now I go for hand-held, long lens, wobbly shots. A few years ago, I directed a film called *Atomic, Living in Dread and Promise*, which had music by the great Scottish band Mogwai. It had no filming whatsoever, only archive, but it was a punky expression of our fear that the nuclear age might return. It played in Hiroshima, Chernobyl, Coventry Cathedral and many places around the world.

Atomic felt like a return to the rage of my neo-Nazi film. Was I going backwards? No. I think I'll always have rage, and I'll always want to make films inspired by the gentleness of *Portrait of Ga*. Hate and love. *Women Make Film* has hate and love in it – hate that great female filmmakers are forgotten, love of their work.

I knew the Hollywood icon Lauren Bacall a bit. She once said "the industry's shit, it's the medium of great." How true. Is that another version of hate and love? And what role does documentary play in the great medium of film? It isn't only a genre, like the Western or the road movie. It's many genres.

Documentary is half of cinema.

CHILDREN AND TRAUMA

A talk at a psychology conference.

I was brought up in Belfast, and was five when the war in Northern Ireland went into top gear. I was a nervy little boy anyway, but the war jangled those nerves. We had a glass door with mottled glass in our hall and my mum always told me and my brother – if you see someone standing outside that door, run into the living room.

The war took its toll on the loving world my parents had built for us. Our house was damaged by a bomb, a family friend was murdered.

Yet I had medicine for the fear, a balm to soothe it. That medicine was … imagery. There were no books in our house, and we never went to art galleries, yet, from the age of eight or so, I'd go to the local library, hunker down on the floor and flick through books of Escher prints, Paul Klee drawings and, in particular, Paul Cézanne's watercolours of Mont Sainte Victoire.

Those paintings eased my nervous system. To explain what I mean, have a look at this clip from the British film *Kes*. The boy in the story is Billy. His dad was a waster and disappeared. Mum does her best but is lonely and has her own needs. The family can't afford a sports uniform for Billy, so he's bullied. He's skinny, too, and tired all the time because he has to do a paper round before school.

We join him here, an hour into the movie. We've seen him cowering. But a new teacher has arrived in the school. He's kinder than the others. He listens more. He's leading a class discussion on the difference between fact and fiction. Billy as usual hasn't been paying attention, partly because he's so tired. So the teacher asks him to stand up and tell a story. The only story he can tell is about a kestrel he has befriended and is training.

On the spot, in front of the class, more pressurised than ever before Billy's imagination saves him. We can see his timidity gently disappear and be replaced by the power of his story, his love of the bird. He becomes the teacher, a source of information, a provider, a leader. The world he describes, on the fields behind Bradford, with the bird, is one of freedom and plenitude rather than constraint and scarcity.

What we just saw is what happened to me when I looked at those Cézanne paintings. I didn't escape into a fantasy world, I became the wee boy who, otherwise, was partially hiding. A second self, more alive than the Mark people knew, and more real than him, opened up. When I watch this scene from *Kes* I can't not think of a moment in the film *Billy Elliot* – about another boy called Billy from a mining community from the North of England, who has an absent parent. Billy goes for an audition to the Royal Ballet. He's quizzed by a panel of posh dance experts. He cowers in front of them. One asks, "What does it feel like when you dance?" He says "good". And then he feels the plenitude and says "Light". Billy Elliot felt more himself when he danced. Billy in *Kes* feels more himself, less constrained by life, when he's with Kes. I felt alive when I looked at those books in that library.

What I'm describing is familiar to most parents, I'd say. Kids have always had imaginary friends, or become absorbed in fantasy books like *The Lord of the Rings*. But I don't think my point is one about how kids escape from reality into fantasy. Rather, *Kes* and *Billy Elliot* are about reality being less real than it should be, or incomplete, or having lost something of itself (a parent). They are stories of children who make themselves and their worlds whole. Stephen Spielberg's *E.T.* seems like a pure fantasy film but, as you'll remember, little Elliot's world is incomplete – there's no father, as there aren't in many Spielberg films. His own father was absent.

Through *E.T.*, Elliot comes to inhabit a parallel universe where he is not ignored, where he is listened to and can articulate himself. E.T. almost dies, of course, so Elliot's grief and loss are not the cause of his second world but, rather, are sourced within that world, when his extra-terrestrial friend begins to die. American cinema has constantly returned to this theme. In *The Wizard of Oz*, Dorothy Gale lives with her auntie Em – her parents are gone. When her dog Toto is taken away and then a tornado spins her world, she invents a parallel universe of chromatic excess, diverse friendships and storybook pastorale.

But again I'm not interested in the escapist aspects of these movies so much as how they depict grieving, or damaged or unfulfilled children in the process of becoming whole. Some years ago I had a eureka moment whilst reading the autobiography of Temple Grandin, a farming machinery designer and lecturer in America, who is autistic. Writing of her childhood autism, Temple describes hearing the word "underneath" and not understanding it until she imagined a table, and herself getting under it. "I ran a video of this in my head", she wrote. As I read I was shocked because, to a degree, that's what I did and still do. Because I'm not great at words, because they are opaque to me, I turn them into videos and run them in my head. As I read Grandin's words I thought back to me in that library gazing, fascinated, at the Cézanne paintings. And I thought of the shadow behind the mottled glass door and I realise, of course, imagery brought things into focus for me. It removed the blurriness of life. I was one of those kids who didn't understand something until I drew it. Go see the Picasso exhibition in Edinburgh and you watch him understand the essence of a bull or a rearing horse by drawing its structure, its key elements.

A famous example from Rudolph Arnheim's book *Visual Thinking*, further illustrates the point. The first image is a painting by Corot. The third is a sculpture by Henry Moore. For me, and people like me – those who understand, figure out and, therefore, get better because of pictures rather than words – and the art schools are full of us, and the engineering, plumbing, joinery, gardening and many other professions

— we understand the Corot picture by seeing its basic structure — a wee blob on the left and a bigger blob on the right leaning towards and around the wee blob, protectively.

I know that not everyone is like this. Visual people are probably in a minority. But I believe that lessons can be learnt from visual people, and the way they think visually and understand imagery. And perhaps those lessons are relevant to those who work with young people who are experiencing loss or grief.

———

Anyway, the story gets more interesting here. By my mid-teens I became a film buff, and then, when I grew up, a filmmaker. Over the years I've come across movies that I think capture the dramas of detachment, loneliness, scarcity, protest, anger, emptiness, reattachment and plenitude that grief and loss can present for young people.

Overall, cinema, especially American cinema, has been crap at capturing the subtleties of childhood loss. The recent example that still disturbs me is Quentin Tarantino's *Kill Bill*, in which a little girl sees her mother brutally shot to pieces, but who seems not to be too affected. If the child actor is in the same shot as the simulated murder, I'd like to know what steps that the filmmakers took to protect her from having nightmares about the apparent blood bath.

Compare that film with one called *Crows*. Polish director Dorota Kędzierzawska saw a nine-year-old on the street, swearing and being brusque, and so she imagined a nine-year-old whose single mum works nights – she might even be a prostitute – and who slumps into bed at dawn. The girl eats alone. Plays alone. The world seems completely empty to her. Adults are on its margins. She begins to see only archetypal aspects of life – a marriage, policing, etc. Her mum becomes spectral. The little girl is lonely, lost, ignored. So what does she do? She steals a three-year-old girl. We join them here when the older has put the younger on a boat.

She wants to go to the end of the earth – because perhaps there's some life and love there. She abducts the child for company, of course, but also because she's so curious about her spectral mum that she wants to play-act her. To see what life looks like from the mum's point of view. In the scene we've just watched, she's reckless and endangers the three-year-old but, also, is her provider, carer and rescuer. By role-playing a mum she gets to feel something like a mother's responsibilities and love. She brings the child home.

Whether you are a visual person or not, films like this, and like *Kes* and *Billy Elliot*, enact situations of change and loss which we can all see and understand. The older girl in *Crows* guesses what it feels like to be an adult. Her behaviour looks disobedient but is understandable. She's angry and scared and since there seem to be no rules in the world, no bonds between people, she creates a bond out of nothing. Though *Crows* is about a theft, the girl's act is creative, I think. I love this film and feel that it would perhaps illuminate loss for adults as well as children, and be a great starting point to talk.

Another film that would open up a space to talk about significant change and the creativity it involves is the Czech film *Kolya*. The little boy in this film has no dad, and his mum, a Russian, has moved to the West. His grandmother, to whom he was close, has died. So he's left with the cynical, womanising cello player who married his mother as a business transaction, so that she could get a visa. The cellist speaks little Russian and the boy speaks little Czech. The adult wants nothing to do with the boy who, in turn, is reluctant to form an attachment to this cold, distant man. Slowly, though, they begin to get used to each other. Touch is important in *Kolya*, and we're moved when, suddenly, the boy takes the hand of the man as they cross a road.

Then they are in the underground railway system in Prague, and this happens: so soon after Kolya bonds with the cellist, the adult loses him in one of the most terrifying places for kids, a subway, packed with people. The shock of the scene shows to man and boy how much each has come to need the other and leads to the intensely moving bath scene where little Kolya calls his dead granny with the shower head. He does so because he was shaken by getting lost but, also, because he's now comfortable enough in the cellist's house and in his company, to reveal how much he is hurting inside. The film is full of links to elsewhere – birds, trains, etc. – and, especially, telephones.

A later scene in the film is a classic one of funeral play – something you'll know about from your work with kids. The cellist plays music at funerals, so little Kolya has witnessed many coffins gliding behind a screen to be cremated. So he gets a shoe box, draws a cross on it, puts a doll in it, covers it with a pair of black lacy knickers left behind by one of the racy cellist's lovers, and eases it through the proscenium arch of a toy theatre.

Where many of the films about childhood loss and grief are gentle and lyrical, Danny Boyle's movie *Millions* moves like an express train. It's about a seven-year-old Damian (there are more boys than girls in films about childhood loss) whose Mam has died and whose dad, played by James Nesbitt, is trying to put the past behind him and find love again. Just as Billy in *Kes* and Billy Elliot find other worlds that are richer than their own bereft one, so does Damian. A suitcase full of money literally falls on him, and, being a very religious little boy, he decides that it is a gift from god. His older brother says they should stash the money away but Damian wants to give it people. He spends £168 feeding homeless people at Pizza Hut.

Millions is a parable about giving. Damian creates a world where he is in control of good deeds. It is a world of total plenitude and creativity. Only when it comes to an end, and when Damien realises the money isn't divine, do we get the following scene, in which Damian imagines meeting his dead mother.

Beautiful writing by Frank Cottrell-Boyce. It's very moving to see, dramatised, the imaginary conversation that many kids have with their lost relatives.

And contrast the widescreen gloss of *Millions* to this movie from Iran. In the 1980s, Iran established something with the pompous title Kanoon: Institute for the Intellectual Development of Children and Young Adults. There was nothing pompous about its pioneering work, however, and since then Iran has made the best kids' films in the world. The one I've chosen is amongst the simplest films ever made. Called *The Boot*, and directed in 1992 by Mohammad Ali Talebi, it tells the story of a young war widow and her four-year-old daughter. The daughter plagues her mum, wanting the latest dolls and the latest toys. Maybe this has something to do to the massive change in her life caused by her father's death. She certainly wants more attention than she's getting – her mother works long hours in a garment factory. We join them as mum comes home from a hard day's work ...

I could give you far more examples, but I think the point is made: some kids respond particularly well to imagery and most might be able to use depictions of loss and change on film as ways of understanding their own situation, seeing other kids, similar to themselves, undergo similar experiences.

———

But everything I've said so far has been about consuming imagery and movies for therapeutic purposes. What about kids themselves producing imagery? Art therapy is as old as the hills, and I'm sure you know of many successful examples of it, or have used it in your own work.

I'd like to use one recent project to look at how image production might help with the grieving process. I haven't chosen a drawing – a crayon and paper – project, as not all young people are confident drawers, and some find it intimidating. And though I co-founded a charity 14 years ago called Scottish Kids Are Making Movies, I haven't chosen a filmmaking project because, again, there's a lot of technique involved in making even simple films, which can put youngsters off.

Instead, I was to look at something called Through the Eyes of a Child, a photo camp run jointly by International Medical Corps and *National Geographic*. IMC is an international NGO which responds rapidly to conflict or trauma situations around the world – the tsunami, Darfur, Rwanda, Iraq, etc. – helping set up *in situ* mental health treatment programmes and working, in particular, with kids who have experienced war and/or bereavement.

The photo camp took place over three days, in October 2006, in south-western Uganda, in refugee camps. All the young people involved were orphans, war affected, child heads of family, or HIV-affected. They were given high-end Olympus digital cameras and, in day one, were taught how to use these by famous photographers. The kids worked in small groups, which were overseen by one of the photographers and a mental health worker. The children were asked to take photographs in three categories – My Life in the Camp, My Home and Surroundings, and Self-Portraits. They looked at the results on laptops, chose their favourites, discussed why they took them and why they liked them, and the best were printed into large format prints. These formed an exhibition in the Oxo Gallery in London, and will tour elsewhere in the world.

Last week I interviewed IMC's Dr Lynne Jones, a child psychiatrist who's worked in Bosnia, Darfur, Rwanda, and in the aftermath of the tsunami. She said the aim of the photo camp was to "Give children a chance to use digital photography to document and explore any part of their lives that was significant to them; to encourage their creativity; and increase their self-esteem." She told me that it more than achieved this. Shy and quiet children started taking hundreds of photographs. They were voluble about the results.

Having a camera allowed them to "see" their lives more clearly, from the outside. It helped build relationships with family members, other kids and care workers. It fostered empathy between the kids. It transformed timid children.

Being photographers helped young people with significant losses see their lives in context. In their pictures we can see the pleasure of fixing the fleeting moment, of getting off the express train of emotions that having suffered a loss often entails, and standing still for a second, and looking, really looking.

Many of the details would have been apparent to the child at the moment she or he pressed the shutter release button, but print these pictures up, and look at them again, and you notice detail – fear on your mum's face, or her beauty. The rhythm of dark triangles in an image, etc.

Taking pictures can act like a memory box. You can go and photograph the place where your dad used to take you fishing before he disappeared. Or, when there's an emotional hole in your life, you can take pictures of what's left, what still makes you happy, to bear witness.

———

I was taught that to draw is to understand. Certainly I only finally got how an internal combustion engine worked when I could draw it. I think these photo camp pictures show that to take pictures is to begin to understand. It is to hang a frame around life – its bad and good bits. Billy in *Kes* or the girl in *Crows*, or like Billy Elliot, did something creative that allowed their self to grow a bit, to experience an exciting rush. To make a photo or do a dance or train a kestrel or even to imagine yourself as a mum is to grow, I think, to escape from scarcity and flatness, into a parallel universe where you are more like yourself. The great writer Joseph Campbell said that grief is a revelatory shock. A shock, probably, but revelatory? For kids, as you know better than I, death and loss can be a terrible incursion into their world of fun, imagination and play. That incursion causes great change, of course, and films dramatise the painful twists and turns in that change. Change, as we know, needs to be seen for what it is, and responded to. The best way to respond, I think, is creatively. To name and shame and acclaim the irreversible thing that has happened to you.

If you are an innately visual person, and hesitant about words, then this process is crucial. Revelatory, I'd say, in my case. Even if you aren't, watching films like *Kes*, *Millions*, *The Boot* and *Kolya* can make childhood loss less scary and more bearable.

WIDESCREEN ON TRAUMA

Stephen Spielberg's new film, *War of the Worlds*, is Hollywood's big, veiled, portrait of 9/11. It is surprising, in a way, that it has taken this long. Traumatic experience has been Hollywood's bread and butter for decades now, since the same Mr Spielberg had his main character face death in the form of a great white shark in *Jaws*. Only a matter of weeks ago the number one film at the UK and US box offices was *Batman Begins*, whose wellsprings are two distressing experiences of a young boy – the murder of his parents, and his falling into a nest of bats. Nearly 10 million people around the world have seen this film so far. Another 40 million are likely to in the next few years.

Such examples are not unusual. The intensity of mainstream cinema, its adrenalised, souped-up, turbo-charged quality have explained its licence to print money for decades now. Hollywood is, let's face it, a kind of traumaland, a Disneyland of distressing events.

Sometimes it's interested in the impact of such events. The climax of Alfred Hitchcock's film *Marnie*, for example, depicted *in vivo exposure*: to find out what is causing his wife's sexually unresponsive, kleptomaniac behaviour, Sean Connery's character takes her back to her mother's house where, he's come to believe, she witnessed something mentally disruptive.

Marnie at least had a crack at depicting the cause and effect of mental life in a grown-up way, but it was still in some ways unconvincing. Mature filmic treatments of trauma events such as the recent bombings of London are to be found elsewhere. In the world of documentary, John Huston's *Let There Be Light* (1946) and Kim Longinotto's *The Day I Will Never Forget* (2002), to take just two examples, brilliantly conveyed the treatment of traumatised World War Two GIs and the agonies of female genital circumcision, respectively. Forget traumaland; forget the roller-coaster ride of sensation that is mainstream cinema for a moment. These and many other documentaries showed that filmed imagery could render painful human experience indelible for those who watch it.

The best example I know in fiction cinema is Elem Klimov's *Come and See*. Filmed in the then Soviet Union in 1985, it is set in Belarus in 1944, as the Nazis sweep eastwards, sacking villages as they go. One 15-year-old boy's whole family has been murdered.

The film shows his flight through peat bogs, his disorientation and tinnitus, the way his head seems to flood with panic and mental noise, with unforgettable precision.

Such films allow us to stand on the threshold of terrifying experience, and watch it unfold before our eyes. But it's not enough to say that cinema at its best, its most innovative, its most morally serious, can depict traumatic experience like nothing else.

No. I believe that not only can it *mirror* those experiences; it, cinema, is actually *structured* like them.

Sidney Lumet's *The Pawnbroker* helps explain what I mean. Made in 1964, it depicts the dull, repetitive life of New York City pawnbroker Sol Nazerman, played by Rod Steiger. We see him at his store every day, talking to his customers in monotone, saying how much he will give them for their candlesticks or guitars – usually two dollars.

Then mental images of Nazerman's days in Auschwitz-Birkenau intrude silently, quickly, then more persistently into his numb daily life. Psychologists call these intrusions flashbacks. So do filmmakers. This isn't an accident of terminology. Just as traumatic memory is discrepant and non-linear, so is film editing. No other art form can jump about in time and space as film can. There are no flashbacks in Shakespeare.

As well as shock intrusions into apparently ordinary life, the medium of film is naturally capable of depicting the more permanently altered states in which traumatised people sometimes feel that they live. Krzysztof Kieślowski's *Three Colours: Blue* portrayed Juliette Binoche's grief at her husband and daughter's death as a somnambulance interrupted by a series of losses of consciousness, signified by fades to black and musical intrusions. Most of these involved close-ups of Binoche. Right from the earliest movies and especially at the time of silent cinema with its huge close-ups of Greta Garbo, it became clear that the magnified human face was distinctly new in human culture. Never before had human beings been offered the chance to inspect faces like their own in lit, flickering, available close-up.

But even if we accept that cinema and traumatic experience are close to the contours of each other, does that mean that movies can help, in any way, with treatment?

No clinical studies have asked this question, so as yet the answer can only be circumspect. On the one hand, movies, the art of being there, have this brilliant, almost off-hand ability to depict experience in a direct way. They are almost like living. But they're not like living, of course, because in life you have to deal with the consequences of a terrible event, where in a movie you see it, feel it, watch its repercussions

– then the credits roll and you're out the door and on the bus home.

But what's the difference between this and the catharsis any good drama can provide?

What's so special about cinema? The answer lies in the paradox at the core of the medium of film. Films like *Three Colours: Blue* or *Come and See* don't simply make us feel closer to the flame of life. They also make us feel safe in getting close. They combine reality and safeness in a unique way. Movies allow us to enter disturbing experiences in a uniquely vivid way without breaking down, or hyperventilating, or having feelings of being unable to cope – then movies are, at their best, like the moment at that a traumatised person feels that they are beginning to recover.

If this is even possibly so, then the closeness of cinema and trauma should be explored. Films take us on the trauma ride and let us see where that ride goes, without being hurt. People who have never been traumatised can enjoy them and perhaps have their eyes opened. The question is whether cinema can be of any therapeutic use. What is certainly true is this: if any art can help, movies can. They, more than any, plot the path to recovery, show that it is possible, that people have traversed it, that it is safe, though scary, of course.

That, in a small way, could be valuable.

FILM FESTIVAL FORM:
A MANIFESTO

The Oberhausen Manifesto helped launch the New German Cinema, and the Danish Dogme manifesto brought new ideas to, and detoxed, nineties cinema.

The film festival circuit could do with a manifesto too …

1.

In Italy in the 1930s, Mussolini's associates launched the world's first film festival – the Venice Film Festival – to celebrate fascist ideas and aesthetics. To counter this, two alternative film festivals were launched, one in a former fishing town called Cannes, and one in the Athens of the North, a centre of the Enlightenment, Edinburgh in Scotland.

2.

Now there are thousands of film festivals. They are a cultural idea that is spreading like a meme.

3.

As the elite of the festival circuit clink another glass of champagne at another party to salute a venerable old festival or the launch of a new one, it would be no surprise if their smiles were a little strained. Masked by glamour and ubiquity, the world of film festivals is, in fact, in crisis.

4.

There are too many of them chasing world premieres and film celebrities.

5.

But they are also chasing a too-narrow idea of what a film festival can be.

6.

Marco Muller says that film festivals should "reveal what the markets hide". Toronto International Film Festival's Piers Handling called this counter-market an "alternative distribution network". In his recent book *European Cinema: Face to Face with Hollywood*, Thomas

Elsaesser says that this network has created "symbolic agoras of a new democracy."

7.

Muller, Handling and Elsaesser each think that the purpose of a film festival is to act counter to the mainstream, cookie-cutter cinema that prevails in most parts. To show a broader geographic, stylistic and thematic range of films than is usually available to audiences.

8.

GREAT!

9.

Except that that's the *content* of a film festival, just as the content of Picasso's *Guernica* is the bombing of a town, like the content of the Smiths' "There is a Light That Never Goes Out" is the suicidal intensity of love, like the content of *Singin' in the Rain* is the rapture of love.

10.

What's exciting about *Guernica* is how its black and white, graphic, epic, mythic imagery shows us the tragedy in a new way. What's exciting about the Smiths' song is the daring of the word and music cadences and ironies ("to die by your side, what a heavenly way to die"). What's exciting about *Singin' in the Rain* is that camera rising up to look down, from where the rain is coming, from where we think of the spirit to be, at this man who is so in love that night-time rain feels great.

11.

In other words, what's exciting is their form.

12.

Film festivals are undergoing formal torpor. Too many of them use the same techniques – a main competition, sidebars, awards, late-night genre cinema, prizes, VIP areas, photo-calls, etc.

13.

There's a simple way of shaking film festivals out of this torpor: we should think of them as authored, just as films are authored. Think of them as narratives – stories lasting ten days or two weeks, just as films are narratives. Think of them as shows being produced on stages (cities, former fishing villages on the Côte d'Azur, etc.) – in which, thus, each has a *mise-en-scène* just as a film has a *mise-en-scène*. A film festival is a shape, a response to the lay of land and light of a city, or to a flood in Pakistan or the threat to bomb Iran.

14.

The people who run film festivals must think of themselves as storytellers and stylists. They must ask themselves what the narrative structure of their event is, and its aesthetic. Most of all they must, as the best filmmakers do, challenge themselves to *do things differently*.

15.

It's about time that, in the spirit of Dionysius, or Guy Debord, or Rilke, or Patti Smith or Djibril Diop Mambéty or Ritwik Ghatak or Samira Makhmalbaf, film festivals realise that they are poetry not prose.

16.

Too many film festivals in the world are enthralled by their function as the alternative shop window for film industries. Film festivals should be more sceptical about business and industry. They should be the conscience of the film world.

17.

There should, therefore, be no red carpets at film festivals. No limos. No VIP rooms.

18.

These things will begin to strip out the excess and ponciness of film festivals — their mannerism — and return them to something purer and more beautiful, inclusive and alive.

19.

Festival directors should use their most discrepant ideas: their funniest, most moving, sexiest thoughts about films. Start a film in one cinema and finish it in another – the audience runs between. Get Godard to recut Spielberg.

20.

Festivals should be radically about joy, about countering alienation, about telling the world of money and commodity that – ha ha – it doesn't know the secrets of the human heart or the inexpressible, stupendous need to be with other human beings.

21.

Film festivals should be naked in front of the innovative, divine, political, honest facts of life. They should lob a thought bomb to show that cynicism is a false lead, art is amazing, cinema is, as Roland Barthes sort of said, "Light from a distant star".

22.

And there's the whole issue of festivity itself to restore to the centre of the world of film festivals. Like music festivals, film festivals should realise that, especially in the age of online, it's the offline communality of film festivals, the fact that we are all getting together to do the same thing, that is part of the source of their joy.

— 2020 —

HALFWAY TO PARADISE

There have been film festivals for more than seven decades. In that time they've told a great story of cinema, but they are everywhere now and too many of them are similar. They need to innovate a bit, dream a bit. Here's one idea.

Venue: as it's not currently in use as the UK Government's Houses of Parliament, The Palace of Westminster, London, England.

Format: a 100-day film festival, which starts with one 57-second film and, on each subsequent day, adds two more.

Opening Night: no red carpet, no VIP area. Alice Guy-Blaché's 57-second silent film *Avenue de l'Opéra* is screened in one of the old parliament's prestigious rooms. On a loop. In another room we hear a 45-minute song by legendary Egyptian singer Umm Kulthum. Somewhere in a distant third room, Billy Fury's song

"Halfway to Paradise" plays. People show up and wander around for free.

Food: from day one, the kitchens are open and free food is given. People can bring and make food.

Subsequent Days: the 57-second film and the music continue to play, but on day two more films are added. They are chosen by Indian economist Amartya Sen and Dolly Parton. Each sent a bed sheet to the festival, and the films are projected onto the sheets, in other rooms of the Palace of Westminster. Other elements are added in other rooms – radio interviews with Marlon Brando and Lena Horne. The music of Scottish band Altered Images and the soundtrack of *The Umbrellas of Cherbourg* begin to play, too.

On day three, the chosen films of Robert Pattinson and Awkwafina are added. Again they are projected onto their bed sheets. The songs of Brazilian musician and philosopher Tiganá Santana begin to play in another room, and we hear a long interview with Bette Davis. On day four, French thinker and writer Hélène Cixous chooses her favourite North African film, and Cher's selected film plays. Albert Lamorisse's *The Red Balloon* and Jafar Panahi's Iranian film *The White Balloon* are added.

The films, songs and interviews repeat and repeat. Films selected by members of the public are added. In the main debating chamber, on a huge screen, Ritwik

Ghatak's *The Cloud-Capped Star*, about the partition of Bengal and consequential refugees, plays.

Surprises: the daily additions are never announced. Each one is a surprise. The selectors send video messages or are there in person. Hundreds, and then thousands, of people show up every day, to see the place, its transformation, its millefeuille of films, music, and cinema sounds. The room that shows Astrid Henning-Jensen's *Palle Alone in the World*, about a small boy who has the world to himself, is full of wonder. Next to it, Peter Ramsay, the co-director of *Spider-Man: Into the Spiderverse*, has chosen his favourite animations.

Judi Dench and Thandiwe Newton are in conversation, and then serve fish pie. Ryan Coogler and Iranian human rights lawyer Shirin Ebadi choose the forty-ninth and fiftieth films. In one of the rooms, unannounced, is the premiere of a new short film by Steven Soderbergh. Also embedded in the labyrinth are premieres by Almodóvar and Apichatpong. People dance in three different rooms.

International: each day, six roving cameras livestream "Halfway to Paradise", capturing its sounds, films, visitors, rooms, adventures.

Switch off: on the one-hundredth day, a team of film fans cleans the kitchen and, one by one, switches off the music, audio and 199 films.

The palace goes quiet except for one film, which will play there forever: Mohammad Ali Talebi's *Bag of Rice*, about a determined little girl's adventure across a city.

Then "Halfway to Paradise" moves to another city, another major building.

DRAG IT INWARDS:
A CHALLENGE TO
SELF-EXPRESSION

Where do movies come from? Before we go to the money people and say "I have an idea for a film", what causes the idea?

I thought about this again last night whilst flopped on my sofa watching a documentary about musician Keith Jarrett. He said "babies don't come from babies." This made me laugh, but also reminded me of converse advice Martin Scorsese gives to filmmakers: watch the old master directors. He means Howard Hawks, Hitchcock, Fellini, etc. Doing so enriches your palette. Jarrett's saying the opposite of Scorsese. His music comes from unmusical things. He drags experiences and feelings from outwith music into his musical software, thereby converting it into music.

Of course, as an altar boy in the church of cinema, I'm all for Scorsese's advice, but I'm increasingly aware of how many un-filmic things beyond the movie pale are jump leads for me. For example, I was in my campervan in St Andrews in Scotland a few years ago, reading a book about the great Scottish painter Wilhelmina Barns-Graham. I tweeted a picture of the cover of the book against a cornfield where she lived. Soon afterwards, the Barns-Graham Trust tweeted me, asking if I'd like to see more of her paintings. I jumped at the chance, visited the Trust, saw scores of her pictures and was ... what's the word when a new idea or enthusiasm seems to take you over? In these Covid times I'll say infected. And I knew I had to make a film about her.

There's nothing unusual in this story, but hold it up against the conventional wisdom about creativity and you get a bit of a mismatch. In Europe since the Romantic period it's been assumed that an artist has things inside her – experiences, a vision – which need to come out. Self-expression is a process so taken for granted (and the basis of lots of art education) that it seems truculent to reject it.

I've had a lot of formative experiences (a few days I spent in Naples in 1990 are a film in itself!) and like you I'm a work in progress, but I don't think that I've accrued an increasingly complex inner life.

It's my outer life – my centrifugal imagination – that has been honed.

If I jump to other filmmakers it becomes clearer what I mean. Take one of the most distinctive, personal voices in movies, Pedro Almodóvar. Can we fully say that he's "expressing himself" onscreen in his female, colour-saturated worlds? Of course many people had similar Spanish/counter-cultural/gender/visual experiences as he did and there's only one Pedro that we know of, but we can say that, like Keith Jarrett in music, it wasn't cinema that made Almodóvar. A lot of it was Spain in the sixties and seventies, which he dragged into cinema.

Move from Pedro to Agnès Varda and my point becomes clearer. She's seen as such a personal artist – and yes her films are full of her friends, family, streets, travels, etc. – and yet one of her signature films, *The Gleaners and I*, reveals how outwardly directed she was. As you'll know, a gleaner is a gatherer, someone with their eyes open, someone hungry. In the film we see how hungry Varda was for new places, discoveries, people, accidents, images. Her films came substantially from the outside.

I know this isn't the conventional way of seeing her great films, and I can feel you saying, "yes but what about David Lynch or Alfred Hitchcock or Yazujirō Ozu? Surely their remarkable worlds are great examples of self-expression?" And you are right. My point is that we need to dial down the "self-expression" idea a bit and learn from Varda and Almodóvar (and Radu Jude, Samira Makhmalbaf, Andrea Arnold, Patricio Guzmán, Ben Sharrock and Céline Sciamma) who are receivers.

Receivers. The American writer Gertrude Stein understood this idea of a receiver (though she's terrible on some subjects). In her *Autobiography of Alice B. Toklas* she says that creativity is observation plus construction. In other words, you start by seeing something remarkable in the world, drag it inwards (like Varda or Jarrett), then shape it. For years this has been my mantra. I saw something that excited me in Wilhelmina Barns-Graham – her unstoppability, her feel for form, her fascination with maths – and then filtered it through my sense of form, of imagery and of story. Other practical things played a role: Twitter, the miniaturisation of film equipment so I can film on almost no budget, etc. These things made it easier to drag the idea inwards.

What I'm saying is that, for me, the question isn't really "what have I to express?" It is "from what do I build the film's world?" Of course it's relevant here that I make mostly non-fiction films, but my movies are very different from journalism and don't use many of the standard documentary techniques. And I think that the best filmmakers ask "from what do I build my world?"

In film schools, art colleges and everyday life, directors should hone their receptors. Which raises the question of whether director is the right word for the job?

SIGHT AND SOUND:
ON CONTROL

Am I controlling this article, these next 900 words, or are they controlling me? The answer seems obvious. I'm doing the typing. The page is blank, and I'm filling it. But my aim is to steer myself, and you, into an area which takes us both by surprise. I want to take us to a felt place, a kind of forest which has its own atmospherics, which has a topography that will start to steer us. Topics have structures. I want to find the structure, then let it take over.

There are other metaphors that refer to what the trip to the forest refers to, the purposeful road to submission, to perdition. David Lynch talks about it as a fishing trip. You go to the river, drop in your line, then wait for the idea to bite. Federico Fellini described it as turning the tuning dial on an old-fashioned radio, past the noise until, suddenly, you hear voices or music:

ideas, emotions, a structure, the joy of submitting to that structure. And control was the main melody of Freud and Marx. What is desire, Freud's life's obsession, but control or/and its flip side? Theodor Adorno and the unlaughing cavaliers at the Frankfurt School said that popular culture is controlling us, that we must wrest back the steering wheel.

Film is in the forest. By jumping on my bike, cycling to a cinema, buying my ticket and sitting down in the dark, I am saying to the film, or its director, *here, have two hours of my time and access to my emotions – do something to me. I'll make it easy for you. I'll just sit here. I'll unbutton a bit.*

And what does the film do to me? It shows me, in *Some Like It Hot*, a beautiful blonde woman submitting her barely concealed body and heartache to the camera as she sings "Through With Love". I submit to her submission. In *Singin' in the Rain* I see a guy in the navy suit sing and dance at night, in a downpour. The camera follows his every move, enslaved to his liberty, his abandon, so much so that when his spirit soars, the camera does too, as if his happiness has entered it like the devil entered Regan in *The Exorcist*.

Such scenes earn my submission. I look at films by the great Asian gradualists Lav Diaz, Apichatpong Weerasethakul, Tsai Ming-liang or Hou Hsiao-hsien and see that they control time like iron. Their long-held shots and slowly revealed stories insist and persist, require and conspire. The languor of their films is almost painful at times, but exquisite too, because of the conviction of their directors, their slowing of the heartbeat, the contrast with the rat race outside the cinema, and the way they say – *I'm in charge. I'll give you pleasure, but on my terms.*

This makes the forest sound like a heady place, and so it is. Movie-going is masochistic. In their different ways, the films of Alfred Hitchcock, Fritz Lang, Brian De Palma, Chantal Akerman and Abbas Kiarostami all show this. Hollywood is totally fucked-up on the subject of control. It wants to make everything easy for us, to suck up to us, to be the big nipple, as Bernardo Bertolucci once called LA, and yet many of its greatest films (*The Searchers*, *Johnny Guitar*, *Touch of Evil*, *Pat Garret and Billy the Kid*, *Raging Bull*, etc.) do the opposite of sucking. They spit.

So. Where are we? I'm lost. When I started writing this (46 minutes ago), I knew that I was interested in a duopoly, one of life's big duopolies: control and the lack thereof. Then I wrote the word "forest" and, as a result, realised (a word that already implies submission) that I should try to write this with feeling. As I did so, I noticed (a word which, like realised, implies something happening to me) that my words were flushed. Suggestive of sex. That's lack of control for you. It takes you places.

I think I know why this happened. In two days' time, I head off to Sweden to shoot my next film. It stars Neneh Cherry and is shot by Chris Doyle. I'm hoping that it will be atmospheric, like the forest. I'm hoping that I won't have to steer it the whole way through, that it will take over, that I can be its stenographer, like I was for the last few paragraphs. The pleasure of such stenography is one of the great things in my life. The forest is so alive – all you have to do is notice that life.

Wish me luck in Stockholm. When the film comes out in a year or so, you'll see if *it* happened. Directing a film is one of the most controlling jobs in the world. You are god for a while. I will even make it snow inside a building. Then I will come home again, and I think I know what I will do to relax after filming. I will go to see a film. It seems mad to escape filming with a film, but the former is all control, the latter is the opposite.

This makes the forest exciting.

I forgot to mention what most writing about cinema mentions these days – digital and interactivity. As you know, both are about us, not it. The digital age is the era of sucking up – you get what you want, when you want it, as you want it, at the pace you want it. And you can pause it to have a pizza. What's interesting about that?

Z

Whenever I'm asked for filmmaking advice by a new director, I always say "remember the z-axis". The x-axis is up and down, the y is left and right, the z is in and out, the relationship between foreground and background. When they're filming a dialogue scene, for example, not enough directors consider what might happen in front of or behind it.

There've been books and thousands of articles on the z-axis, what's usually called deep staging and/or deep focus. It was the signature tune of Orson Welles; it's the dimension that gives William Wyler's *The Best Years of Our Lives* its dimension; it's what makes Béla Tarr movies cavernous and clear; Omar Sharif's spectacular camel ride towards the camera in *Lawrence of Arabia* is z to the power of z; and, in French critic André Bazin, film had a patron saint of zedness. In cinema's sister art, painting, Vermeer presents us with the domestics of z; Mantegna puts us at Christ's feet and lays his body backwards, like tram lines; Canaletto does z with a set square. You could argue that Western Renaissance painting in general was the rediscovery of the illusion and coherence of z.

Z came easy to the movies and was the source of its startle. The train arriving at La Ciotat, and all those phantom rides, showed the thrill of z, the mother of all *trompe-l'œils*. As movie modes started to emerge and separate, it became clear that some were better at zedness than others. Musicals, for example, were mostly y – Fred and Ginger were side by side – and comedy is mostly y (all those double-acts and comedy mid-shots, the exceptions are filmmakers like Tati and Keaton). However, the fact that in horror movies we want to shout "behind you" shows that that that genre is more zeddy. One of the pleasures of John Carpenter's *Halloween*, for example, is that Michael Myers is in the scene, advancing along the z. We can see him, but poor Jamie Lee can't. And if horror movies are zeddy, road movies are even more so. They're entranced by z, in love with it, turned on by it. And such things are not only the concern of a film director. Script editors should, I think, always ask screenwriters "so what's happening in the z?"

If *Sight and Sound* could be printed in 3D, I'd ask you to put on the glasses here to emphasise the obvious point that zedness these days isn't only a question for film geeks. Whether we like it or not, 3D cinema is now a part of the multiplex business plan. The aesthetic zedness of Welles-Wyler-Bazin-Béla has become a staging imperative in kids' and action cinema these days. Z is what we pay the extra three quid for.

Move beyond such mucky money stuff, however, and the idea of z begins to resonate and open up. If z has poetics (Welles etc.), generics (horror etc.), and economics (the multiplex's 3D), it also has what you could call empathics. In the y-axis, people talk to each other, sing, dance or kiss. Y is the social axis, the plane in which people already know each other or get to know each other. X is, you could argue if you're into such things, the god axis. Religious people in Pasolini and Bruno Dumont movies levitate a bit, Buddhist monks in King Hu's *A Touch of Zen* defy gravity. In comparison to these two, the z-axis is a human plane but one in which people leave what they know, their own community or family, and head towards the horizon, over the rainbow, to another world. Zedness is reaching out beyond what you know, it's wanderlust, curiosity. In film terms, it's the axis on which many of the best documentaries work. Zedness is empathy.

Whilst on holiday on Skye recently, I started thinking of making a film about zedness. I took my camera out and filmed a horse. It walked straight towards me, along the z. Then, at dusk, in azure blue light, I filmed a highland cow. The light was so low that the focus was really shallow, but the cow walked towards me, along the z. As it did, the autofocus on my camera adjusted to keep the cow sharp, along the z. We talk about "pulling" focus. Zedness is push and pull.

On Skye I realised that Z is everywhere. It's a visual thing, a filmic thing, a staging thing, a money thing, an optics thing. Maybe most of all, it's a people thing.

— 2016 —

DORSAL VENTRAL

What and Where.

"Ma heid's mince"[*] is what I often say to my editor Timo after a long day cutting, when my brain has stopped working.

The discoveries of neuroscientists, the great explorers of the mince, are changing how we think of the arts. In the twentieth century the avant-garde was a bunch of non-conformists who changed the form of their art; in the twenty-first century they are people with enhanced bits of brain. Formalists were anti-social stylists; now they are people with atypical neuron activity. Sentiment was (and often is) considered an excess or weakness in storytelling; now it can be traced to affect-specific areas of the brain.

You can raise an eyebrow at some of this, but how about the following. Studies of the brains of people and monkeys have suggested that they use somewhat different streams within the brain's rear visual cortex when they are assessing what something is and where it is. The "what?" stream, the ventral, tells you that the thing coming at you as you cross the road is a motorbike. The "where?" stream, the dorsal, which is a bit higher up, tells you where the bike is and how long you have to avoid it.

The dorsal and ventral systems are far from independent, but the distinction reconfigures film history. On one hand we have the ventral objectivists: Alfred Hitchcock, whose things – the key in *Notorious*, the shower head in *Psycho*, the chignon hair in *Vertigo* – seem to hypnotise his camera. He lets us stare or glide towards these things, as if we are to reach out and touch them. David Lynch films are also ventral – think of the ear in *Blue Velvet* and the strange worm-foetus in *Eraserhead*. We don't just glance at them and then look away. It's as if we are committing them to memory by taking the time to let them burn into our consciousness.

There's a slowness and centrality to the ventral object. In Claire Denis' *Beau Travail*, we see Denis Levant's pulse in a vein in his arm, a tiny detail seldom shown (and hard to film). Denis's movie doesn't whip past that detail, it lingers. In Taiwan, Tsai Ming-liang is the ventral modern master of lingering. His shots stay in rooms longer than most, immobile, staring at people or water. They're not continually assessing the moving position of objects, because those objects are not moving much. Ditto, in a way, the things in Yasujirō Ozu's ventral movie world. Kettles just sit there and boil; a jug is filmed without movement; and at the end of *Late Spring*, a man simply peels an apple. In the films of Terence Davies, the camera will be slowly drawn to a photo on a wall, like a tractor beam, or it will gaze at a carpet or slowly arrive at a face. In most of the movies of Robert Bresson, it's the object that matters – a wallet to be pickpocketed, for example, or blank faces. Bresson saw his actors as objects.

Compare this type of film with dorsal seeing, where the objects are less reified, and it's their movement which excites. Perhaps the greatest dorsal film-maker is Hong Kongese Tsui Hark. Many of his scenes are vortices in which his cameras, actors and sets (curtains, doors, etc.) swirl around each other. Their whatness is less important than their whereness. His is an art of relative velocity. Ditto John Woo, in whose films to stop is to fail or disappear. Paul Greengrass' Bourne films are dorsal, too, in that they are a scurried montage of vectors, the tripod often abandoned. In the way that the camera keeps swooping through space, and the films cut on the move, the Orson Welles of *Othello* and *Chimes at Midnight* is dorsal. And Gareth Evans' *The Raid* is one of the most dorsal films ever made.

This isn't just to separate action movies from the rest. The films of John Ford, Kira Muratova and George

Cukor aren't action/dorsal cinema, but neither are they as object-focussed as pure ventral filmmaking. And more intriguingly, neuroscience has found that the ventral and dorsal streams differ in how they relate to other things that are strongly relevant to cinema. The where/dorsal is, as you'd expect of something so integral to our fight or flight mechanisms, fast. It is stored for a shorter time in that it is constantly overwritten, and so is less available to memory. Also it is relatively unconscious. The what/ventral stream is slower, stores for longer, and so is more memorised, and is higher up in consciousness. Neuroscience is conforming what Hitchcock and John Woo instinctively knew – that we'd remember Kim Novak's chignon, and that our panic buttons are pressed by multiple moving cameras.

Beyond cinema the dorsal-ventral divergence is also revealing. The pipe, bowler hats, combs and apples in the paintings of René Magritte are redolent of the ventral stream, as is the solidity of the pictures of Poussin. By contrast, the flickering impressionism of Monet, in which things seem to dissolve, and the swirling compositions and non-primary colours of Tintoretto (Tsui Hark in sixteenth-century Venice) make them dorsal indeed. Timeless and timeful, solid and melting.

My head is mincemeat, if you don't understand Scots.

World of Cinema

THE WILD BUNCH

Imagine a gigantic kineopolis, a repository of all films from all nations, an Alexandrian library of movies. Picture yourself walking through this cavernous San Simeon and fancy, if you will, that the movies call down at you from cans on shelves and servers in niches, like cockatiels in eucalyptus trees and monkeys in banyans.

Which films would have the loudest, most distinctive calls? Not those by William Wyler, Jean Renoir or Bresson – Bazin's boys – or by Frears, Jia Zhangke, Margarethe von Trotta, Hou Hsiao-hsien, George Cukor or Ang Lee, surely. No, above these we'd hear the stylistic roar of Jodorowsky's *Santa Sangre*, and then Tsukamoto's *Tetsuo*, then maybe Tod Browning's *Freaks*, Josef von Sternberg's *The Devil is a Woman*, the fingernails on a blackboard that is Żuławski, Cammell and Roeg, every frame of Fellini and the imagistic tourettes of Lars von Trier.

And then you notice that these first raised voices you hear in the kineopolis are all from those who scuba down into the unconscious. None of this first lot are much interested in the rational or social. The same could be said for Cronenberg and Catherine Breillat, David Lynch and Matthew Barney, not the loudest kids on the block sonically, but boy do their images from down there echo up.

We're talking here about "wild" filmmakers. They come from all decades and places but prick up your ears to them in the kineopolis and you notice some trends: think of the production values of the films of Marcel L'Herbier, Erich von Stroheim, Pastrone in *Cabiria*, Cecil B. DeMille and Buster Keaton in *The General* and you realise that the 1910s and twenties were years when there was a flight from tameness in cinema. Then notice the megaphone passion of Ritwik Ghatak, the intensity of longing in Gulzar (who got an Oscar for *Slumdog Millionaire* after decades of great films) and the fact that many Indian films derived from what were called mythologicals and can't resist lifting off the ground of realism into the gulf stream of musical fantasy and you clock that most of Hindi (what's called Bollywood) cinema has a wild excess of expression, a vocality and throw.

And then consider that swollen period of film history, the 1950s, when Youssef Chahine in Egypt,

Kenneth Anger in the USA, Xie Jin in China and Ghatak (again) in India were pump-priming their movies with rage and you might decide that liberation movements around the world, and Eisenhowerian conformism, caused film form to scream.

A decade later, the new permissiveness allowed existing wildies to go further – think Pasolini with *Salò* – and opened the floodgates for Dušan Makavejev, Walerian Borowczyk, Ken Russell, Mario Bava, Alberto Cavallone, and Yasuzō Masumura. From the early seventies, their *dance macabre* flickered and frolicked in grindhouses and the Midnight Movie fleapits of New York, and in the Scala in London.

Finally, hark how some directors – Pasolini, Shōhei Imamura, Djibril Diop Mambéty in Senegal, Japanese documentarist Shinsuke Ogawa and their latter-day patron saint Werner Herzog – all believed that society was so stale or doomed that they yelled about Rousseauean sublime worlds.

But do these filmmakers have anything in common beyond the fact of their attention-grabbing? I think so. Firstly, they are mostly impatient with the Aristotelian unities of time and space. They prefer their settings to be baroque, extended into multiple realms. Secondly, they're not ones for categories – think of Baz Luhrman's masala of disco, Shakespeare, Bollywood and

Sergio Leone, or the bisexuality and populism of Paul Verhoeven. Thirdly, they are all people for whom the birth of an idea in the mind's eye is basically a violent or feverish event. Unlike the great movies of, say, Tapan Sinha, who died in January, or Henry Hathaway, form is not servile to content for them. Rather, it is monstrous, or "exploding, like the eruption of Mount St Helens" as David Lynch once told me in an interview. Each of these directors has a psychic energy that is manic to a degree and might well be fuelled by sexual rage, or colonial exploitation, or a Marxist hatred of consumerism or historical events like partition or a fear of modernity or the body (Tsukamoto we salute you), but that energy in turn fuels a will to form that is so feral that it makes the act of filmmaking look feverish, and fairness to content an anaemic propriety.

Such energy makes for electrifying movie-going, but if these Mr Hydes have in common the energy of their mental activity or the intensity of their reaction to society, then it should be made clear that neither of these things is purely filmic. And so it's no surprise to discover that Pasolini's writing is just as hysterical as his filmmaking, or that our hallucinated cage rattlers have much in common with R. D. Laing, Jean-Jacques Rousseau, Edvard Munch, Wilhelm Reich, Yukio Mishima, and Vincent van Gogh, to name just a few. If Aeschylus could sashay forth from classical time and watch a

Bresson and Parajanov double bill, he'd easily recognise the spirit of Apollo in the first and Dionysus in the second. The idea that the creative act is also a violent act occurs throughout human thought, nowhere more than in Hinduism. Kali, the goddess of both creation and destruction, would be a fitting patron saint of the Wild Bunch (she could be impersonated by Kenneth Anger in slap).

Mention of Kali and Mr Hyde raises the question of how male is this tendency in cinema, how much of a stag night. The first lists of directors compiled for this issue were mostly men. But Věra Chytilová clearly fits, and Riefenstahl, Breillat, Claire Denis, Sally Potter, Mae West, Jane Arden and Liliana Cavani. Jane Campion told me recently that the unconscious is like a shy animal that must be teased out through gentleness – which is miles away from the cage rattlers, and with which I agree – and might we accept that the loud voices in the kineopolis might be more valued by male critics?

And there is another caveat. Do the wild bunch Dionysians outstay their welcome? Too much Borowczyk or Abel Ferrara sends me running to Ozu. Still, I love most of these directors. They seem to need cinema, or creative expression, more than other filmmakers. They are not using cinema, it's using them. Such helplessness is touching. As a result, I think they do more R and D than other directors. They sculpt film. They meld it in their furnace. They expose their hearts like Jesus exposes his in the last temptation of Christ.

In the era of DVD, the lurid, burlesque, baroque, melodramatic, enraged and discrepant in cinema is more available than ever. So pray silence for the Wild Bunch. To get in the spirit, read this issue of *Sight and Sound* naked on the bus.

Mark Cousins (naked as I write)

— 2014 —

SIX DESIRES:
D. H. LAWRENCE
AND SARDINIA

Words for a film starring
D. H. LAWRENCE, HIS MIND
AND BODY AND SARDEGNA

Co-starring
FRIEDA VON RICHTHOFEN

With appearances by
PAUL CÉZANNE, SAINT ANTHONY THE ABBOT,
ANTONIO GRAMSCI, PIER PAOLO PASOLINI,
BENITO MUSSOLINI, SHEEP, THE *MONA LISA*,
MARIO SIRONI, GRAZIA DELEDDA, HÉLÈNE
CIXOUS, PJ HARVEY, MADAME CÉZANNE
AND THE MAMUTHONES OF MAMOIADA

Dear D. H. Lawrence,

It's dawn here. This ship is gliding from Rome to Sardinia. It sailed all night on the Mediterranean and now, as the sun rises, it's arriving in Cagliari, on Sardinia's south coast. It's January, so there'll be no hot ferocity to the day, nor many tourists. We're almost alone.

Do you recognise this place, Bert? Can I call you Bert? Your family did. I guess I can call you what I want since you're long-dead, so can't complain.

Do you recognise these gorgeous waters, Bert? This alba? This arrival? This harbour? This expectation? This off-peak beauty?

Of course you do, because you saw these things when you arrived here in January 1921.

Into this world of 1921, this picture, this morning, came a creature as alive as seagulls. You. What's that look on your face Bert? Are you wary of this day, this trip, this film? A bit sceptical?

Don't be. We're just trying to see what you saw, and how you saw Sardinia when you came here. You wrote a book about it, of course. A vivid book called *Sea and Sardinia*.

And you weren't alone. You were with this stately woman. Your wife. Frieda von Richthofen. You called her the woman of a lifetime. She was an aristocrat but wanted to sleep in haystacks.

We imagine that you are the woman and man in this film, *Cenere*, which is set in Sardinia and was made in the year that you were there, 1921.

You wrote of you and Frieda:

> We sat under the magnificent heavens, wrapped together in the old shepherd's shawl, for which I have blessed, so often, a Scottish friend, half sheltered from the night and wind.

Yet, in *Sea and Sardinia*, you call her the q-b, the queen bee. An odd name for your lover, your second pair of eyes, your sounding board, your woman under the blanket.

You two had been together for twelve years, by 1921.

1921. What a year, Bert. What a time to be alive and thinking and looking.

Revolutionaries in Russia tried to level history's playing field. They used searchlights, diagonal compositions and bold captions to excite us about Lenin and his new world order.

The atom was split.

And so were we. Freud told us that we dreamt what we denied. *The Cabinet of Dr Caligari* painted shadows on sets to show what our unconscious lives might look like.

Our movies showed us fantasies of women like Pola Negri turning towards the light, unfurling their wings like birds, maybe birds of prey. Women got the vote in the US.

In the book you write this:

> Ah the trembling of never ended space, as one moves in flight. Not to be clogged to the land any more ... Why come to anchor? There is nothing to anchor for. Land has no answer to the soul anymore. It has gone inert ... Let me wander aimless across this vivid outer world, the world empty of man, where space flies happily.

What a wanderlust! What desire. Desire was your middle name, Bert, or maybe your first. Maybe that's what the D stands for. Let's make our story about that D – Desire. What made you tremble. Maybe what makes us tremble.

This silhouette of traffic on Cagliari's main road, the Via Roma, makes us think of your first desire.

The reason you came here in the first place – your desperate need to escape England.

On the train from Rome yesterday, as we looked out of the window, we saw so much that you hated. Industry. Concrete. Modern life.

You called England "A Banquet of Vomit". The Edwardian period was just ending. Life was all corsets and tight collars. You wanted to escape what you saw as the primness and the rationality of the twenties, of industrial life. By railing against it, you wanted to return England back to what it was.

Did you ever see this picture, Bert? It was painted by Mario Sironi, who was born here in Sardinia. It was painted when you were here, in the early 1920s. The man on the white horse is like you, Bert. *Heading away from the factories*, the regimented life.

———

And what did you and Frieda do here, on your first day in Cagliari, your place of escape?

You went to café on this street, and wrote:

> At the tables were mostly seated men, taking coffee or vermouth or aqua vitae, all famil-iar and easy, without the modern self-con-sciousness. There was ... something of a feudal free-and-easiness.

You lament that such men are dying out, Bert, leav-ing "Only rabid equality-mongrels ... The old, hardy, indomitable male is gone ... how detestable."

Wow. That's fighting talk, Bert. Equality's ruining men?

You and Frieda walked up the hill to this place, the hotel where you stayed. You talked of how many steps there are in Cagliari. Thousands. Did you know that one of the world's great architects of steps, Francesco Boffo, was born here in Cagliari? He designed the famous steps in Odessa that Sergei Eisenstein used in his film *Battleship Potemkin*.

Eisenstein's rhythmic editing made them seem even taller than they are, a movie conveyer belt, a killing field.

And then you and Frieda went to the market here, and you describe it like the colour palette of a painter:

> the intense deep green of spinach seemed to predominate, and out of that came the monuments of curd-white and black-purple cauliflowers ... then the long, slim, grey-purple buds of artichokes, ... scarlet peppers in trumpets, magnificent fennels so white and big and succulent ... the green and vivid-coloured world of fruit-gleams, I have never seen in such splendour.

> the vast market house fairly glows with eggs ... eggs glowing warm white ... they give a warm, pearly effulgence into the air ...

And you and Frieda climbed to the cathedral, about which you write: "it has come, as it were, through the mincing machine of the ages, and oozed out baroque and sausagey."

And talking of colour and light, look at this woman, the Hollywood actress Pier Angeli. She was born here in Cagliari. Her make-up's perfect, her dress of turquoise satin, beautifully contrast with the matt brown walls. The camera flows. All so Hollywood. And yet her song seems to comment on where we are. It's Spanish, as was Sardinia for many years, and it's called "Port Afrique". Port Africa.

You realised, Bert, that we are close to Africa here. You wrote:

> Africa!, showing her coast on clear days. Africa the dreaded ... this great, red, trumpet-flaring sunset had something African, half sinister, upon the sea.

Sinister? Is that the best word you could use, Bert?

Some Sardinians still say that Cagliari is African. Arab.

Up at the top of the city, we start to feel that we are seeing your frame, Bert, your point of view.

The sun begins to set. We stand where you stood to watch it, and read what you wrote:

> From the terrace just below the fortress, above the town, we stand and look at the sunset. It is all terrible. Taking place beyond the knotted, serpent crested hills that lie, bluey and velvety, beyond the waist lagoons. Dark, sultry … hanging sinisterly, with those gloomy blue cloud bars.

That night. A dream. Of velvet. You are a lamplight on a pier. Alone and loving it. But then, towards you glides the future, the twentieth century, everything you are dreading. It carries with it, the stuff of the twentieth century – TV, bright lights, teenagers. We glimpse into its rooms and see rock and roll, beat literature, Nazism, nuclear war, gay rights, motorways, the Berlin Wall, Chairman Mao, space travel, decolonialisation, pop art, Black Power, punk, the internet, the virtual world.

Next morning.

We head north, to the small town of Mandas. You went there by train, we'll go by car. It rains. You say that the countryside here looks English and you're right.

We're looking at these sheep but then birds swoop and soar and land on a wire.

We drive through the town of San Sperate, which has roads like mirrors. The great artist Pinuccio Sciola cycles past us. So we follow him. And he shows us his art. He cuts stone, and then rubs his hands on it and, without amplification, it makes this music. He says that the rocks have memories. That the sound is born of a caress.

He's speaking your language, Bert. This is music to your ears, isn't it?

In Mandas, we see the train station that you write about.

A woman here asked you if you are socialists. You smiled. Frieda said "there's too much socialism everywhere." The woman said "one wants a tiny bit of socialism in the world … but not too much … at present there is much too much."

And do you remember the Mandas station bar, Bert?

Here's what you wrote, it makes me laugh …

> A quite pleasant woman behind the little bar.
> A brown woman with brown parted hair and
> brownish eyes and brownish tanned complex-
> ion and tight brown velveteen bodice.

Then there's a sunburst!

Night falls, and we find that the restaurant in town,
Osteria La Fourchetta, has a Menu Lawrence, based
on what you ate here.

> *Creamed cabbage with cream of sea urchin.*
> *Red onion ravioli with braised wild boar.*
> *Pork boiled with creamed tomato.*
> *Ricotta and honey mousse.*

You ate well, amigo.

———

Before dawn in Mandas, as you did, we go for a walk.
Wow. A mistland, a smeared world. As we walk, we
think of what you wrote:

Wonderful the blueish cold air. And things standing up in cold distance ... this bleakness and touch of frost in the ringing morning goes to my soul like an intoxication. I am so glad on this lonely naked road. I don't know what to do with myself.

Wonderful to go out on a frozen road, to see the grass in the shadow bluish with hoar frost, to see the grass in the yellow winter-sun-rise beams melting and going cold-twinkly.

And then an El Greco sky.

And then we leave Mandas. And drive into the hills.

And see scenes from *Don Quixote*. Sardinia starts to look Mediterranean. And we realise that this was your second desire. The desire for the sun, the South. You came here to look at scenes like this. And feel the sun on your skin.

The desire for the South is like this old love song, "Non Potho Reposare", I cannot rest, by Maria Carta: she sings "I'm thinking of you all the time. Don't be sad, golden jewel."

Goethe's and Nietzsche's lives were changed by Italy. You write:

> Whenever one is in italy, either one is conscious of the present, or the medieval influences, or of the far mysterious gods of the early Mediterranean ... Man has lived there and brought forth his consciousness there.

Did this place bring forth your consciousness, Bert? We think so.

You write:

> for us to go to italy and to penetrate into italy is like a most fascinating act of self-discovery – back, back down the old ways of time. Strange and wonderful chords awake in us, and vibrate again after many hundreds of years ... Italy has given me back I know not what of myself, but a very very great deal.

And of course, we're in Sardinia which, in a way, doesn't feel like Italy.

Later we see this old movie footage of Sardinia in the 1920s. A tilt down a beautiful Romanesque church.

Three women walk inside.

And lurking in the foreground is a man. Watching. Loving it. Is he you?

We get to Sorgono.

At first you called it a magic little town.

It's famous for its trees and you love them. Later on the island, we heard four men sing the extraordinary "Stabat Mater", the standing mother.

The trees are like the "Stabat Mater".

You wrote:

> The famous woods begin to appear ... a stream-bed opens a little and shows a marvellous cluster of naked poplars. They have a ghostly, almost phosphorescent luminousness ... myriad cold-glowing twigs, gleaming strangely. If I were a painter, I'd paint them.

But you are a painter, Bert. You go on:

And the cork trees! I see slim, oaky looking trees that are stripped quite naked below the boughs, standing brown-ruddy ...They have a naked suavity, skin bare and intense coffee-red.

The trees seemed to draw you in. Make your focus shallow.

Us too. We see *Arburtus*, *Erica arborea* (used to make bowls for pipes), hazelnut.

This makes it sound that you liked Sorgono, Bert, but of course you hated it. It made you gag. You were rude to its people.

You stayed here. You met a man who thought that World War One had finished, but wasn't sure. Three years after it had done so. Incredible. There's a war memorial here now, Bert.

Was it that man's lack of knowledge that made you write about Sorgono as if it is a puddle, a circle isolated from the world? You say of its people:

> Each of them is pivoted and limited to himself. The fascination of what is beyond them has not seized on them. Their life is centripetal,

pivoted inside itself, and does not run outwards to others and to mankind.

We found them amongst the friendliest on our whole
trip.

At dusk, you and Frieda went for a walk. You wrote:

> No denying it was beautiful ... but I was in
> too great a temper to admit it ... the sun
> immediately went right down ... the village
> began to send forth blue wood smoke ... the
> last red was smouldering beyond the lost,
> thin-wooded hills of the interior. A fleece of
> blue, half luminous smoke floated over the
> obscure village.

Frieda shouted at you.

> Why are you so indignant? You petrify that
> man in the inn by the very way you speak to
> him, SUCH condemnation. Why don't you
> take it as it *comes*? It's all life.

Nice one Frieda. High five Frieda.

———

Next morning, we get the frost that you got the previous day in Mandas.

And that frost is magical.

The morning's like a horse after a gallop.

We talk about this great Sardinian film, *Bandits of Orgosolo*, which was filmed here, in these famous mountains, the Barbagia.

These are real shepherds. They're shot against the sky, to make them look elemental. The camera's amongst them, amongst the wood, the bonfires. It's hand-held. It follows their eye movements. You agree with this film that these men are ancient, don't you Bert? It's what you said about the guys in the coffee shop in Cagliari.

You write that they have medieval faces.

You write of one man: "How handsome he is. And so beautifully male."

You look at men you met here the way the filmmaker photographs these Sardinian fishermen in the fifties.

They're filmed low down, against the sky again. All effort and muscle. You worshiped such virility. You wrote: "How beautiful maleness is if it is in its fullest expression — and how perfectly ridiculous it is in modern clothes."

This great filmmaker and poet, Pier Paolo Pasolini, who was born about a year after your trip to Sardinia, Bert, would heartily agree.

Your line "One realises with horror that the race of men is almost extinct in Europe" could have been written by him. Like you, he felt that modern life and consumerism was making men — men — less hardy, less handsome, less desirable.

And this is your third desire, I think, Bert.

Your desire for bodies.

We think of your paintings. A naked man, in the sunshine, pissing. Looking down at his own urine. His arm casts a shadow, but his piss doesn't.

And what about this painting of yours, Bert? A rape scene? An orgy? Bodies, not faces.

And what were you trying to show in this painting? A man, maybe a shepherd, lies in a field. His sheep are behind him. He's naked and erect. Three women, maybe nuns, look on, shocked. Is the man asleep? Is it a dream? Or a fantasy? Are you the man or the women in the picture, Bert? Is your desire to be him or them?

And, wait to you hear this Bert: 39 years after you died, your book *Women in Love* was filmed. You had two men wrestle naked in the aftermath of a drowning, so this is a shock and recovery scene. But their nakedness is like Sardinia, in contrast to the fancy architecture.

Clothes are for wimps. This is a furnace. They are smelted. They're in the zone. Do you like this scene, Bert? You could have directed it.

And what sort of pictures did Mario Sironi, who painted the man on the white horse escaping industry, go on to do?

Did you ever see this painting by Gustave Courbet?

It was painted in the year you were born. It seems right up your street. Very *Lady Chatterley*. If you saw it, did you like it? It's called *The Origin of the World*. Is it one of the most beautiful pictures in the world?

Your desire for bodies doesn't seem to be a desire for female bodies, Bert. It seems less sexual than that. Your essay on this great painter, Paul Cézanne, might help explain. You said that Cézanne:

> wanted to touch the world of substance once more with intuitive touch ... If the human being is going to be primarily an apple, as for Cézanne it was, then you are going to have a new world of men: a world which has very little to say, men that sit still and just be physically there.

You wanted men to be naked, because it is more honest, like an apple.

We drive on.

And head to this place. Mamoiada. You saw a great event from these mountain tops, Bert.

You write that on a ridge you:

> Saw a glitter of scarlet and white. It was in slow motion. It was a far-off procession ... In a strange, brief, staccato monody chanted the

men ... The priest in his robes, his boys near
him, was leading the chanting.

But we saw more of the event than you did. If our film
catches fire anywhere, it'll be here. We've talked about
Mamoiada for days. People are flocking to Mamoiada.
You can't tell. It looks so peaceful.

We drive into the village.

Is this woman sweeping up for some special occasion?

We start to see piles of twisted wood and roots.

And then come across the grandest of the piles, outside the Church of the Blessed Virgin Mary and Saint
Anthony.

Suddenly, we hear that the bonfires are being lit.

The reason why we're here begins. Lighting the fire
begins the celebrations of the feast of Sant'Antonio,
Saint Anthony.

From the bit of the feast that you glimpsed on the
mountain ridge, you thought that they were celebrating
St Anthony of Padua. A monk from Portugal, who lived

at the turn of the thirteenth century. Like you, he was great with words and, so, 30 years after he died, they dug up his remains. His body had crumbled to dust but, the legend goes, his tongue was preserved and moist. Maybe your tongue would be, too, Bert.

But St Anthony of Padua wasn't like these men, your kind of men, virile men. He was delicate. You wrote that he looked like a male Madonna.

The truth is that the event you witnessed, and that's cranking up before our eyes now, wasn't the feast of Saint Anthony of Padua, it was the feast of a far more ancient Saint Anthony, Sant'Antonio Abate, who lived 800 years earlier, in what's now Libya.

A more archaic guy, the sort of guy you wanted to be. He's the patron saint of fire. Something you'd understand, with all that fire in your belly.

The fires conjure the saint. We hear that he'll arrive, but see no sign of him yet. The men give us wine. The women give us cakes. But something even more ancient happens in this town. These men, Bert, start to dress up.

They're the Mamuthones of Mamoiada.

More wine. At last, Sant'Antonio makes an appearance.

The Mamuthones are fully transformed into something archaic now, and go out into the town. They're the candy man. The bogey man.

The performed self. Decked with sheep bells which look like muscle shells.

The priest blesses the fire.

The holy procession circles it.

So does the unholy procession.

The Mamuthones represent death, ashes, the old year dying and being buried. The guys in red coats, the Issohadores, represent the New Year. Life. Life calls the tune, death dances to it. The future calls forth the past. The priests and the old ladies who follow them — where do they fit in? Are they already thinking beyond life? The afterlife?

The death and life an afterlife seem to spark off each other. Another kind of smelting.

This clashing of past and present makes us think of a scene in a film that you'd love.

DON'T LOOK NOW SEX SCENE.

A woman puts on her grey top.

Her man takes it off. On, off. On. No sound, except the click of a hanger. Just love and buttoning and unbuttoning, and opening and closing, and the camera rolls and they roll, and so does time, thanks to editing on movement, graphic matching.

You and Frieda, Frieda and you. Then and now. Now and then. Love is a mosaic, Bert. Life is a mosaic.

Sardinia is a mosaic.

It remembers many things, from many times, at once. It is what it was.

This St Anthony, the old one, was born rich, but gave his money to the poor. He lived alone in a Roman fort in Libya for twenty years. Barricaded himself in. Two decades later he emerged fit and radiant.

As in this picture, he'd been focussed on something beyond life. He's been looking elsewhere.

In the middle of all this tonight, can we say that the thing that we like about you is that you didn't look elsewhere. When you were here you were here.

Did I mention that this is our last night with you and Frieda?

Tomorrow, we're going our separate ways.

—

The embers are still burning the next morning, and will go on for days, Bert.

We seem to see you in a new light. We realised last night that what we like about you, despite all that we're not sure about, and despite what Sant'Antonio Abate thought, is that when you were here, you knew that life isn't elsewhere.

That's the biggie. Life is right here, the ongoing moment. Or as Frieda told you back in Sorgono, take life as it comes!

We've been using the word "we" a lot, Bert, and often the most-lively bit of a film shoot, is what happens behind the camera, off screen, in the car between locations, or after wine in the evenings, so, in the spirit of you, of life not being elsewhere, here's our here and now.

Enrico's been driving all the time. He washes the wind-screen with alcohol for me each morning, so that I can film. Now that you're leaving us, he washes it again, and we see clearly now.

Enrico's Sardinian, studying humanities. He's young – 24 – yet drives gently.

Gill did the sound on this film. She's a psychotherapist. In Rome on the way here, she went back to this mil-lennia-painted underground garden. She cried when she first saw it in 2001.

Laura is a Sardinian with family in Scotland. This film was her idea and she's one of its producers. When she was growing up, she was told to hide her Sardinian accent. Now she's searching for roots. She could study Sardinia for the rest of her life, and wants to get a house here, in which she could pick capers in the morning. In Mandas, when we heard that the town mayor was coming to meet us, she suddenly put on lipstick. She hadn't put it on for us.

We were hurt.

Luca is a Sardinian psychiatrist who takes his patients into the mountains. He has cousins in every town we visit. His name alone opens doors. In one of the B&Bs where we stayed, I slept in the same room as him. He woke us up by playing "These Boots Are Made for Walkin'" and dancing, wearing only briefs. This is him, minutes later, lost in thought.

I'm wearing a silly high-visibility jacket. Laura insisted on it because I've been filming on very narrow roads. I'm hoping to use PJ Harvey's song "Happy and Bleeding" at the end of this film, because it's inspired by a D. H. Lawrence song.

Notice that Laura's wearing lipstick in the car here. She must be expecting to meet someone important. Not us.

We eat Fruit Joy sweets in the car. They sum up our mood. We are happy, Bert. A famous five, on a grand tour in B&Bs.

So we drive on.

We realise that the fourth desire of this film, lurking in it all along, has been the desire to be with you and Frieda. To see how you get on.   .

To hear you use words, to see your rage.

But we can't, of course, so we drop your frame, Bert. We drop you. These trees seem to make a new frame.

We're on our own now.

We like it. We start to ask what you didn't see, to look for what you didn't see, or understand.

We head towards Nuoro.

Its road sign, like many here, has been shot at by hunters.

In the film *Cenere*, which is set in Nuoro, there's this lovely shot, which feels like an arrival. The camera tracks right, keeping its distance. Italy was famous for such shots.

We get to Nuoro.

You said of it, Bert, that its "morning was of a bell-like beauty."

As we're in a bigger place now, Luca gets a satnav out.

It starts to talk to us a bit like the computer HAL in *2001: A Space Odyssey*, but in a female voice, and I realise how travelling with you has felt very male, and that all movies should turn into something else. So what if this film became more female? We joke that the satnav could narrate the rest of this film.

And we fantasise that a great actress, Claudia Cardinale, could speak the rest of the film.

FEMALE VOICE FROM HERE ON.

But we settle for this. That's better, Bert. A takeover.

We go to the home of Grazia Deledda.

She was born in Nuoro, as you know. The second woman ever to win a Nobel Prize for Literature, in 1926, five years after you were here, for her 33 novels.

This is her garden.

She called Nuoro "a bronze age village".

She wrote about tragedies, what she called "These internal struggles, these storms in one's brain." The sea shimmers in her work, the hills hold secrets like the Mamuthones, like the fact that life is unbearable.

Her first piece was about a woman who pushes a man over a cliff. The magazine that published it was burnt. People in Nuoro thought that she was mocking them. Her family were pilloried.

She wrote:

> Even if I changed my life, I would always remain the same. And perhaps homesickness, that exclusive misfortune of Sardinians, would not let me enjoy it.

Her 1916 novel *Cenere* (*Ashes*), was about a woman who gives up her illegitimate child. It was turned into a movie.

The Nobel Prize Committee cited her "inspired writings which with plastic clarity picture the life on her native island and with depth and sympathy deal with human problems in general."

She got breast cancer and died aged 65. She was buried, in Rome, in the dress she wore to the Nobel ceremony in Stockholm. But by 1956, Sardinia thought better of her and, so, had her reburied here in Nuoro.

This is her coffin.

This is her voice.

Deledda's is another frame.

In 1950, Giuseppe Dessì wrote:

> I think of our women as many Penelopes with-out Ulysses ... Let's learn from our women to create all that ... we should have done for centuries. Because it is not enough just to be proud and manly, in order to be husbands to Penelope.

And, still thinking of frames outwith yours, Bert, how about this woman, Hélène Cixous.

She's a philosopher, critic, poet and playwright. She was born in Algeria, so is African, which is way beyond your frame. Where St Anthony looked slightly off to another world, and you looked at us quizzically, she looks far left. Somewhere much removed from where you looked. And when she writes about naked bodies, it's so different to you.

In her brilliant essay on this painting, *Bathsheba*, by Rembrandt, she says:

> This female nude is not nude. She whom we see is not the mortal object. Not the object of desire ... what there is not in Rembrandt: there is no Da Vinci. Not the smile ... Of what secret hearts are we made? Of what densities ...

Cixous says that Rembrandt takes:

> the red staircase, down to the bottom of ourselves ... Ah, so that's what's gripping my heart. The young woman is in the process of aging. The future is spreading through her limbs ... It isn't with the appetite of desire that Rembrandt paints Bathsheba. It is with the attentive love for ... the sober splendour of the ordinary.

Wow, Bert. Were you ever without the appetite of desire?

Look at how Paul Cézanne, about whom you wrote so well, painted his wife. Head tilted slightly to one side. Hair like parting curtains. She looks right at us. Less superior than Sant'Antonio. Less determined than Hélène Cixous. Her heart isn't beating fast, like Lady Chatterley's does. She's no stormy sea.

We imagine your Frieda looking at her, jealous, perhaps, of how much Madame Cézanne held her husband's attention, the lack of swell of her waves.

And talking of quietude, did you ever see the paintings by Giorgio Morandi, the Bolognese artist who was doing some of his best work in 1921, when you were in Sardinia? Where you had wanderlust and travelled the world, he hardly went anywhere. For decades he painted the same jugs, vases and bowls.

Their shadows. Very little colour. He saw the whole world in these everyday objects. The calmness of his work, the lack of adventure, the lack of desire, would have driven you nuts. Some of the greatest art was still life, but your life wasn't still.

And when we're looking at life in ways that you didn't, at things that were beyond your frame, at things you didn't understand, we need to look at the darkest thing, Bert.

In his autobiography, Morandi wrote: "I had much faith in fascism from the beginning ... faith that never wavered, even during its most sad and tempestuous days."

What did he mean, and what's that to do with you?

We imagine that this field in Sardinia is the island, or Italy, in the 1920s, thirties and forties. People move up it across the years, towards the future.

Within months of you being here, Bert, Benito Mussolini came to power in Italy.

He was born just two years before you. In 1914, he formed the fascist party. He said that "a million sheep will always be dispersed by the force of one lion." By 1919, two years before you were here, the fascists were arguing that the whole of the Mediterranean was a *spazio vitale*, a special place that belonged to Italy. In 1920, the fascists argued, in public, that it would be OK to sacrifice 500,000 Slav people, whom they saw as barbaric, for the sake of 50,000 Italians.

Did you know of this, Bert? If so, did it not ring alarm bells?

The fascists said that Africans were inferior. Did you hear them do so? You admired the writer Gabriele D'Annunzio, Mussolini's troubadour, his role model. When 40,000 Libyans died in Italian internment camps, what was D'Annunzio's response? He commissioned a gold and ivory medal in celebration. Fascism was a cult of beauty and death.

You don't mention Mussolini in *Sea and Sardinia*. In 1928, you wrote "I don't care about right and wrong, politics, fascism, abstract liberty or anything of the sort."

Mario Sironi, who painted the man on the white horse and the nude woman against the tree, was a big supporter of the fascists.

As life went on for ordinary Italians, a man born right here in Sardinia in 1891 tried to lead them in a different direction.

In Rome on the way here, we saw his face painted on an underpass, so his ideas must be still alive.

He said that Sardinia showed the injustices of the world in microcosm.

You don't mention Antonio Gramsci, Bert.

He wrote widely, from 1914.

He argued that the very people you saw on your trip, deserved proper education in order to see that mass society, capitalism and fascism were treating them like … well … sheep. Wouldn't you have liked him, Bert? Couldn't you and he have had a few *mirto digestivo*, and talked about the working classes?

Gramsci developed the idea of *hegemonia*, hegemony, to try to explain why people conform, and how capitalism legitimises itself.

Look at the way he looks. It's like we've said no to him. It's as if he's disappointed in us.

Antonio Gramsci was arrested by the fascists in 1926. He spent most of the rest of his life in prison.

His namesake, the other Antonio, Sant'Antonio Abate, imprisoned himself, of course. Both were disappointed by life. But Gramsci holds our stare more.

What you couldn't know, Bert, and what few people knew, is that as the twenties turned into the thirties, Mussolini started hanging out with someone else who loved blood and soil. Together they agreed that destruction is renewal, that war purifies. In the forties, on the horizon of these times, places like Auschwitz were the end of their line of thought. As you didn't live long enough to hear the word Auschwitz, we won't trouble you with what it was.

Shall we leave this lovely place?

———

We drive to somewhere you didn't go. The village of Lodine.

Look what we find.

Murals of Mandela and Muhammad Ali.

Gandhi.

Footballer Gianfranco Zola.

Anti-mafia magistrates Falcone and Borsalino.

And, check by jowl ... Deledda and Gramsci!

We're delighted.

We go to another place you didn't see, Castelsardo.

It's like a cubist painting, or one by Magritte. Out of season.

We hope to see its famous altarpiece, *Madonna with Child*, by the Maestro di Castelsardo. First we see the *Madonna in Heaven*.

Standing on the heads of angels, as you do. The chapel is wintry dark. And, oh no, because it's the feast of St Anthony, he's standing in front of the famous Madonna.

We're not even supposed to be filming here. But we get the last postcard left of her. She's got her own string quartet, and hair to her waist, and a faraway look. Composure, patterning, foresight, hiding her dread. The picture's even better than we hope.

Lights flicker, night falls.

———

We're up before sunup, to film Castelsardo. It's still a bit too dark.

In the semi-dark, the rock looks almost abstract, like a pure shape, and so I angle the camera a bit, to make the old town a diagonal.

As we do so, we realise that we're thinking about the sixth and last desire in this film.

The desire for form.

We've been reading Sigmund Freud on desire and on Leonardo da Vinci. He says that da Vinci had his mother's smile but, after it went, he tried to recapture it. The half-smile in the *Mona Lisa* is a half capture.

Da Vinci had the talent, the will to form, to paint that smile.

You have the same, Bert. In your book *Sea and Sardinia* we can see that you can feel that you can write. Form is like a piano in a room. You know you can play it and so you do. Your ability to write, your will to form, is like a credit card in your pocket. You want to spend with it. It's like there's a cock between your legs. You want to fuck with it.

Your sense of the form of a sentence burns a hole in your pocket. You can't stop playing, spending, fucking. You travel more to play, spend, fuck more.

There's your talent and there's Sardinia, and they met and hit it off. Sparks flew. They were terminals on a battery. If there's a gap, a desire gap, a voltage, a spark jumps between world and art.

This film isn't in the end about your wanderlust or sexuality or politics, it's about that electricity.

—

We go one last place Bert, another place you didn't go.

Up this road and round to the left a bit, is one of the most beautiful things we've ever seen.

It's a 3-4,000-year-old olive tree. It's in the centre of a field, as wide as a cumulus cloud. It's nearly as old as the pyramids of Giza, older than Christianity or Islam. It has outlived everything we've talked about.

Leonardo da Vinci. Even Sant'Antonio Abate.

Let me show you it. I pick up my camera and take a few steps forward, but then. No. Wait. A step back again. I put the camera on the road again.

Maybe it's best not to show it.

Not all desire should be satisfied.

In Rome, recently, we filmed this old couple walking away from us, towards young people, a ball game, joggers, a classical façade.

We imagined that it was you and Frieda, Bert. We imagined that you didn't die just nine years after your trip to Sardinia, in 1930, aged just 44. You and Frieda continued travelling – to Ceylon, Australia and New Mexico, where you lived.

We imagine that you and Frieda grow old together. You wrote of the Mediterranean:

"How lovely it must have been to Ulysses."

We look at your old man's walk and think of what you did and were in Sardinia.

You wrote in your book about the malaria on the island. There were an estimated 30,000 people with the illness when you were there. But your book's publication helped alert other countries to the size of the problem, and guess what? More than a decade after you died, The Rockefeller Foundation and others funded malaria's eradication with DDT. By the 1950s, fewer than ten people had the disease.

You played a role in that. Quite a feather in your cap.

———

And, as we leave Sardinia, what else stays with us? That fact that you were so grumpy, so surly.

You did a whole lot of looking on the island, but a lot of magical thinking too, and dodgy longing for a time before the Enlightenment, before reason came along and, for you, spoiled everything.

You were like a prophet, Bert. A John the Baptist, calling forth a new religion. You yelled from the mountain tops that we had lost our souls.

You yearned to return England to itself. Thank god your dreams didn't come true.

But your sensuality lives on.

Thank you, Bert.

You choreographed this week, this work, this walk.

Bye.

D. H. LAWRENCE AND SERGEI EISENSTEIN: AN INTERVIEW

CAPTION, WHITE ON BLACK:

In 1946, two years before his death, the great Soviet film-maker Sergei Eisenstein was interviewed, by an English journalist, about his thoughts on the UK, its literature, art and politics. In this extract, never published, Eisenstein talks about his fascination with the writer D. H. Lawrence, who had died 16 years earlier. The filmmaker, who was always on the move, insisted that the interview take place whilst driving and walking around Moscow. Eisenstein is voiced, here, by Mark Cousins.

MIKHAIL GLINKA'S "LA SÉPARATION,
NOCTURNE IN F MINOR", SLOWED DOWN.

~

SHOTS OF DRIVING AND
WALKING AROUND MOSCOW.

THE QUESTIONS APPEAR AS CAPTIONS.

Mr Eisenstein, did you ever meet the novelist D. H. Lawrence?

No, but I would have liked to. I read his *Lady Chatterley's Lover* on an ocean liner crossing the Atlantic enroute to Hollywood in late 1929. We had numerous shared interests. I would have liked to have argued with him, travelled with him, driven around this city with him, as we're doing now, or gone to Mexico with him.

Might it not have been a difficult encounter, however? You admired his writings, but he famously didn't think much about movies. He might not even have seen your film Battleship Potemkin.

Well that might have been more fun! He liked some Westerns, and wanted *Women in Love* to be filmed, but hated *Ben-Hur*. Remember that he wrote this: "We think a lovely woman must look like Lillian Gish, a handsome man must look like Valentino," but "there is a greater essential beauty in Charlie Chaplin's odd face than there ever was in Valentino's." What insights there are in those few sentences! He saw beyond the fuselage of beauty, into its engine room. He knew that if we see only the clothed surface of beauty, that we are not doing the work of the artist, we are not operating out of time, and beyond ideology.

Beyond, yes, but couldn't you also say that in his written work, and even his paintings, he wanted to get beneath the surface of everyday life?

Beyond, beneath, above. He was Galileo, railing against Copernican conformism. And Lawrence held movies responsible for some of the ersatz qualities of what was then our new twentieth century. In "When I Went to the Film," he says that we see "all the black-and-white feelings that nobody felt," and that the people in the cinemas underwent "emotions that none of them felt". Like me, he knew that the human heart is epic, that emotions have great amplitude. He wanted to excavate. Look how often he uses the

English word naked. He wanted to unclothe his people, their desires.

Here's a drawing I did of a scene in his *Lady Chatterly's Lover*. The man soars above the woman like a great tree, like a thunderous storm cloud, his heel raised like his whole body is raised. I could have made a great opera with this book, an opera staged in Paris.

Can I show you another drawing I did?

Of course, Mr Eisenstein.

It's from Lawrence's story "The Prussian Officer". On the left is the aging captain, who is frustrated by life's experience, and poisonous. In the middle is his younger orderly. The orderly is in love with a woman, but the captain attempts to prevent that love. Angered, the orderly viciously attacks his superior. The result is tragedy, as my drawing of a corpse in the bottom right indicates.

Why did you choose to illustrate these characters from Lawrence?

Well, in my country, we like stories of youthful rebellion, of refusing to be controlled by the elite! But I was attracted very much to the almost Greek theme in the scenario. This is a tragedy. The older man fascinated by the younger's vitality, his beauty even. He peers at the epicene orderly, and resents him. Time is the thing. Time is the property that the captain cannot control or reverse. Lawrence, I think, didn't know his own mind. Without being aware of it, he wanted to reverse time. He had a professed love of the Italian Futurists, their kinesis and fascism, and yet in so much of his writing, he imagines a Rousseauean time before the innovations of the twentieth century. Think of his book *Sea and Sardinia*, in which he grumpily harks after an unspoiled epoch. I like that he contradicts himself. I like that he doesn't know what he thinks. They call that repression, these days! Repression creates a great force, great pressure and, eventually, a baroque explosion. Lawrence's work is just such an explosion.

In December 1943, after my "breakdown" after ninety nights filming *Ivan* in Alma-Ata, I went to rest in the mountains, where I was utterly absorbed by Lawrence's *Short Stories*.

I was interested in what you could call the animal epic running through his novellas. It made me think of, of all things, Disney.

I found the *Short Stories* striking for their abundance of latent action and sheer literary brilliance.

There was a lot latent in his work, wasn't there? Can I turn, now, to landscape? Lawrence's writing is full of depictions of

*the natural world, and his people are often most at home in
the countryside, as if they are figures in a Poussin painting.*

Poussin? No! Too sedate. They are like people in one
of Corot's stormy forests, animated by the passions of
Courbet! And, if I can say this, I think that my consid-
eration of landscape helps explain Lawrence's. I have
written that landscape in fiction is like pathetic fallacy.
I call it Non-Indifferent Nature. The landscape is produced by the person, by their psyche. In Lawrence, the
countryside seems to spring from within.

It is a great shame that Lawrence died so young.

He was only 44 years old! How terrible for his wife,
and for us. And think of the times that he lived in –
we lived in – and what he has missed. His novel *The
Rainbow* was published into the world of Verdun and
Dada. Then Rutherford split the atom and Malevich
astonished the world with his monochrome crosses
and squares. A year later the Austro-Hungarian Empire
was broken into fragments, and new liberties emerged.
And then there was Bauhaus! And they murdered Rosa
Luxemburg. Lawrence was on the wrong side of some
of this, of course, and does he even mention Antonio
Gramsci? Did he register the 1923 Hitler putsch?
There's so much that he seemed unaware of?

Why was he not shaken by James Joyce's *Ulysses*? His *England, My England* came out in the same year as *Mein Kampf*, the year before my *Potemkin*. I found myself in a vanguard. Did he, ever? He was a tumult, yes, but his ferocity was Whitman more than Joyce. The year he died, Gandhi began to stir the spirit of India, and Freud wrote *Civilisation and its Discontents*. That could be the subtitle of many of Lawrence's books!

And your films?

Not at all. Lawrence takes us back, I take us forward.

So you are very different after all?

No. That's the wrong thing to conclude. Look how well Lawrence understood Paul Cézanne. He knew how to look, as I do. He was an omnivore, as I am. I am interested in everything. He was interested in most things.

ADMISSION: No such interview took place — but the quotations from Lawrence are true. And the drawings are real. And Eisenstein was very interested in him.

EISENSTEIN IN NEW YORK

Sergei Eisenstein first went to Manhattan on 8 May 1930. He was 32 years old, exactly the same age as the city of New York itself, if you take its incorporation of Brooklyn and outlying areas as the starting point of its modern idea. By the time of his arrival, movies had already begun to bicycle-pump up the myth of Manhattan. 1930 was two years after King Vidor's *The Crowd* and just three years before *King Kong* had turned the city's skyline into the Alps of their age.

It's not just Manhattan that was mythic. Its visitor was too. At the age of just 27, Eisenstein had released that modernist, shrill, *feu d'artifice Battleship Potemkin*. As a result, the Jazz Age fell for it and him. He was quixotic, a brain-in-a-jar, a Riga-born master of cinema ceremonies.

Though Eisenstein travelled for most of the way to America with Eduard Tisse, the great cinematographer of *Battleship Potemkin*, he carried a film camera himself, and made a tripartite movie about his time in New York. Eight decades later, the film exists only in fragments and Eisenstein, the great sound theorist, never managed to add a soundtrack. Perhaps Manhattan was surpassed in his priorities by the sensory-political assault of Mexico that he experienced on his onward journey. Yet the film is revelatory, a kind of fugue.

Part One, which seems to chart his first impressions of the city, might well have been bitter or low key. Famously, Major Frank Pease welcomed Eisenstein to the US by accusing him of being part of "a Jewish Bolshevik conspiracy to turn American cinema into a communist cesspool." Furthermore, Eisenstein's written accounts of those first days show that he was disappointed with the height of the skyscrapers and, typically, didn't want to go to museums or posh restaurants. The thing that most people find easy about New York City – its street grid – he found hard. The street numbering didn't help him find his bearings. Yet his images are, to use one of his words, ecstatic. He was clearly dazzled by the play of rain on Manhattan's night-time streets. He wrote of the city's advertising boards, that they:

> nullify all perception of real space ... they seem like strips flickering over a flat surface, the black velvet of the night sky ... the

upside-down reflections in puddles destroy our perception of which way is up and which down. All these contribute to forming a similar mirage of light under our feet ... as we make our way through this double world of neon-advertisements.

Talk about Broadway boogie-woogie. He's reminded of René Guilleré's article about jazz age aesthetics, where perspectives in music and painting are multiple. He calls this the "emotional plurality of meaning".

On his first full day, he had to eat artichoke "whose leaves form a cupola and end in a small spike that stick maliciously upwards" and, that night, he stayed at the Savoy Palace Hotel. It's easy to imagine him lying in bed at night, staring at the ceiling, hearing the roar of the city, the honk of horns, and maybe laughter, or a saxophone, outside. How this disparity between what he was seeing and hearing must have reminded him of the Statement of Sound that he, Pudovkin and Alexandrov co-signed just two years earlier. And just months before his Manhattan trip, he met James Joyce, in Gagra, on the Black Sea. He loved how Joyce's interior monologues in *Ulysses* were on a different track to the outside world. If Eisenstein had added sound to Part One of his New York film, it's tempting to imagine that it, too, would have been an interior monologue. Meyerhold had taught him to imagine a theatre production rehearsed with music but performed without it. That's what his night-time images in Part One feel like. Eisenstein would surely have had his ideas about synaesthesia in mind in these sequences, the suggestion that the visual and the auditory are subterraneously linked in culture and the human mind. In attempting a unified theory of art, politics and the senses, he believed that looking, for example, conjured listening. If it has become a cliché, almost, that Manhattan looks like jazz sounds, then the look of the advertising reflected on wet streets, surely, has synaesthetically induced soundscapes.

On his third day in Manhattan, he gave, unshaven, a press conference at the Astoria hotel. In the lobby he met D. W. Griffith, who lived there for many years. Griffith was 55 at the time but looked much older. He also met Douglas Fairbanks who took him to a speakeasy. He filmed neither of these encounters, but there's a fabulous still photograph, by Margaret Bourke-White, of the maestro having a shave on the Chrysler Building, with the Empire State in the background. His mask-like face shows little emotion, but the last images of Part One were probably filmed on that day. His camera pans the skyline, looking, looking.

Part Two of Eisenstein's fugue film — a kind of interlude — seems to have been filmed when he returned to Manhattan, to stay at Theodore Dreiser's house on the Hudson. Dreiser loved Eisenstein's adaptation of his famous novel *An American Tragedy*. David O. Selznick called it the most moving script he'd ever read. Yet it must have been dawning on Eisenstein that it wasn't going to be made. Hollywood's slow no. There are more people in Part Two. Close-ups of faces, framed square on, often shot from a low angle. Eisenstein had seen King Vidor's *The Crowd* by now (and, in Hollywood, had quizzed Vidor about how he's done the famous tracking shot up the skyscraper and into an office window). *The Crowd*, of course, was about anomie. Is that what Eisenstein wanted us to see in these faces in Part Two? At one point he talks of the "emptiness" of American life. The *ex-stasis* of Part One of the film is gone now.

Part Three was probably shot after his long filming trip in Mexico. The drive back to New York took 19 days. This time he saw the Ziegfeld Follies, the Barnum and Bailey circus, nightclubs in Harlem, and a heavyweight boxing match at Madison Square Garden. He loved the non-naturalism of these events, what you could call their emotional contagion. And it's noticeable what he films at them: not so much the spectacle, but the audience. He was, after all, a man of theatre, trained by Meyerhold to direct the audience's attention. Many have argued, convincingly, that his famous montage theories, where he claimed he could get the audience to think, en masse, certain thoughts, came from seeing audience members' heads turn, in unison, to look at something stage left or right.

Watch the tantalising fragments of Eisenstein's film about Manhattan more than once and the thought occurs that it is not a film about a city at all. It's about Eisenstein. His fascinating idea of "non-indifferent nature" suggests that the director is the landscape that she or he films. There is no emotional distance between him and the city in these fragments. He brought himself with himself to Manhattan and found there: ex-stasis, graphic night-time imagery, loneliness, cityscapes conjuring interior monologues.

Eisenstein the non-indifferent, lionising, film genius left Manhattan in April 1932.

—

A CONFESSION: alas, Eisenstein did not film his time in New York. Though all the facts, meetings, locations and quotations above are true, and the ideas are mostly Eisenstein's, the film is a fantasy. Thanks to Robert Robertson's book Eisenstein on the Audiovisual, *and Ronald Bergan's* Eisenstein: A Life in Conflict.

ASSUMING THAT THEY'RE THERE

Questioning Assumptions About Female Filmmakers.

This is a story about getting lost. It veers in a way that seems logical, yet ends up in the wrong place.

It starts with Meryl Streep, Helen Mirren, *Sight and Sound*, me and (I'm assuming) you. All five of us, and lots of others, believe that it's bad that so few women are getting to direct films. We all admire Jane Campion, Kathryn Bigelow, Claire Denis, Lynne Ramsay and many of the other women directors who do make films, but know that gender equality is far from being achieved in film directing. The five of us know why that is. Men select content. Movies are a money game, and the money men favour men, etc. We're angry at this sequestering. Politically, we argue that the result has been a historic loss of voice, a perspective deficit.

So far so uncontentious. Then add into the story our cautiously hopeful assumption that – with Meryl and Helen on our side, and with the growing feeling that men dominating film directing is unacceptable – we might be getting somewhere. The more persistently and inventively we push, the greater the chance that we'll get the numbers up. Again, this is hard to disagree with.

But here's the veer: call "There aren't enough great women directors" proposition A, and "if we push we can win the argument and get more of them" proposition B and we sort of infer a third proposition, C, that movie history hasn't had many great female directors. This is untrue. There are lots of them, but our anger at the fact that there aren't more today (A), and our determination to do something about that (B) leads us, politically, into a false consciousness whereby, accepting that the patriarchy is strong and self-interested, we conclude that its instinct to exclude has been very successful (C). It hasn't.

C is what I call the "assuming that they're not there" position. Take Africa, for example. Many movie lovers might assume that, because they haven't heard of African female directors from the past, women directing film in Africa is relatively new. It's not. Yes, let's argue A and B about Africa, but let's not, then, veer into C. If we do, we forget about great directors like Safi Faye,

Moufida Tlatli, Sarah Maldorer and Assia Djebar. I talk often about these filmmakers, and notice that, when I do, people, if they haven't heard their names, seldom write them down. Why not? Because they don't know how to spell them? Or because they assume that they are very minor figures, that I am scraping the bottom of the barrel? Or is it that the subtly negative effect of C, combined with our proper present political point (A), is to downgrade the heritage of women directors, or assume that they aren't there?

Assuming that it's there is an empowering, enlightenment project. Marie Curie assumed that radium was there. She saw it in her head before she saw it in her test tube. We can borrow this scientific approach, or its converse, which is to try to invalidate the proposition "there are no great female African filmmakers from the 1960s, 1970s and 1980s." If we can't invalidate that, if we can't show that C is rubbish, then maybe it's true.

Luckily, there are lots of people – researchers, curators, festivals, publications – who, now and for many years, have been naming and celebrating the great women directors from the past. Some people are wary of the conservative implications of the word "heritage", but in this case I'm not. Yes, let's get angry about how few women get to direct films, but let's know the heritage. Let's make sure that Kira Muratova, Rakhshān Banietemad, Lois Weber and Helma

Sanders-Brahms are part of the conversation we have when we talk about this. Young directors should be taught about Pirjo Honkasalo and Larisa Shepitko, like they're taught about Richard Leacock and Tarkovsky. When I say that rejecting prop C is empowering, I mean that it gives us a sense that we are standing on strong foundations, or sturdy shoulders. I mean that women directors today don't need to feel solitude. They can ask "How would Forough do it?" How would Elaine May do it? How would Esfir Shub do it? How would Suzanne Osten do it? How would Carol Morley do it?

To ask these questions is to feel unstuck. To ask these questions is to build upon foundations. To ask these questions is to move beyond anger. Despite it being born out of calls to action, prop C is a passive place. It's incurious, too. I say again that I'm describing only a tendency here, and that there are great people who have written histories of women film directors, but prop C draws a veil over that history, and suggests that there's not much behind the veil.

Let's rip it away. Let's assume that they're there.

TARANTINO AND INTERNATIONALISM: A PROPOSAL

For *The Observer*.

The spat between Quentin Tarantino and Tilda Swinton at the opening of the Cannes Film Festival made headlines a few weeks ago, but the substance of their disagreement continues to intrigue.

The bone of contention was what is wrong with the world of cinema and how it can be put right. Tarantino claimed that most countries don't have film industries because they don't have movie stars. The only three which do, he said, are America, India and Hong Kong. The rest are not industries but *boutiques* producing high-quality work on a small scale but incapable, presumably, of replicating blockbusters.

This is only half-true, and Swinton was the first to demur. Querying the idea that we need to move away from boutique cinema to more star-driven movies, she said that in Britain, where multiplexes out-number art cinemas by ten to one, it is the non-American, discrepant, personal or innovative work which is smothered. She has a point. For every twenty people who saw *The Matrix Reloaded* in the UK or the US, for example, only one went to the Mexican film *Y Tu Mamá También*, which was released around the same time and was surely – would anybody disagree? – far more entertaining.

Wherever you stand on this – I want to see both types of movies but agree with Swinton – a throw-away line from Tarantino at the same press conference shows why his vision of cinema is interestingly skew-whiff. Pressed on whether the anti-Bush message of Michael Moore's *Fahrenheit 9/11* would influence the jury's evaluation of it, the director quipped "It's going to fall down on whether we like the movie. Politics be damned."

On the face of it this was no surprise. Tarantino is perhaps the most aesthetic, least reality-oriented, of the North American directors. But not only is politics not damned in Cannes, it is, like Prada and hubris, just about everywhere you look. Particularly global politics. Particularly the relationship between Europe and America. The Festival is supercharged by the American film stars who walk up its famous red steps, so in some ways Tarantino is right. Yet a few minutes later, when the lights go down, a Swintonian boutique film is the most likely to unspool. This combination is political, as a single comment in one of the most daring films of the year – the Iranian movie *10 on Ten* – showed. At one point in it, as he drives along a dusty road, the director Abbas Kiarostami says that American cinema is more dangerous than the American military.

Few would go along with such incendiary talk, but the iniquity of globalisation has become one of the key themes of star and boutique movies these days. The most international art-form is, more than any other, reflecting the concerns of its age. It is doing so with its customary elisions and compromises of course, but some of the new films are outstanding. At Cannes alone, for example, a documentary about the world of wine production, *Mondovino*, sounded like a snore, but turned out to be a brilliant punk-philosophical travelogue about macro-economics. *The Edukators*, the first German film in competition in the festival for eleven years, charted the growing understanding of three politically naïve young adults, a kind of *Jules et Jim* meets Chomsky. And Jean-Luc Godard's *Notre Musique* looked at the impact of global war in a moving triptych: *Hell*, *Purgatory* and *Heaven*.

Whatever the merits of these movies, their attempts to draw the bigger political picture highlight

Tarantino's blind spot. He got into the movie industry partly because, from the age of two, he lived in or around Los Angeles. People with far less talent than he did too, for the same reason, but kids in Liverpool, Cairo, Inverness, Scranton, Warsaw or Osaka who have a real gift for cinema, often do not. For those who are passionate about cinema, this is galling. How do we know that the next Kieślowski, Ōshima or Samira Makhmalbaf will get through? And how do we change things? If Tarantino's star idea is wrong, if his politics be damned is naïve, then what isn't?

How about this for a proposal, unlikely to have been considered by the economic development experts and film industry analysts: we internationalise cinema by stopping the flow of any films internationally. Completely. For some time. If the real problem is not the star-boutique debate but the lack of a level playing field, then might it not work to give each national cinema a period of inwardness – a kind of detox, if you like – during which its own talent and ideas could grow?

It would work like this: for two years, no country would export its own films or import any others'. Audiences would only see movies made at home. Their own national senses of beauty, of fear, longing and mirth, would play on screen for 104 weeks. This year, for example, Chinese audiences would see films like Zhang Yimou's *House of Flying Daggers*, so beautiful that Cannes audiences rapturously clapped individual scenes. The film's star, the astonishing Zhang Ziyi, acts as enigmatically as Garbo and is photographed through as many layers as Dietrich; together director, actress and cinematographer create a work which is about beauty of the decorated, still, scroll-like and perhaps feminine kind, an aesthetic influenced by Confucianism and Buddhism. Distinctively Chinese, it is a star film *and* a boutique one.

Even those who are intrigued by this hypothetical restructuring of world cinema will see that it could not happen immediately. In order to allow national film industries to prepare for such radical changes, the mutually agreed closure of borders would need to take place five years in the future rather than now, to give film people time to prepare. The closure should be for two years, 2009 and 2010, to allow the detox time to work and producers and audiences time to change the way they think.

The argument for such a period of inwardness starts to sound less pie in the sky when you look at three periods of film history: Germany in the late 1910s, Russia in the 1910s and twenties and Iran in the eighties and nineties. Only when Germany isolated its film production between 1916 and 1921 did its filmmakers begin to become distinctive. Unable to rely on international influence, they became more think-tanky and, within a few years, world-class talents such as Fritz Lang, Robert Wiene, F. W. Murnau, and G. W. Pabst, emerged. Some will say that this blossoming was more to do with the fact that oppressive regimes often inspire great artists, but if it was the spirit of opposition alone which fuelled these talents, then they would have made their masterpieces before the new leftist politics of 1918. The far more rational explanation is that it was being forced to invent and being faced with screens not filled with work from other countries, which did the trick.

This is what I mean by detox, the equivalent of a writer sitting down at a keyboard and asking her or himself the question, "What do I really think?" German filmmakers asked themselves what they really thought. Despite the coercions of Bolshevism, that is what the Russian and Soviet directors did too. Again, the detail proves the point: before 1914, Russian cinema was dominated by French product. When the country entered World War One, most international film companies closed their Moscow offices. Almost immediately, the country's filmmaking became more distinctive. After the Revolution and inspired by its iconoclasm, a group of now famous directors – Kuleshov, Vertov, Eisenstein, Pudovkin, etc. – together changed the way films are edited by asking the question, "How can we make our national cinema different from others'?"

After the Islamic Revolution in 1979, Iranian directors saw few films from the West. Instead, the most innovative of them drew on the traditions of Persian poetry and philosophy and came up with a series of fable-like stories of remarkable allegorical and philosophical power, work such as Kiarostami's Koker trilogy, Mohsen Makhmalbaf's *A Moment of Innocence*, and his daughter Samira's *The Apple*.

The very idea of such isolationism would make many people – particularly maestro Tarantino – bristle, but no permanent arrangement is being proposed, just a temporary disavowal, a period of celibacy. The effect on twenty-first-century cinema would be as great as that on Germany, Russia and Iran in the twentieth. Without its imports from the US, the British film industry would have four times as much screen time to fill and, assuming that people continued to go to the movies – a big assumption, I know – up to four times the income. Pessimists will argue that the result would be the same lowering of standards as seen when television went satellite, but if you accept that the reality of UK film culture today is some stalled talent unable to get on, then surely that talent would blossom? Small scale, personal digital production would accelerate the process. The British equivalent of the Coen brothers could emerge. To our boutique films would be added star-driven ones. The big *James Bond* sound stages could be given over to Stephen Frears, Danny Boyle, Gurinder Chadha, Michael Winterbottom, Bernardo Bertolucci, Terence Davies, Marc Evans and Lynne Ramsay, who would have five years to plan big, imaginative, entertaining films.

Nearly every other European country would undergo a similar change. Australasian cinema's two heydays were in the seventies and nineties, when filmmakers, boosted by a new film school and some public money, confidently turned to a diverse range of questions about racism, landscape, theology, and sexuality. Faced with the imaginative and commercial gap left by the temporary disappearance of US, Asian and European movies, that continent's filmmakers would again be forced to look at their own societies and pleasures and find stories and styles to express them. Ditto South American cinema. The commercial sectors of the film industries of Taiwan, South Korea, Hong Kong, China and Japan would be strengthened and, though the arthouse directors would initially suffer from the loss of their international advocates, filmmakers like Wong Kar-wai, whose new work *2046* is a virtual remake of *In the Mood for Love*, would be forced onto new subject areas.

India and Iran would remain unaffected. Though the former exports to the Middle East and now Europe, its lower production budgets and complex regionalism has made it almost self-sufficient. In Iran, where there are more women directors than in many other countries, audiences flock to popular melodramas and art-house directors are amongst the best in the world. Tarantino and Swinton would approve. If only US cinema would take a leaf from that country's book.

Since America is a vast net-exporter of cinema, it would be the first and most powerful country to veto the two-year detox. This would be a shame because it too could benefit. It has been noticed for some years that the US movies which do best at the international box office are the Ur-action ones – the high body count, high-octane, Arnie and Stallone vehicles which exist in parallel universes of killing machines and abstract power. Given five years to anticipate the cessation of revenue from these, the studios would need to look to other markets within their own country. Middle-aged and old people, middle-class Hispanic, Black and Asian audiences, even intellectuals. US independent cinema addresses these to some degree, but a blurring of the line between independent and mainstream would occur. Multiplexes would be forced to broaden the range of people they attract through their portals, becoming boutiques as well as superstores. This maturing of audiences and themes would prepare movie-goers for the return of international film in 2010.

The bonus of my proposal would come on 1 January 2011. After two years of denial, imagine the pleasures of rediscovery and acquaintance. Immediately after World War Two, French moviegoers were able, in the single month of July 1946, to catch up on the treasures of American cinema, seeing *Citizen Kane*, *The Best Years of Our Lives*, *The Maltese Falcon*, *Double Indemnity* and *The Little Foxes*. January 2011 could be even better. We would all see the new Zhang Yimou, Wong Kar-wai and Kiarostami movies, and they'd see the new ones by Frears, Boyle and Winterbottom.

And the medium of film might, conceivably, have improved.

AFRICA

For *Vertigo*.

The 1960s are rightly considered a time of upheaval in world cinema, but not until the early 1970s did film history become as dramatic as political theatre. So striking were the events of the new decade that it seemed as if a playwright with a keen sense of irony and a penchant for ideas was behind the twists and turns of cinematic fortune. Take this striking concurrence, which no film history book I know mentions: in the single year of 1974, no less than four key figures in world cinema were in prison. Turkey's Yilmaz Güney had been so since 1972; Georgia's Sergei Parajanov began a four-year sentence in the same year on charges of fraud, homosexuality and incitement to suicide; documentary director Carlos Alvarez had been incarcerated for more than a year by then; and the Iranian

Mohsen Makhmalbaf had begun his formative four-year imprisonment at the same time.

Each of these situations had discreet explanations, of course, but together they suggest that state anxiety about the disruptive power of film had internationalised in the 1970s. Never before had such disparate countries felt so threatened by filmmakers that they tried to silence them under the law. Though Makhmalbaf was still to become a director he, like Güney, Parajanov and Alvarez, argued new ideas about the role of identity in politics. These ideas were unsettling the world of film in these crucial years, and questioning the relationship between entertainment and social change.

The seeds of this political upheaval were planted by the now famous meeting of 29 Asian and African countries in Bandung in Indonesia in 1955. The purpose of the Bandung Conference was to forge economic and cultural links between countries such as India, China, Japan, Egypt and Algeria. Eventually these, together with Yugoslavia, Indonesia and many African and Latin American states, formed the Non-Aligned Movement. Crucial to their co-operation was that they were allied neither to the "first" capitalist world of North America, Europe and Australasia nor to the "second" Communist world of the USSR and the Communist Bloc. Bandung identified not just a third point on the political triangle, but a third point on the map of the politics of film style. Mehboob's *Mother India* (1957) and Youssef Chahine's *Cairo Station* (1958) were landmark attempts to articulate such a third possibility.

This discrepant, third, non-aligned vision of cinema took root and grew throughout the 1960s. Its next theoretical boost came in 1969 when two Argentinean filmmakers wrote a manifesto which built on the writings of Mario Vargas Llosa, Gabriel García Márquez and Ngũgĩ wa Thiong'o, and the radical film work of Brazilian and Cuban directors of the sixties, and called it: "Towards a Third Cinema: Notes and Experiences for the Development of a Cinema of Liberation in the Third World." Fernando Solanas and Octavio Getino argued that the medium of film had so far been a commodity. Directors in the developing world should reject this history and start again, treating cinema as a weapon to fight oppression, a revolutionary tool. If early-seventies cinema was a piece of theatre, this article was its inciting incident. Solanas and Getino's cultural Marxism was not new, of course, but somewhat confusingly, a tripartite analysis rather different from Bandung's emerged: First Cinema was industrial and commercial, lasting between from the earliest days of narrative film until around 1958. Second Cinema was the modernist art movies of individual creative directors like Godard, Antonioni, Bergman and Fellini and had its heyday between 1959 and 1969. Third Cinema was political modernism, opposed to both industrial and autobiographical art cinema. This new idea of Third Cinema was the stage on which the full cinematic ironies of the period would play.

African, South American and Middle Eastern cinema of the seventies would all be affected by this new idea of thirdness, but it is on Francophone West Africa that I wish to dwell. This is because of the possibilities afforded in the comparison between the film world of Dakar, Senegal at this period and that of another city in the desert whose achievements at this time have been as fetishised as Dakar's have been ignored. Of all the ironies of early seventies cinema there is no greater one than this: every aspect of the Los Angeles film world of the time has been poured over, every stone unturned, every seminal filmmaking dinner reported on, every drug-fuelled party detailed, every aesthetic advance celebrated. Yet at exactly the same time that Scorsese, Coppola, Friedkin and Bogdanovich were storming the citadel of Hollywood, in Dakar, thousands of miles away from the swimming pools of Southern California, an equally vibrant film culture was blossoming. Striking films made by passionate and complex directors in this promontory city of 1.7 million people were released in such rapid succession that it was hard to keep up, yet the same film historians who have lionised the

US Movie Brats have largely ignored their African contemporaries.

African cinema had long had characters as fascinating as Martin Scorsese and the rest. At the first Carthage Film Festival in Tunisia in 1966 Egyptian Youssef Chahine said "Freedom of Expression is not given, it is taken", later adding, "I'm the first world, I've been here for 7,000 years." One of the continent's first black features *Black Girl* was made by Ousmane Sembène, a former Citroën factory worker and novelist, in Dakar in 1966, three years *before* the first widely-distributed American film directed by a black person. The story of a black housemaid in a white family who becomes depressed and commits suicide, it used an interior monologue spoken by a different voice to that of the actress, the first of many experimental techniques used in African cinema in the following two decades.

Foremost amongst the experimenters was Djibril Diop Mambéty who, like founding father Sembène, was born in Dakar – in 1945 – and raised by a strict father who taught him to look beyond materialism. At the age of 28 he released *Touki Bouki* (Senegal, 1973), an African *À bout de souffle* or *Easy Rider*, about two ironic young dropouts who swank around and swindle money in order to go to Paris. The man, Mory, works in a slaughterhouse but drives a motorbike with oxen horns on his handlebars. Anta, his partner, is a political worker. Mystical scenes of their ritual love-making are intercut with the blood sacrifice of a goat and open mockery of locals, village life and colonialism. In a key scene of ironic defiance, Mory strips and rides naked in a car, fist held high, making a mock political speech to a cavalcade of black Citroëns, the vehicle of choice of the colonialists.

The historian of African cinema Manthia Diawara wrote that *Touki Bouki* "tears up the screen with fantasies of African modernity never before seen in film or literature." Its assertion of youthfulness and cinematic irreverence was a door opener for new African filmmakers. Its title means "journey of the hyenas" in Mambéty's local language Wolof, and throughout his career he would use hyenas to symbolise the viciousness of human beings, in one instance pulling out a stuffed one to illustrate his point. It would be twenty years before he made his next feature, itself called *Hyenas* (1993), by which time the vision of this innovative director had darkened considerably.

This combination of Senegalese father figure and radical son was augmented further by Safi Faye, Africa's first important female director, when she made *Letter From My Village / Kaddu Beykat* in 1975. The first indigenous black African feature-length film to train its focus on the cultural details of village life, it documented the impact on farmers of the fall in the market value of their peanut crop, using a letter about a day in the life of villagers as its narrational device. At one point the letter writer says "I have often wondered why we live and die without any pleasure." European anthropologists like Jean Rouche had long made documentary films about Africa; Faye's went further than any of these.

In the same year as *Peasant Letter*, Sembène released his follow up to *Black Girl, Xala* (Senegal, 1974); it was almost as caustic as, and had been influenced by, *Touki Bouki*. Sembène's subject this time was the temporary sexual impotence of a black businessman in an unnamed African country who so co-operates with the colonisers that he even washes his limousine with mineral water. Where *Xala* was funny and popular, Sembène's next film *Ceddo* (Senegal, 1976) used a simple style to tell a symbolic and controversial tale about the impact of Islam in Africa. Featuring horrific slave branding scenes, it argued that the future of Africa relies on its refusal of the imposition of any monotheistic religion. Its ending, in which a princess slays a Muslin Imam, was considered scandalous, and the film was banned in its own country for eight years.

In these four films alone we begin to see a key element in the evolution of cinematic creativity: a filmmaking community. Whilst Sembène casts at least as long a paternal shadow as, say, Francis Coppola; where Mambéty's innovation and rebelliousness make him some kind of amalgam of Martin Scorsese and Dennis Hopper; and where Safi Faye as a woman has no parallel in Los Angeles, this community under-known by Western critics and audiences. I have seen their films and read what I can about these directors but cannot offer a detailed account of their influences on each other because the research on this has not yet been done or is not fully available. Why is this? One answer certainly involves the fact that to enter the world of Los Angeles in 1973 poses fewer intellectual challenges for a Western critic than to write and think about Dakar. To do the latter, after all, one needs to understand Senegalese writer Léopold Sédar Senghor's idea of *négritude*, a theory of opposition to French cultural imposition. In contrast, the fervour of the US directors of the 1970s is simpler to grasp.

A more disturbing explanation for the invisibility of Dakar is that Western commentators and audiences identify with the psychodrama of LA circa 1973 and don't with Dakar at the same time. If this is true, then a spade needs to be called a spade: the undervaluation of Senegalese cinema is racist.

AFRICAN REVENGE

Where would movies be without the fire and phlegm of revenge? It's the driving force in Quentin Tarantino's *Kill Bill* and *Death Proof*. Reprisal is a dish served cold in Korean director Park Chan-wook's trilogy *Oldboy*, *Sympathy for Mr Vengeance* and *Sympathy for Lady Vengeance*. *Gladiator* kicked off the new millennium with Old Testament revenge. And it was the same further back. A sixties Western like *Once Upon a Time in the West* is a retaliation opera. *The Godfather* trilogy is a Rembrandtesque study in vengeance. The films of Don Siegal, Jean-Pierre Melville and Robert Siodmak are cratered with revenge. The first commandment of genres like martial arts, horror, grindhouse, gangster, and rape revenge is an eye for an eye. Grindhouse and horror seem high on it. Retaliation, in these genres, is narcotic.

It's in pop songs and novels, theatre and opera too. And it's surely no surprise. The desire to hurt someone who's hurt you is a primitive impulse; its moderation or otherwise is the stuff of the great religions.

But in cinema revenge is particularly prevalent, because it has a movie *shape*. A cruel act – a false imprisonment, say, or the murder of a relative – sparks a quest for retribution that is suspenseful because its conclusion will be violent. Revenge isn't multiple, like novels are multiple, but singular, like classic movies.

So how do we explain the fact that the continent of Africa, which has rather more reason to be vengeful than the Anglophone world because of the iniquities of colonialism, hasn't produced many films about getting its own back? Lots of wonderful movies have been made in Africa since the 1960s yet, unlike Tarantino or Sergio Leone or Park Chan-wook, its great movie makers don't seem excited by the idea of filming people hunting down and hurting those who have hurt them. You'd expect centuries of oppression, humiliation and exploitation to have a caused a continent-wide psychological need for catharsis and, indeed, African life has been tragically bloody for decades now. But its movies don't really reflect this.

Take *Daratt*, for example, the latest African film released in the UK, made in Chad by Mahamat-Saleh Haroun. In it, a sixteen-year-old youth sets off to find and murder the man who killed his father. He takes a job in a bakery owned by the murderer, watching him every day, choosing his moment. Surely this is a classic revenge situation? Yes, the film broods with *andante* suspense, but in the end the son only pretends to kill the assassin, so *Daratt* is about the dissolution of the impulse to avenge. It looks at retaliation through a fresher lens than bravura Western directors like Tarantino.

But what, then, about *Bamako*, a previous African film shown in the UK, in which a trial is held in a courtyard in Mali's capital city? In it, African society is the plaintiff and the legacy of colonialism and the world financial institutions are in the dock. Again the stage is set for a revenge story – the film stares the evils of colonialism squarely in the eye – but what unfolds is witness-bearing, not vengeance.

And, further back in the history of African film, when the wounds of colonialism were still raw and so cinematic retaliation might be both more expected and excusable, it doesn't regularly appear either. Even those classic African films that seem to be about vengeance, or look as if they will depict it, aren't quite and don't. Med Hondo's *Sarraounia*, for example, made in Burkina Faso and Mauritania in 1986, is one of the continent's angriest movies. It is set in 1899 in the Sudan, amidst French atrocities committed against locals. But it shows resistance to, rather than vengeance for, those crimes. It lacks a time lag and, therefore, doesn't deal with the psychology of delayed anger. The plot of the late

Senegalese director Ousmane Sembène's masterpiece *Ceddo* (1977) similarly sounds like a springboard for retribution: in an unspecified past, the Ceddo tribe are threatened by the spiritual colonisation of Arab-Islam and Euro-Christianity, and physical slavery. They must choose between insurrection or integration. Sembène is too busy charting the implications of this choice to look at belated bloodletting.

Egyptian director Youssef Chahine's state of the nation film *The Sparrow* (1972), which I've mentioned before, climaxes with Nasser's shock announcement of the loss of the Sinai during the Six-Day War. His characters are stunned. The matriarch of the film, Bahiyya, runs into the streets, overwhelmed and yelling "We won't accept defeat!" Chahine's tracking shots of her are amongst the greatest moments in world cinema – passionately melodramatic and moving – yet his film stops short of vengeance.

I could go on, but the point is clear. Neither new African cinema nor the great films by founding fathers Sembène and Chahine nor mid-period master directors like Hondo are much about retaliation. Why not? As many of the great African films – and there are loads of them – are co-funded by the French government, it's tempting to think that the former oppressors have baulked at financing films in which wrongdoing is avenged. This may be so – only an analysis of African film projects rejected for French funding would show whether it is – but even if it were, it would only be a partial explanation.

More relevant, I think, is the fact that, with the exception of Egypt, Nigeria and South Africa, the continent's most acclaimed movies have been closer to what we in Europe think of as art cinema, and so have not been an expression of populist rage and resentment.

This is not to say that there's no fury in African movies, just that they aren't, on the whole, populist. It's certainly there – few filmmakers in the world were more militant than Sembène and his brilliant compatriot Djibril Diop Mambéty. But instead of that fury being embodied by lone avengers like Clint Eastwood or Jimmy Cagney, their angry people are likely to be women, in the case of Sembène, or the tone of their movies is likely to be wildly satirical, like Mambéty's *Touki Bouki* (1973) or *Hyenas* (1992) or Sembène's *Xala* (1975). *Hyenas* seems to be about rage – a jilted former lover, who has since become "richer than the world bank", returns to her home village to punish the man she loved by promising the villagers that, if they kill him, she will give them all the consumer goods they want. But it is the locals' greed that vexes director Mambéty, not the woman's ire. And the story itself is European, adapted from by play by Friedrich Dürrenmatt. After an hour or more of crisp gender satire in Sembène's *Xala*, a troupe of disabled people do circle in on the movie's greedy and self-important central character. They enact a revenge of sorts by spitting on him, the shock of the act coming from the very fact that it is so rare in African movies. Both films are about women, in many ways, and women are just as capable of wanting revenge as men, of course, but the target of their ire in African cinema is as likely to be obdurate black men as domineering white states, so their narratives do not usually have nice clean vengeance contours. And the influence of *griots* – storytellers – on African film stops them being clean-cut eye-for-an-eye movies too. From the mid-seventies onwards, such griots have woven their way through African cinema, turning fact into fable, and interpreting events. This takes some of the raw anger out of the plots, rendering them mythic.

All of the above are relevant but the real answer to why African films are less vengeful than ours comes from Sembène again. In his great book on the director, David Murphy quotes him as saying "you don't tell a story for revenge but rather to understand your place in the world." Surely that's it. African cinema is angry, yes, and driven, but not by the need to retaliate. *Daratt* and *Bamako*, *Touki Bouki*, *Hyenas* and Souleymane Cissé's *Yeelen*, *Ceddo* and *The Sparrow* are too busy working out how Africans should live with other Africans – what

Edward Said called the move from filiation to affiliation – to deal with the almost decadent matter of revenge. Vengeance is for people with time on their hands. Eastwood and Cagney, Oh Dae-su in *Oldboy* and Charles Bronson's harmonica man in *Once Upon a Time in the West* had bags of time. African movies in the seventies looked around at the rubble left by colonialism and said – *OK, now that we've shook them off, where do we go from here?* In the eighties they turned the clock backwards and told stories of precolonial times, to ask *Where were we before they came? And can we pick up a thread from those times?* These were such brilliant and relevant questions that, in comparison, vengeance stories were for wusses.

Back in the Anglophone West, we have begun a cycle of Iraq movies – *The Kingdom*, Brian De Palma's *Redacted*, etc. – that have the feel of apology and atonement about them. It's right to say sorry, of course, but maybe our filmmakers could take a leaf out of Africa's book by not only saying gotcha or sorry, but by making dazzling films about finding a place in the world.

DENNIS HOPPER OBIT

As I sit down to write about Dennis Hopper, a man I knew a bit, a discrepant cowboy hipster who grew up in old Hollywood and helped create New Hollywood, the BBC is running a breaking news roller at the bottom of my TV screen: "Hollywood Actor Dennis Hopper, star of *Easy Rider* and *Apocalypse Now*, has died."

It's not a great log line. It should at least have said that he *directed Easy Rider*, the film whose jaggy trippiness mocked Hollywood's squareness in 1969. What else about the man should we recall?

Firstly, that he was indeed a Stetson-wearing cowboy of sorts, born in Dodge City of all places, in 1936. And, as if to prove the point, he was in *Gunfight at the O.K. Corral* and *True Grit* with John Wayne, and worked with Western director Henry Hathaway. But add to this his friendship with James Dean, which fired him like no other: Hopper was in *Rebel Without a Cause* and *Giant* with Dean in the fifties, as the latter burnt brightly and Hopper was just warming up. He worshipped Dean. The young actor's Freudian, unravelling, modernism set Hopper directly against the world of Wayne.

In fact "against" was a key word for Hopper. He was against his times and himself. As we walked around his "Art Barn" Frank Gehry house in Venice, CA, he told me with real pride that he was one of the first people in California to buy an Andy Warhol. His eyes burned as he quoted one of his favourite ideas, "if you could not create would you die?" Yes, was his answer, as if directing and acting was what kept him alive. You'd think the blinding success of his directorial debut *Easy Rider* in 1969 would have kept him alive for a bit but, instead, almost to sabotage its success, he made his second film *The Last Movie*, a brilliant, impenetrable movie about how filming messes with people's heads. The critics slaughtered it. Hopper moved to New Mexico, and started drinking like a fish. By the time I met him in the late-nineties, he'd long stopped doing so but, like a samurai, passed its lore onto me, teaching me how to order a martini – Tanqueray gin, straight up, olives.

Out of his New Mexican exile – manic, peyote-fuelled – came his best seventies work, his brilliant snooker-playing cowboy Ripley in Wim Wenders' *The American Friend*, his astonishing, wild portrait of soldier returning from Vietnam in Henry Jaglom's *Tracks*, and his manic photographer in *Apocalypse Now*. Gone were the fifties good looks, and the sixties concern with social change. Instead, something close to psychosis had come into view, daredevilling, the sort of acting without a safety net that would lead to the hammy excess of his late performances in films like *The Texas Chainsaw Massacre 2*. Hopper was never far away from horror cinema, acting in his best films in the seventies but then, as if to pull the carpet out from under himself *again*, he played a daft, psychotic photographer in Robert Altman's trite *O. C. and Stiggs*, mocking the one in *Apocalypse Now*.

Around about then he kicked the martini habit, and the many other habits and, cleaned up, at 50 he looked 40. He read the screenplay of *Blue Velvet* and famously told David Lynch that he *was* Frank Booth. The rapist-fetishist Booth took the mania of Hooper's seventies characters up a gear but, set in Lynch's Eisenhower-textured world, he looked like one of the most terrifying characters in the history of the movies.

This led to typecasting, of course – *Dennis give us some more snarling* – but, again, the contrarian in the man made sure that he didn't become samey. The rebel without a cause, the easy rider came out as a supporter of Reagan and Bush número uno, which ruffled the feathers of his hippie comrades. And, to rub salt in the wounds, he did an advert for Ford Cougar in which, to the tune of "Born To Be Wild", he drove past his idealistic motorbike in *Easy Rider*.

The hearts of millions sank at the sight of this sell out, this political reversal, but the image of overtaking yourself, is a decent metaphor for the gleeful lack of sentimentality in Hopper's life and work and the amplitude of its reversals.

He was given the Cougar by Ford, of course, and it sat in his house in Venice, an art object amongst the Warhols. Hopper went to Scotland a lot to play golf, so I gave him a book about the great artist Ian Hamilton Finlay's Scottish garden, Little Sparta. Hopper flicked it for a while, then said "will you take me?" I never got to. I'll remember his handsomeness, his high shoulders, his insistence that I smoke a Havana cigar, and the tears in his eyes when he acted out, with his hands, the position of the cars in the crash that killed James Dean. Most of all I'll remember his question to himself – "if you could not create, would you die?"

AMY ADAMS

The silent era had Garbo. The 1940s had Greer Garson. The fifties had Ingrid Bergman. In the 1960s and seventies, there were Ellen Burstyn, Gena Rowlands and Sissy Spacek. The eighties and since have had Meryl Streep, Jessica Lange, Susan Sarandon and Cate Blanchett.

American cinema has always needed new women to embody the disappointment and sadness that it sometimes allows itself to admit to or evince. Judging by the back-to-back releases of Tom Ford's Hitchcockian guilt drama *Nocturnal Animals* and Denis Villeneuve's misty close encounter parable *Arrival*, a new American lightning rod for tristesse is Amy Adams.

In these films, Adams is neither girl nor gamin; no Audrey, Winona or Natalie Portman. Godard wouldn't know what to do with her. She doesn't just submit to the dejection in the films' storylines, nor is she simply a function of their disconsolations. She's not in them to be admired. Instead, she seems to colour them and give them their tones. Perhaps that's how sadness works – it radiates.

Part of the pleasure of seeing Adams onscreen these days is the contrast with what she's done before. In her first lead role, in Disney's self-parodying *Enchanted*, she's all ribbons and bows: Snow White stepped out of the drawn world into the real world. In an early interview she said she was "attracted to characters who are positive and come from a very innocent place." But then she played the wife of the preacher-healer in Paul Thomas Anderson's *The Master*. Hair up, we could see that lantern face more purely than before, and the determination therein. Born into a Mormon military family, real life had tested her. "I didn't have a huge skill-set coming out of school, and I was my sole provider . . . a bootstrap kid." We could see the bootstrap kid in *The Master* and, also, those eyes, which were wider than the norm (the opposite of Kirsten Dunst's) and whose pupils are small. Bowie and Kim Novak had eyes that helped shape their careers. Adams' are piercing and, so, it's fitting that Tim Burton give her the lead in *Big Eyes*.

After *The Master* she played Lois Lane and, then, Sydney in David O. Russell's *American Hustle*. Watch how she dances to Donna Summer in its club scene. Look at her braless outfits, and those dresses that show the underside of her breasts. She'd replaced bootstraps for seventies silver slingbacks, but her performance was the sexiest in American cinema in years – strutting, Dionysian, innovating. Again the film's tone – inebriated, desperate, and songful (Adams was a restaurant singer before she got into movies) – is set by her performance.

"It's a strange transition to come from a survivalist place to a more artistic place," said Adams of her increasing power in the industry in these years. She clocked that increase as it was happening and is using it as wisely as Julie Christie did, decades earlier. By the time of *Nocturnal Animals* and *Arrival*, extra things were happening with her on screen. In movies now she seems like she's in a Virginia Woolf novel. Directors can't help but film her in close-up, to get nearer to those eyes. Unlike John Wayne or Marilyn Monroe, her walk isn't very distinctive – a walking shot in a car park in *Arrival* is used to show her ordinariness – but the closer you get the more you feel the Woolfian TARDIS, the way that she's bigger on the inside. Adams is better at looking than being looked at, and great at slowness and blanching. She's often in minimal make-up but seems sadder still in lipstick and eyeshadow, as if they are admissions of defeat, or another manifestation of the bootstrap.

Some say that *Nocturnal Animals* is anti-woman, but I don't agree. She treated a weak man badly in it and now the guilt means that she can hardly sleep.

It's an anti-*femme fatale* film. *Arrival*, based on a story by Seattle-based writer Ted Chiang, is a *quai des brumes*. The weather in it is misty, the light is soft, the colours muted, the contrast low. Adams' Louise Banks has echoes of another LB in another misty place, Laura Baxter, played by Julie Christie in the Venice-set *Don't Look Now*. Perhaps it's inevitable that an actor's best work will happen in a great film, but *Arrival* is such a thing. Her face has never been more lantern-like, her melancholia never better calibrated. The film's anti-bellicosity is moving at a moment when we have someone called President-Elect Trump. There's a hint in Adams' walk into shot, towards a wall-window, to pour herself a glass of wine at what looks like dusk, that the moment is the fount of the whole film.

Amy Adams is a fount for American cinema at the moment, and that's great news. Todd Haynes doesn't need her – he's got Julianne Moore and Cate Blanchett. But imagine if the Coen brothers or Tarantino or the Wachowski's worked with her, and what Chantal Akerman would have made of her, and vice versa.

CHANNING TATUM

Channing Tatum, or is it Tatum Channing? He looks like either. Unless he has a side parting, as in *Hail, Caesar!*, his face is precisely symmetrical, his brow and eye lines horizontal. A geometric face with a mid-distance look.

But that's the thing about movie stars. Their faces should be enigmatic. When those close-ups come, and they seldom do for Tatum, too much expression makes them noisy. A close-up should be quiet.

What shouldn't be quiet is the body. Chaplin's wasn't, nor was Cyd Charisse's or Rita Hayworth's, Louise Brooks' or Marlon Brando's. Nor is Tatum's. In *21 Jump Street*, he's a cop who wants car chases but only gets to rescue Frisbees. He's crap at policing and has to go under cover as someone "really stupid, so you should blend right in". His body's ahead of his head, like a teenager's, and he plays it beautifully, this boy-man who's frustrated or humiliated.

Which brings the politics in. Tatum comes from a working-class background. He went from roofer to stripper. He's great at anti-Michael Bay men who aren't pumped by their own ego. Class, poverty and gentleness have stopped them getting to that hypermasculine place that Hollywood seems – just – to believe in, despite the collateral damage it does. In *Magic Mike*, which is based on some of his own experiences, his character knows where his power lies, and where it doesn't. He has a body and moves, and makes the best of both, as they won't last forever, and he knows it. So he shines for as long as he can shine, but isn't Icarus, isn't one of those Tennessee Williams characters who suddenly find themselves alone because they thought they had it all and didn't look ahead. If you're working-class and pretty and bright, you know the clock is ticking and that when the looks go the tide will go out and you'll be left where you started.

If we didn't know where to fit Tatum into movie history, *Hail, Caesar!* showed us. His dance scene was like an outtake from *On the Town*, but it's the Gene Kelly of *Singin' in the Rain* or even *It's Always Fair Weather* that seemed to come alive in that Coens number. Kelly's face was *identikit*, too, but his body polyglot, like Tatum's: put it on a movie screen and you've got life. Think of other aspects of fifties cinema and we can refine who Channing Tatum is. Is he a king actor like

John Wayne or Orson Welles? No way. In *Foxcatcher* he was a supplicant. No great lawmaker, he. But nor is he much of a detective driven by scepticism in a world where the law is dead. He's a pawn, moved around by others – social forces, or rich women – and he's not enraged by that. Far from it. His characters might vote Bernie (or even Trump?) because they're the bottom of the heap, and so outside politics, but they know how to enjoy things now.

Anxious fifties actors like Montgomery Clift or James Dean always wanted to escape, the moment, the agony, their own skin. Tatum is the opposite of that. There's a short film, *The Trap*, in which he has a simple scene. He's at the top of a trapeze ladder, a woman climbs it. She's terrified, and for more than three minutes, he just reassures and comforts her. And enjoys it. Hypermasculinity can't stand being around women, but Tatum's characters clearly love it – not to boss them, just because of the attraction, the feeling of being intimate, useful and entertaining. For the discourse.

In the scene in question, Tatum is topless, a state of undress to which he is not averse. You could say that this is the fifties thing too – think of Victor Mature and all those peplum films – but Tatum's nakedness is more Ewan McGregor than Charlton Heston (another of those names that could be reversed). Back then, men seemed to display their bodies unconsciously.

They didn't get, or pretended they didn't get, any pleasure from being looked at. Ewan McGregor was really clear: *yes I love getting my ass out, and love you looking at it.* Tatum is equally cool on this. It's not polished, like metrosexual is polished. It's more euphoric than that, and far less controlled.

To say this makes me realise who Channing Tatum really resembles. Don't laugh: Jane Russell. I knew her a bit and she was un-neurotic, funny and up for a laugh. If Tatum is a woman's man, Russell was a man's woman – she had loads of brothers, and behaved like a cowgirl. Despite being religious, you can see in her movies what unfettered pleasure she took in her own body. If you haven't seen her "Lookin' for Trouble" number in *The French Line*, look it up on YouTube. It's sexy, outré, complicit and probably censorable. She's as comfortable in her body, in its sexuality, and the humour of that, as Tatum, and the scene reminds me of one of the *Magic Mike* routines.

As some critics raved about *Magic Mike 2*, I saw it and regretted it. I was bored. But Channing Tatum was once again Jane Russell and Ewan McGregor.

NICOLE

She turns 50 in June, and was in four films in Cannes. A milestone and a deluge. Who is she, this Nicole Kidman that we see so often or, rather, what kind of movie person is she? Imagine that her best films — *To Die For*, *The Portrait of a Lady*, *Eyes Wide Shut*, *Moulin Rouge!*, *The Hours*, *Dogville*, *The Paperboy*, *Top of the Lake* — are a deck of cards. Flick them and what would you see? Is there a composite or centre of gravity in them?

Yes. In the flick book we see a stander. She's usually shot full height, like Fred Astaire. She's not much of a sitter or sloucher. She's tall, central, white and frontal, the same composition as Botticelli's *Venus*. If films are a graphic art, why would you ignore all that height? You'd film her hieratically, like she's always on a staircase, like the red carpet steps in Cannes. It's easy to imagine her doing Streisand's "Hello, Dolly!" number, or on the stairway to paradise in *An American in Paris* or — how this for a head fuck? — on the Odessa Steps.

Stop flicking the cards and look at them one by one and you start to see the dead calm in Kidman, even in an operatic character like the courtesan Satine in Luhrmann's Parisian reverie. As a girl she did ballet and you can still see the poise, the spotting. Of course in some parts she must lose control but even when she does, you never fear that she's going to unravel or explode. She's more Tilda Swinton than Oprah, Jack Nicholson or Bette Davis. She says she's shy, and that rings true. On the one time that I was in the same restaurant with her, everyone seems to move more than she.

Is this why a greatest moment in film is that long held shot in Jonathan Glazer's *Birth*, when she's in the theatre and the camera is on her face and doesn't cut? Jane Campion plays her best and swishes her around most, I think, but Glazer got the ballet spotting thing and made her look for ages, as the wee boy looks in Herz Frank's masterpiece *Ten Minutes Older*. That stare in *Birth* is her Garbo moment, her *Queen Christina*. Her husband has died, a boy is now claiming to be him, and time is running backwards behind those glassy eyes. The eyes are framed by those brows, which are at such an angle that they look like horn-rimmed glasses. It's hard for Kidman not to look quizzical.

Composition, emotion, spotting, irony, but what of her choices? The list of directors she works with, and styles of film she makes, is a powerful actor's semaphore, her colour palette. Kidman has made some very bad films, but they don't seem cynically bad. They're sincerely bad. Flick that pack of cards again and you notice the wow-factor of her genre and tonal range. *To Die For*'s a deadpan comedy, but she's done minimal (*Birth*), maximal (*Moulin Rouge*), camp (*The Paperboy*), experimental (*Dogville*), eros (*Eyes Wide Shut*), surrealism (*Top of the Lake*) and much more. This can't just be chance. She obviously enjoys sky-jumping into different tone-worlds. She holds back tears in many of these films, but with different degrees of realism or irony.

And the choice of *Dogville* still seems remarkable. It's hard to imagine many names submitting to something so full of abjection, blame, suspicion of America, and stylistic dissidence. Given that von Trier had never been to America, his film could so easily have been awful, pretentious and inauthentic, and the lack of sets and locations could have been absurd, and yet she went for it with, as I say, submission. I have no access to Kidman's thought processes, but my hunch is that she did it because it sounded exciting and dangerous. Only a person who loves cinema (lots of actors don't) and theatre, would have taken such a risk.

What about the future? Will she become like Katharine Hepburn? Will we say of her *My she was yar*? I think she's more Myrna Loy than Hepburn. Loy had grace and naughtiness, as does Kidman. *The Paperboy* got some stinking reviews but it, in a way, was as daring as *Dogville*. I'd love to see her directed by dancer Michael Clarke, or musician PJ Harvey (who would make a very good filmmaker, I reckon). And it's a shame that Poussin is dead, because what a painting he's do of Kidman — hieratic again, and completely un-flickering.

AGNÈS VARDA'S TENT

Some filmmakers seem to hold cinema up, like poles hold a tent up. It's hard to imagine the scale and welcome of movies without, say, Buster Keaton, Orson Welles, Ernst Lubitsch, Kira Muratova or Akira Kurosawa.

Belgian-French Agnès Varda was such a tent pole. Over seven decades and three continents, she elevated the movies, and made them hospitable. Her film voice was her own, but you could hear traces in it of French essayist Chris Marker in it, and Frida Kahlo's self-portraiture, the writing of Virginia Woolf, the activism of Jane Fonda, and the legerdemain of Montaigne.

Her very first feature, 1955's *La Pointe Courte*, raised the movie game by modernising French cinema and helping create the idea of the French New Wave. Once there's a new space, you inhabit it, which is exactly what Varda did. Her next feature, *Cleo from 5 to 7* (1962) was about a woman walking a city. The title character, Cleo, had just had a cancer diagnosis. She was a flâneuse. Many such films about women walking had been made in Japan, and Katharine Hepburn's loneliness pushed her through the streets of Venice in David Lean's *Summertime*, but Varda's film was more innovative. It was about Cleo's looking.

Three years later, Varda extended cinema again; *Le Bonheur* (1965) was about a golden, happy couple, but he has an affair and she kills herself. Its gilded tragedy was one of the most tonally complex films of its time. In 1977, with *One Sings, the Other Doesn't*, Varda showed that you could make a happy musical about, of all things, abortion. How much further could the tent be extended? Certainly to 1991's *Jacquot de Nantes*, her autobiographical film about someone else's life (her husband, Jacques Demy's). More daring combinations of subject and style, another leap of the imagination.

As Varda's remarkable career progressed, and despite being undervalued in comparison to great directors like Jean-Luc Godard or Martin Scorsese, it became clear that a tent is one useful way to understand her. The French title of her acclaimed 1985 film *Vagabond / Sans toit ni loi* (no roof, no law) points to Varda's interest in homelessness, rootlessness and temporary living. The film's central character has no fixed abode, no bricks and mortar, and Varda's heart goes out to her. *Vagabond* was a film about drifting, but its many tracking shots were amongst the most planned and beautiful in film history: another contradiction, perhaps, like the tonal contradictions in *Le Bonheur*. Varda has extended the movie tent once more.

And still she pushed onwards, outwards. In 2000 she made another film that captured the mendicant, hand-to-mouth nature of many people's lives. Again its French title – *Les Glaneurs et la Glaneuse* – is revealing: "the gatherers and the gathering woman." In her film we see gleaners gathering discarded fruit and vegetables in city markets, and potatoes that supermarkets don't want. It was moving, revealing filmmaking, but Varda realised that she too is a gatherer. Her emphasis on documentary, her outwardly-directed imagination, her cinematic welcome made her a kind of potato-gatherer, a finder as much as an inventor. Or, rather, she found things in the world (tenderness, complexity) and reshaped those things into dazzling, often rigorous film form.

By this stage, 45 years after her first feature, it was clear that Agnès Varda was raising, extending and rethinking the movie tent, the empathic and aesthetic space of cinema, like few others, but she wasn't always credited with this. Frequently you'd meet movie-lovers and critics who'd casually say that they hadn't seen any of her films. They were in the tent, but didn't know who'd helped build it. If this upset Varda (and she could be rightly bullish with festival directors who undervalued her), the very belated honorary Oscar she received in 2017 will have helped. In receiving it, she danced with Angelina Jolie, an echo of Stanley Donen's honorary Oscar in 1997, when he danced and sang Irving Berlin's "Cheek to Cheek". "Heaven, I'm in heaven", sang Donen, and Varda seemed to be in heaven too but, also, her dance reminded us that her cinema was essentially joyous.

She saw the arrival of video cameras and digital cinema as joyous. Her productivity increased in the late 1990s, when she hit her sixties. And she made another kind of tent. As there was no longer any need for lots of 35mm film copies of her films – they could now be projected digitally – she made art installations of them, using the film strips to create the walls of movie sheds which looked a bit like garden sheds. Shelter again, temporary again, welcoming again, innovative again, Varda again.

The refugee crisis in Europe and on the USA's southern border means that we need the humanity of Varda more than ever. We need her heart and innovation. A few months after she died, I had to introduce her new film, *Varda by Agnès*, which gets a North American premiere in Telluride. I did so with potatoes – she loved potatoes – and with a French song, "*Comment te dire adieu?*" "How do you say goodbye?"

With gratitude and a broken heart.

AFTERWORD:
THE FUTURE OF CINEMA

So here we are, at the end of this book. Thank you for reading it. Did you skip "Rupture"?

Now it's time to listen to Shania Twain or watch Béla Tarr's *Sátántangó*. How great that life contains both. How great that we can ride the dissonance, as Cornel West suggests.

Is this book dissonant? As the pieces were written over nearly two decades, on different continents, for several reasons (or none), they don't ask to harmonise, but there are recurring themes: looking, travel, feminism, form, Orson Welles, bodies, childhood, etc. I hope that you found some warmth in the book and a lack of snobbery about cinema, that affordable sublime.

In the photo on the cover, which was taken by Phoebe Grigor, I'm lying in a cinema, across seats, lit by the movie screen. We tried to make an image that was a bit dreamlike, submissive, floating. I didn't want to be sitting up, paying attention. You've encountered some of my thinking in this book, but of course life is more than thinking. It's a sensory assault, a kind of meteor storm.

I'm often asked about Netflix, Amazon Prime, Mubi and the other streamers – or video games – and how they are changing film culture and movie-going. When I answer I think of a meteor storm. I enjoy lying on my sofa, eating pizza and watching Netflix as much as anyone. And I know that for people with reduced mobility, the enhancement of home entertainment is a marvel. But I think back to the asteroid field sequence in *Star Wars: The Empire Strikes Back*, which I saw when I was 15. It enveloped me. The asteroids flew towards me at great speed, but the Millennium Falcon dodged them. We all want comfort and control in our lives, the ease of pizza and Amazon Prime, but we are also hard-wired for something else, the kid-old wildness and ceding of control that I mentioned elsewhere in this book. At times we need to get out of ourselves, we need the mosh pit, to climb the Alps.

This is why cinema will last, because its sublime is affordable (though ticket prices are getting too high in big cities). You spend two hours in Barbie's pinkosphere, its gender Möbius strip, and then you're back in your cream living room that you know so well. The transition from knowing to knowing is lovely, but you turn on a streamer and you scroll and scroll and suddenly you realise that home entertainment is a small-scale meteor storm. It comes at you constantly, without end. It's hard to decide what to watch. Your brain says *almost, not quite, not now. I fancy something lighter, newer, more familiar or recent.* And after half an hour you start to question what you want, and the meteors keep coming, their blandishments like rain in your face. And so you turn to TikTok and watch someone eat egg-fried noodles, or dance to Dua Lipa. And these things are lovely, simple, alive, and you realise that that's what you want – *alive*.

Yasujirō Ozu's films are gently about this, and in Wim Wenders' *Perfect Days*, a guy who cleans toilets in Tokyo feels alive when he looks up at the light through the trees. The film shows that cinema doesn't need to be wild like *Star Wars* to entrance. It needs other things – concentration and scale. That's what I'm looking for when I go out to my local cinemas, usually in the afternoon. I want – need – to block out the distractions, to go into the dark, to look forward and up at a crafted, luminous, landscape, cityscape, time-machine where I can look at human faces massively magnified, available for inspection, and clothes and trees and sunsets and fear and rapture and anger and ... what? What's the extra thing? Visual thinking.

It's been said before, but there's a way of understanding all this in Islam. People have their prayer mats at home, their domestic form of worship. But then there's the Friday Mosque which is much bigger, more collective, an event, a pilgrimage.

ACKNOWLEDGEMENTS

For years Nick James gave me a space to write about cinema in *Sight and Sound* magazine. I'd never have detailed my thoughts on Channing Tatum or Nicole Kidman if not for him and Isabel Stevens. Mike Williams continued that to some extent; if you love movies and don't read *Sight and Sound*, put it on your Christmas list.

In *Prospect* magazine, Alexander Linklater and David Goodhart took an earlier risk by giving me a monthly column when I had yet to understand the form of a column. I'm grateful for their incubation.

Others overruled my reluctance to write. Chris Agee at *Irish Pages* suggested that it was worth compiling these pieces (my previous collection is *Watching Real People Elsewhere*).

Thank you so much to everyone at The Irish Pages Press / Cló An Mhíl Bhuí who worked so diligently on *Dear Orson Welles & Other Essays*: Chris Agee, Milena Williamson, Jacob Agee and the design team at RV.

And to GLM I say two words: Gladys Knight.

Mark Cousins
Over the Atlantic
About to watch a documentary
about Ennio Morricone